Web
Designer's

Guide to

Style
Sheets

Hayden
Books

Steven Mulder

President
Richard Swadley

Associate Publisher
John Pierce

Publishing Manager
Laurie Petrycki

Managing Editor
Lisa Wilson

Marketing Manager
Kelli Spencer

Development Editor
Jim Chalex

Technical Editor
Jeffrey Veen

Copy Editor
Jeff Durham

Production Editors
Kevin Laseau
Terrie Deemer

Publishing Coordinator
Karen Flowers

Cover Designer
Aren Howell

Book Designer
Sandra Schroeder

Manufacturing Coordinator
Brook Farling

Production Team Supervisors
Laurie Casey
Joe Millay

Production Team
Aleata Howard
Malinda Kuhn
Christopher Morris
Beth Rago

Indexer
Chris Barrick

Web Designer's Guide to Style Sheets

©1997 Hayden Books

Library of Congress Catalog Number: 96-78279
ISBN: 1-56830-306-8

Copyright © 1997 Hayden Books

Printed in the United States of America 1 2 3 4 5 6 7 8 9 0

Warning and Disclaimer

This book is dedicated to...

```
becky { love: 100%;
        beauty: unparalleled;
        fun: everlasting }
```

About the Author

When not scouring used bookstores in search of gorgeous, musty-smelling old media, Steven Mulder delights in cavorting in the electronic fields of new media. Until discovering style sheets, he worked *way* too hard at making HTML do things it was never supposed to do.

In his non-spare time, Steve is a Product Development Specialist at Hayden Books, which is to say that when he isn't writing, he's wreaking havoc on the writing of others. Or he's inventing ideas for books that will have more readers than his Master's thesis on John Steinbeck's *East of Eden* as postmodernist metafiction. And when he isn't doing that, he's attempting to keep the Hayden Web site sparkling and fresh.

And no, he is neither an agent for the FBI nor an unsolved X-File.

```
http://www.mcp.com/people/mulder/
```

Acknowledgments

Thanks…

…to Laurie Petrycki, Jim Chalex, and others at Hayden Books for finally letting me create a book instead of just complaining about how great *my* book would be if *I* could ever write one.

…to Jeff Veen for being picky, caustic, and generally mean-spirited with his neurotic editing of my so-called facts. :-) His dedication to quality made this book a reality. His dedication to digital style helps make the Web a fun place to be.

…to the wise sages at the World Wide Web Consortium for first inventing the wonder that is style sheets and then practically stalking the folks at Microsoft and Netscape until they supported style sheets in their browsers.

…to Netscape and Microsoft for creating software that crashes my computer just enough to keep me on my toes, but not quite enough to make me stop wanting to wander the Web.

…to Becky and the cats for enduring my giddy laughter and agonized screams when things did work and didn't, reminding me occasionally that the real world doesn't have an Undo command (sigh), and generally purring and smiling at me each step of the way.

Hayden Books

The staff of Hayden Books is committed to bringing you the best computer books. What our readers think of Hayden is important to our ability to serve our customers. If you have any comments, no matter how great or how small, we'd appreciate your taking the time to send us a note.

You can reach Hayden Books at the following:

Hayden Books
201 West 103rd Street
Indianapolis, IN 46290
317–581–3833

Email addresses:

America Online: Hayden Bks
Internet: hayden@hayden.com

Visit the Hayden Books Web site at `http://www.hayden.com`

And visit the Web site devoted to this book at `http://www.hayden.com/internet/style/`

Trademark Acknowledgments

All terms mentioned in this book that are known to be trademarks or services marks have been appropriately capitalized. Hayden Books cannot attest to the accuracy of this information. Use of a term in this book should not be regarded as affecting the validity of any trademark or service mark.

Contents at a Glance

Table of Contents

Using this Book

You're welcome to use this book any way you want; that's up to you. But you should know that diving right into the individual style sheet properties (Chapters 4–9) will cause you to miss out on information that is essential to using style sheets effectively. Chapters 2 and 3 are vital for learning how to compose style sheet rules and incorporate them into your HTML documents.

This book contains everything that the World Wide Web Consortium's official Cascading Style Sheets recommendation (level 1) contains—all the properties and options. It also covers the newer "Positioning HTML Elements with Cascading Style Sheets" document cowritten by Microsoft and Netscape (see Chapter 8). But as we all know from the world of HTML, what's in the official spec is not nearly as important as what the *browsers* actually support. That's why you'll see notes and examples throughout the book about what Netscape Navigator and Internet Explorer support and what they don't. What about other Web browsers? Frankly, I don't think they're important enough to spend time on; Navigator and Internet Explorer swallow up the vast majority of market share. So, in this book I focus on them.

Watch for these notes on what isn't supported by Microsoft's Internet Explorer browser, or what strange behavior results in certain situations. You'll see info on Internet Explorer 3.0.1 for Windows 95 and for Macintosh, as well as info on the latest version as of this writing. (I was able to test things using beta 1 of Explorer 4.0 for Windows 95; see the notes throughout.)

Watch for these notes on what isn't supported by the latest version of Netscape Navigator, which is part of the Netscape Communicator suite. I used Preview Release 3 of Navigator

4.0, both Windows 95 and Macintosh, for testing.

Last Minute note

For the latest updates on style sheets support in the 4.0 browsers, check in regularly at this book's Web site: `http://www.hayden.com/internet/style/`.

Check out these notes for last-minute information discovered just before this book went to press.

Syntax and Notation

Chapters 4–9 concentrate on the various properties you can set using style sheets. Each begins with a line showing the syntax you must use for that property. This syntax is the same one used in the official style sheets specification. Here's a quick guide to translating it:

➡ `<xyz>`

Words within brackets give a type of value. Examples include `<length>`, `<color>`, and `<percentage>`. In place of these you might put `2in`, `red`, and `50%`. Many of these units are explained in Appendix A.

➡ `x y z`

When several words or numbers appear in a certain order, all of them need to appear (in that order) in the final style sheet rule you create.

➡ `x ¦ y ¦ z`

A bar means that *just one* of the elements separated by the bar must appear. Above, either x or y or z must appear, not more than one.

➡ `x ¦¦ y ¦¦ z`

A double bar means that *at least one* of the elements must appear, either x or y or z or any combination of them, and in any order.

➡ [x ¦ y] z

Brackets are for grouping, so you know what's decided by the Web browser before anything else. Bracketed items are most important. The above syntax must have either x or y, and it must have z. Without the brackets, the meaning would be different (either x or both y and z).

For judging what gets the most priority: juxtaposition (x y z) is more important than the double bar, which in turn is more important than the bar. So, a b ¦ c ¦¦ d e is the same thing as saying [a b] ¦ [c ¦¦ [d e]].

➡ x*

An asterisk means that the preceding type, word, or group is repeated zero or more times (zero meaning that the element in question is optional).

➡ x+

A plus sign means that the preceding type, word, or group is repeated one or more times.

➡ x?

A question mark means that the preceding type, word, or group is optional. It doesn't have to appear.

➡ {x,y}

A pair of numbers in curly braces means that the preceding type, word, or group is repeated at least x times and at most y times.

➡ /

The slash must always appear in the final style sheet rule exactly where and how it appears in the syntax.

You'll also see other keywords that must appear as-is, without brackets or quotation marks.

I promise: It's less confusing when you see the syntax for actual properties, followed by explanations and examples, in Chapters 4 through 9.

Every Web page and example of style sheets discussed in this book is online at the book's Web site, which is located at `http://www.hayden.com/internet/style/`. Drop by!

CHAPTER 1

Why Style Sheets?

You bought this book (I presume), so apparently you already know part of the answer to this question. But I think it's important to step back and explore all the potential benefits of this new Web language/technology, so we know how best to take advantage of it.

Style sheets is not a new idea. It has been around for quite some time in other venues. In word processing and desktop publishing, for example, applications use style sheets for improved efficiency. In Microsoft Word, you can create a specific style and then apply it to whatever elements of text you like. If you want a style called "Big Headline" that calls for 36-point bold type set in the Times font face, then you simply create a new style and call it "Big Headline." You label each line of text in your document with this "Big Headline" style, and instantly these lines take on all of those characteristics. And here's the cool part: If you decide later you would rather use Garamond instead of Times, you simply change the style itself, and instantly *all* of the instances of those headlines change to Garamond. You don't have to change each one individually.

Wouldn't that be great to do on the Web? Wouldn't it be amazing to be able to declare that all normal <P> text be 14-point Helvetica, instead of *constantly* having to specify that with the dreaded <FONT FACE> HTML tag? With style sheets, you can. And it's easy.

Note

Really, style sheets has existed on the Web all along. Each Web browser ships with its own style sheet that determines how it displays the various elements on a page. Netscape Navigator, for instance, uses a style sheet that defines the background as a light gray and the default text font as Times. Internet Explorer has a similar (though slightly different) built-in style sheet.

Cascading Style Sheets is basically a mechanism to (finally!) enable Web designers to override these default browser style sheets.

But before we get to the *how* of using style sheets, let's look at the *why*. Basically, style sheets is something to get excited about because of the following reasons:

➡ Style sheets enables you to separate the *structure* of the content on your page from the *form* or appearance of that content.

➡ Style sheets gives you never-before-possible control of exact page appearance, from precise layout to specific fonts and styles.

➡ Style sheets is bandwidth-friendly.

➡ Style sheets is the easiest way to change and maintain Web pages, especially if you deal with many pages.

➡ Style sheets is friendly to all browsers. (It may not always work correctly, but it doesn't crash any browsers or display as gibberish.)

Let's take them one at a time, and you'll see what I mean.

Separation of Form and Structure

HTML was originally conceived as a language that defined structure. The idea was that with HTML you could define the various parts of a document (such as headings, body text, emphasized text, and so on), but not the appearance of those parts. HTML simply said to the Web browser, "This is a level-one heading," and then let the browser figure out what font, size, color, and so forth to use when displaying that heading text on-screen.

And that's what browsers did. And they all went about it differently too. That's why the same level-one heading looked different depending on what browser you used. For designers and for companies wanting to create precise, branded Web sites, this was a disaster. How could you do careful, thoughtful design on the Web if the display of a Web page was more or less out of your control?

Then Netscape came along, and with its Web browser introduced new HTML tags that it invented out of thin air. But designers loved them because they finally enabled a little more control over page appearance. Now you could center text and align images. Finally you could create margins with complicated table tags, and even specify what fonts and text sizes to use through the <FONT> tag.

There were a couple of problems with this "solution." First, in the process of all of these new HTML tags being introduced by Netscape (and Microsoft), the original intent of HTML was getting lost. HTML didn't define just structure anymore. Form and function were intermingled. Thus, it became a lot harder to easily move content from print (or database) to the Web. And a lot harder to create content from scratch. You had to go in and manually insert all the new appearance tags within your content. (Well, you didn't have to. But then you ended up with bland-looking pages.)

The second problem was that coding Web pages was becoming ridiculously complicated. To create a simple margin, you had to use an array of table tags that were never intended to create margins. There were more creative workarounds and "cheats" to HTML every time you turned around. Web page code got longer and longer, and messier and messier. That adds up to more time creating pages and more time maintaining them.

Style sheets changes all that. Style sheets is based on the principle of separating form and structure. When you use style sheets, your content exists in a nice clean form, uncluttered by workaround HTML tags. Style is treated separately and applied to that content, as if from a distance. As we'll see, this makes page creation easier and faster, because there's less coding and less frustration. It also makes content conversion to the Web easier, because you can convert the content first and worry about styling it later.

Content and style are separate, so you can also easily change one or the other at any time. You don't like how the content looks across 100 pages? Change the style once, and the look changes (see Figures 1.1 through 1.3). Want to replace the content but keep the style? It's just as easy. Read on.

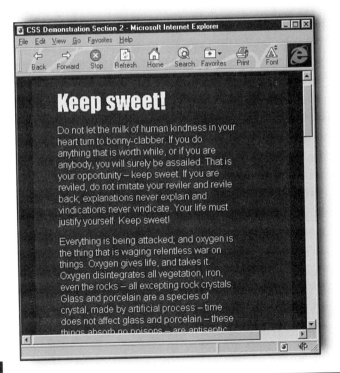

Figure 1.1

You can take the content of any page and change just the style.

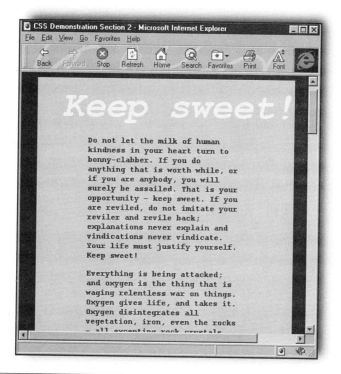

Figure 1.2

Same content, different style.

Improved Control over Page Layout

As far as immediate, visible evidence of the wonder of style sheets, this is the big benefit. With style sheets, you have more precise control than ever before over how your Web pages look. Here are just a few of the possibilities:

➡ Text set in the font of your choice.

➡ Specify the size of text in points, pixels, and many other units.

➡ Set specific top, bottom, left, and right margins on text or images.

➡ Add any color or background color to elements.

➡ Set a background image behind specific elements, and control where it's located and how or if it tiles.

➡ Control the leading (the space between the lines) of text.

➡ Easily align text left, center, right, or justified.

➡ Add text effects like small caps, indents, and strikethrough.

➡ Float text or images and wrap text around them.

➡ Precisely position images or text down to the exact pixel.

➡ Overlap text and images for cool layering effects.

You can do a few of these things already. But you have to resort to clunky HTML workarounds that take too much time to code. Or you have to use GIF files that make your page slower to download. But with style sheets, control of such things as margins is easy. And as you can see, you can also do a lot more that isn't possible in HTML now (see Figures 1.3 and 1.4).

Figure 1.3

Font, sizing, and margin control are at your fingertips.

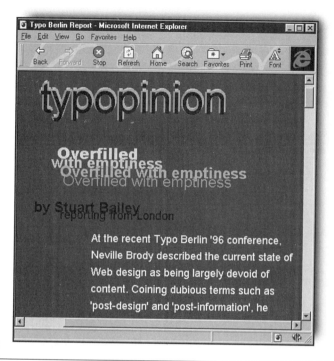

Figure 1.4

Special effects can mean a site that better expresses what you're all about.

Finally, we have some control over the layout of a Web page (not as much as we can control the layout of a printed page, but we're getting there). And this is just the beginning. Read on.

Bandwidth-Friendly

All of what I just listed is now possible, and the wondrous thing is that it's the most bandwidth-friendly approach to accomplishing these kinds of results. A style sheet is just ordinary ASCII text. It's just like HTML. Just write your code, save it as a common text file, and upload it like you upload an HTML page.

When visitors come to your styled page, all they download is text and code. Style sheets don't require huge GIFs, Shockwave, compiled Java applets that take forever to run, and so on. No plug-ins are necessary. All your styles download just as fast as the content you're styling (see Figure 1.5).

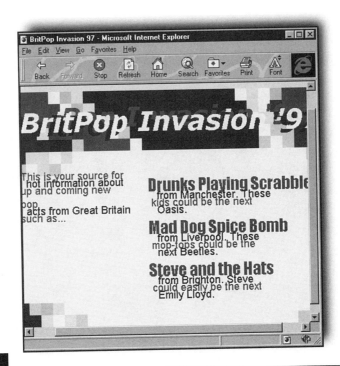

Figure 1.5

Looks like a lot of graphics, right? No, not one. The whole page is 9K.

Of course, this also means that you don't need any special application to create style sheets. All you need is a simple text editor. Creating style sheets is easy. Read on.

Easier to Change and Maintain

As we're all painfully aware, if you want to change something like a font or margin across multiple pages, you have to open every one and change it manually. This is the burdensome result of having form and structure intermingled instead of separated.

With style sheets, part of the magic is that one style sheet can be used for multiple pages. And if you set your font and margins in that one style sheet document, it can control the appearance of as many pages as you want. So if you want to make a change across hundreds of pages, just change the one style sheet document, and the effects of that change will immediately trickle down to each and every page (see Figure 1.6).

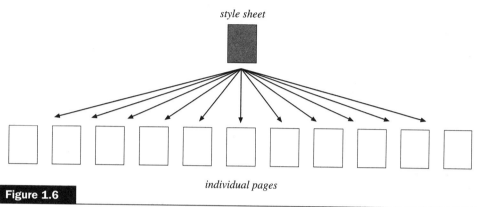

Figure 1.6

One style sheet can set the appearance of many Web pages.

Now you can see why it's so much more attractive to use style sheets for a big site: Instead of manually changing hundreds of documents, you can control everything with just *one* document.

To extend this benefit even further, you can use several different style sheet documents to affect your pages.

Let's say you want to create a Web page about a new product that comes from your department. You can't start from scratch, because your division already has some guidelines about what Web pages should look like, and so does your overall company. From now on, these guidelines can take the form of style sheet documents. Perhaps the company style sheet defines the fonts and colors to use. And maybe the division style sheet defines the margins and text sizes. Finally, you can create a department style sheet that specifies the placement of your department logo. Point to all of those style sheets from the new pages you create, and the browser will use them all to create a stunning final page (see Figure 1.7). And you save a tremendous amount of time, because you don't have to redo work that's already been done.

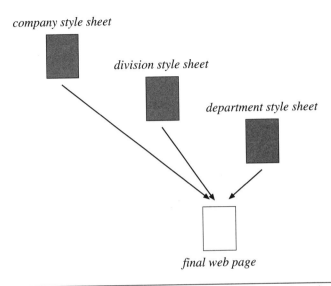

company style sheet

division style sheet

department style sheet

final web page

Figure 1.7

Multiple style sheets can set the appearance of a single Web page.

Not only that, but your bosses and their bosses no longer have to worry about maintaining a consistent look across the entire company Web site. The style sheets guarantee it. And everyone smiles confidently because the style sheets work well across browsers and platforms. Read on.

Scale Well Across All Browsers

If you use a Shockwave file on your site to create a cool effect, visitors without the Shockwave plug-in will get an ugly broken icon symbol. We know it all too well. If you use proprietary tags such as Netscape's <SPACER> to control layout, many browsers will not be able to follow those instructions. The result? Your page looks like a grenade hit it. It's ugly.

Style sheets scale and degrade well. That means that if you use style sheets effectively, your pages can look great even in older browsers that don't support style sheets. You won't get any broken icons or ugly messes. Your page won't look as great as it does in a better browser, but it will still look fine (see Figures 1.8 and 1.9). Just think: no need to create two sets of pages!

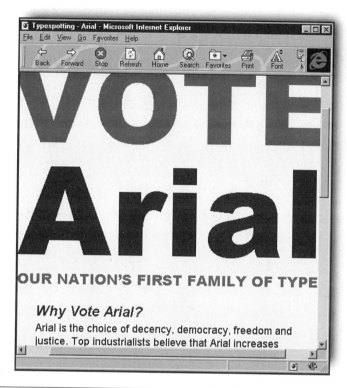

Figure 1.8

A beautiful, styled page.

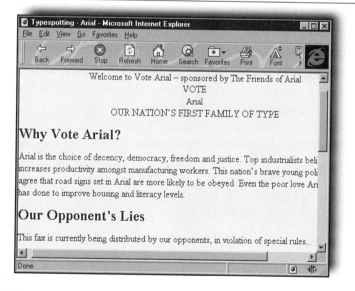

Figure 1.9

The same page with style sheets turned off. Not as beautiful, but definitely still readable.

A Little Background

Okay, so now we're all in agreement about how wise you were to buy this book and decide to learn style sheets. :·)

Style sheets is an evolving language, just like HTML, so it's appropriate that we keep track of where it came from so that we can also see where it's going and how to best use it and make long-term plans.

People figured out a long time ago that style sheets on the Web was a good idea. In particular, a group of people at the World Wide Web Consortium (W3C) got together and started talking about how Web style sheets could actually work. They developed a draft of style sheet properties and syntax, and created it so it would work well with existing HTML standards. This document became known as "Cascading Style Sheets, level 1."

Note

> The World Wide Web Consortium (`http://www.w3.org`) is a standards body that develops and recommends new languages and technologies for use on the Web. The people at W3C often work with companies such as Microsoft and Netscape to create and implement open standards that everyone can work from. At least that's the idea. The reality is sometimes more challenging, as companies race to establish their own "standards" before those proprietary solutions can be examined and endorsed by the W3C.

Throughout all of 1995 and 1996, work on this draft specification continued. New drafts were published on the organization's Web site, and public feedback enabled the group to refine the style sheet syntax even further.

Of course, no Web browser could *see* anything done in style sheets (well, except a little-used browser called Amaya that the group improved for the purpose of testing the style sheet properties). That all changed in the Fall of '96, when Internet Explorer

3.0 debuted. Microsoft's browser offered the first real (though somewhat buggy) style sheet support, and finally a lot of people started to see the exciting possibilities style sheets represented.

By December of 1996, the Cascading Style Sheets (CSS) specification was finalized and became an official Recommendation of the W3C. Stabilizing the specification was important so that the browser companies could support it more completely.

In the spring and summer of '97, with Version 4.0 of the two major browsers, Netscape Navigator and Microsoft Internet Explorer, support for style sheets is beginning to improve and stabilize.

Note

> Note the word "beginning." Unfortunately, both browsers have significant problems with their style sheet support. And I'll document those shortcomings along the way in the coming chapters. I just wanted to prepare you for some disappointment. But we're used to that already in the world of HTML, right?
>
> Version 5.0, we can all pray, will probably be better yet.

Other Varieties of Style Sheets

On the Web, of course, the entire universe gets turned upside down every week or so. There are more hot new technologies than there are Web sites. And therefore it's not a surprise that there are various kinds of style sheets (or something related) evolving, or at least being talked about. Let's look at a couple.

JavaScript-Accessible Style Sheets

With Navigator 4, Netscape introduced support for Cascading Style Sheets as well as for something it called JavaScript-Accessible Style Sheets (or Dynamic Style Sheets). JASS essentially offers the same capabilities as CSS, only it ties the CSS syntax in with JavaScript and thus makes style sheets scriptable.

Why would you use the JavaScript version of style sheets instead of the more standard version? For most Web sites, you wouldn't. You can have the same kind of layout control through CSS, and CSS is easier to implement. And while CSS is support by both Navigator *and* Internet Explorer, JASS is supported only by Navigator. Not good.

But where JASS could come in handy is if you want to make your styled page more dynamic. In essence, JASS enables you to animate and dynamically change existing style elements. Let's say you want layered images to move around or change color when the user rolls her mouse over a specific location. With CSS, you can't do this. With JASS, you can. JASS enables you to change styles and elements on-the-fly, *after* the page has loaded. Potentially very cool.

This book focuses exclusively on Cascading Style Sheets, however, because only it is supported in *both* of the major browsers.

> **Note**   If you really want to learn more about JavaScript-Accessible Style Sheets, visit the Netscape Web site. The documentation is there, ready and waiting.

Dynamic HTML

Dynamic HTML is a term introduced by both Netscape and Microsoft to describe new capabilities in their Version 4 browsers. Unfortunately, the companies are using it to describe different things.

For Netscape, Dynamic HTML is essentially CSS, JASS, and some new layering and positioning HTML tags that are proprietary and not supported by any other browser.

For Microsoft, Dynamic HTML is also CSS, but it's also a collection of new tags and scripting options that are proprietary to *its* browser. The same kinds of dynamic styles and pages are possible as I described for JASS, though through different code and syntax. The details are still emerging as of this writing.

The bottom line? All these new technologies and languages sound cool. Rather, they will be eventually. Right now, they can't do too much, and they don't work on both browsers. Cascading Style Sheets, however, is supported by *both* browsers. For me, that's reason enough to use it over anything similar.

The Future of Style Sheets

Where is style sheets going? With any luck, the dynamic nature of JASS and Dynamic HTML will become standardized and integrated with CSS, so we can all work from a single standard set of rules to create truly dynamic, interactive pages. That would be heavenly.

Of course, CSS itself will evolve to new standards. We'll have more and more control over exact positioning, layering, and formatting. We'll be able to easily create things like drop shadows and drop caps without resorting to GIFs. We'll be able to use fonts that users don't have installed on their systems.

We'll also see other creative uses of style sheets. For example, a specification called "Aural Cascading Style Sheets" is in the works that could make spoken Web pages much more comprehensible.

And soon, authoring tools such as FrontPage and NetObjects Fusion will undoubtedly support style sheets, so we won't have to code them by hand.

In other words, CSS is just the beginning. But for now, it's revolutionizing the way we create Web sites. So read on.

CHAPTER 2

The Basics

If you have used styles in Microsoft Word, PageMaker, or another similar application, you already have a good idea how style sheets work. A style sheet is a set of rules that tells the program how to display text, and to a certain extent, how to display images. For example, if you create a style in Word called "Heading" and define that style as 24-point Helvetica bold, then every line of text you set to be "Heading" style will automatically be 24-point Helvetica bold. Change the style definition later to 18-point, and every "Heading" line of text will change automatically.

Web style sheets work in much the same way, only in style sheets, the style names are HTML tags with which you are already familiar. You can easily define the <H1> tag on a page to be Helvetica, and all text within <H1> tags on your page will be in that font. Here is what the main code looks like:

```
H1 { font-family: helvetica }
```

This example is a basic style sheet consisting of one rule. Put this line into your HTML document properly, and all text within <H1>s will suddenly be displayed in Helvetica, (assuming your computer has Helvetica installed, of course), as you can see in Figure 2.1.

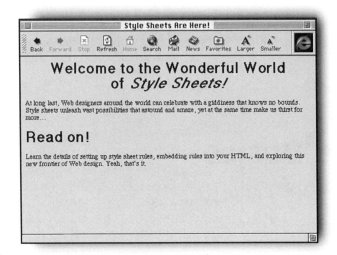

Figure 2.1

A page with headings defined by style sheets.

> Remember that all of the examples throughout the book can be viewed on the Web via the *Web Designer's Guide to Style Sheets* home page: `http://www.hayden.com/internet/style/`.

The rest of this chapter provides the essential bits of information you need so you can start to create your own style sheets and add them to Web pages.

Setting Up Rules

A style sheet rule, like the one we just illustrated, consists of two parts: the selector and the declaration.

The *selector* is the "name" of the style, if we think of it in terms that Word users will understand. It is what links the style to the HTML document. Let's return to the simple example:

```
H1 { font-family: helvetica }
```

In this rule, `H1` is the selector.

The *declaration* defines what the style is, and consists of two parts: property and value. In the example, `font-family` is the property, and `helvetica` is its value.

Other rules can be set up similarly, with each rule using everyday HTML tags as selectors. With these kinds of rules, you can easily make all `<CODE>` text bold, all `<LI>` text with a 100-pixel margin, and all normal text green (by using `P` as a selector). One thing to remember is that `<P>` is officially a double tag: `<P>` and `</P>`.

Note

To avoid confusion, use `</P>` as much as possible. Many people (including me) often don't bother closing the `<P>` tag because it's not required by most browsers. With style sheets, things can go awry if you don't close the `<P>`. For example, Internet Explorer 3.0 *nests* block-level elements such as `<H1>` and `<P>`. If you don't close with `</P>` before starting a `<H1>`, then the `<H1>` text will be considered *part* of the preceding paragraph. This can mess up styles you want to establish.

Tip

Avoid setting up rules on implied tags. For example, if you define a rule for `<BODY>`, make sure you actually use the `<BODY>` tag in your HTML.

Using `<SPAN>` as a Selector

New to HTML 3.2, the `<SPAN>` tag can come in handy if you want to apply a style to certain text, but not affect its structural role (like `<H2>` or `<LI>` would) or its default appearance (like `<I>` or `<B>` would). Putting text within `<SPAN>` has no effect unless style sheet rules are used.

```
SPAN { font-family: helvetica }
```

Using the above style rule, a Web browser would display any text within `<SPAN></SPAN>` in Helvetica, regardless of where it occurs. You can use `<SPAN>` anywhere that you'd be able to use `<EM>` or `<I>`.

Grouping

You can set up rules that have more than one selector or declaration. Selectors and declarations can be grouped to work together.

Here is a more interesting example:

```
H1                { font-family: helvetica;
                    font-weight: bold;
                    font-size: 24pt;
                    color: blue }
BLOCKQUOTE, EM, I { color: red }
```

Here we have a style sheet consisting of two rules. The first tells the browser that all text within <H1> should be displayed in 24-point, blue Helvetica bold. Note that you have to separate multiple declarations with a semicolon.

Note

> As with HTML, it doesn't matter how you break your lines (or even add spaces, for the most part). The browser will parse this code as it does HTML and ignore extra spaces. But as with HTML, code that's easier to read is also easier to revise later. That's why you'll see my code "lined up" as it is.

The second rule defines three different selectors. Any text in the Web page that occurs within <BLOCKQUOTE>, <EM>, or <I> will appear red. Note that multiple selectors must be separated by a comma.

You can also group selectors and declarations at the same time. Here's an example:

```
H1, H2, BLOCKQUOTE { font-family: helvetica;
                     font-weight: bold;
                     font-size: 24pt;
                     color: blue }
```

So now you've seen examples of the basic syntax of style sheet rules. In addition, there are some properties that have their own unique grouping syntax. Here's an example:

```
H1 { font: 24pt/26pt helvetica }
```

This is a shorthand way of setting the `font-size`, `line-height` (leading), and `font-family` properties all at once. Keep your eyes open in Chapters 4 through 9 for properties that have this kind of shorthand.

Maybe you have already asked this question: What happens if two rules conflict? What if we have a blue-defined `<I>` tag within a red-defined `<H1>` tag? The text can't be both blue and red!

True. That's where the "cascading" aspect of style sheets comes in. We'll look at that in more detail in Chapter 3.

Inheritance

The best way to understand inheritance is through an example. Suppose you set up the following style sheet in your HTML document:

```
H1 { color: green }
```

All the text within a level-one heading will appear in green. But then suppose you want to put a phrase in italics via HTML:

```
<H1>
Style sheets are here, so Web designers better <I>get with it!</I>
</H1>
```

`<I>` hasn't been defined by a style sheet rule, so how will it display? Well, in this example `<I>` occurs within `<H1></H1>`, so it *inherits* the declarations that `<H1>` (its "parent") has. So the phrase "get with it!" would appear in italics and in green (see Figure 2.2).

Figure 2.2

<I> *inherits the green color from* <H1>, *so the whole line appears green.*

Inheritance starts at the top–level elements in HTML, so the <HTML> tag has the ultimate say, followed by the <BODY> tag. After those tags come the heading tags (<H1>, <H2>, and so on) and other block–level tags (tags that create their own line breaks, such as <BLOCKQUOTE> and <TABLE>), followed by the "flow" tags such as <B> and <I>.

Note

You can even set up a style sheet rule using BODY as the selector. The following code would make *all* text on the page 14-point Helvetica bold, from <P> text to <H1> text:

```
BODY { font-family: helvetica;
       font-weight: bold;
       font-size: 14pt }
```

As an upper-level tag, <BODY> has more "authority" than tags like <P>, so normal text would inherit <BODY>'s declarations. In effect, setting up a rule for BODY creates "default" style properties for that Web page (see Figure 2.3) because <BODY> is the "ultimate" block-level tag.

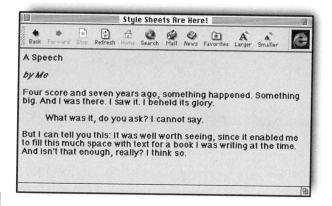

Figure 2.3

In one fell swoop, BODY can define the style of the whole page. Here, all text looks the same, even though several tags are used.

Note

If you set up a rule for BODY, make sure the <BODY> tag actually appears in your HTML! Otherwise the style sheet won't work.

To sum up, if "children" have no rules to follow, then any "parent" can at any time tell them what to do. Just like life. Well...

There are some style properties that are not inherited from parent to child. For example, it makes sense that the background property does not inherit, because once you've set the overall background, there's no need to do so over and over.

Inheritance can also occur when the value of one property is dependent on that of another property. Consider this example:

```
H1 { font-size: 20pt }
H1 { line-height: 150% }
```

Here, leading (line-height) for H1 is defined as 150% of the font size, or 30 point. In Chapters 4 through 9 you'll see which properties allow percentage values, as well as exactly what property each percentage value refers to as its reference.

> **Note**
>
> A technical detail: In this example, "children" of H1 (like an <I> within the <H1>) will inherit the computed value of the line-height (30 point), not the percentage.

Problem Tags

Unfortunately, the current browsers don't support style sheets completely, as you'll be discovering again and again throughout this book. Theoretically, you should be able to use *any* HTML tag as a selector in a style sheet rule. But alas, there are some tags that don't currently accept styles in Netscape Navigator and/or Internet Explorer.

Here are commonly used tags that have problems:

➡ <HR>: Horizontal rules can be styled in Explorer, but not in Navigator.

➡ <A>: Navigator treats styles on the anchor tag inconsistently. Sometimes Navigator will act correctly the first time the page displays, but then "forget" the style if you come back to or reload that page.

➡ Table tags style fine in Explorer, but behave strangely in Navigator. In Navigator, when <TABLE> is styled, <TH>, <TR>, and <TD> inherit just some of those styles (for example, background works, but not font-family). But if you try to style <TH>, <TR>, and <TD> individually, and not style <TABLE>, then Navigator actually crashes (on both platforms)! In other words, when mixing styles and tables, test everything carefully.

➡ In Explorer 3, some styles work (for example, font-family) for <MARQUEE>, but some don't (for example, color, background). Explorer 4 corrects this bug.

➡ Forms can be styled somewhat through the <FORM> tag, but none of <FORM>'s children (such as <INPUT>, <SELECT>, and

<TEXTAREA>) can be fully styled (though Explorer for Windows allows some styling).

Netscape
Navigator

> Navigator exhibits another disturbing inconsistency. Sometimes when you want to change the style of a phrase in the middle of a paragraph, Navigator will add *line returns* at the beginning and end of that phrase. This can destroy the intended appearance, of course. Test carefully whenever you attach style to flow tags such as <I>, <EM>, and so on.

Netscape
Navigator

> Keep in mind that Navigator 4 is in beta release as I write this, and that some of these bugs might be worked out by the product's final release. Check this book's Web site for updates (`http://www.hayden.com/internet/style/`).

Adding Styles to Web Pages

We've talked about setting up basic style rules. So how do you actually insert these rules into your HTML? Use one of the following methods:

➡ Embed a style sheet within your HTML document

➡ Link to an external style sheet from your HTML document

➡ Import one style sheet into another style sheet

➡ Add styles inline in your HTML document

Before I dive into each option, I want to point out that adding style sheet code to your HTML documents is as simple as it sounds. Style sheet rules are text-only and live right alongside your HTML tags. No extra application or compiling or mystical spells required. Just type 'em in.

Can you combine these methods for adding style to Web pages? For example, can you link to an external style sheet as well as add styles inline? Definitely, and with powerful results. See the next chapter for details.

Embedding a Style Sheet

If you want the most control over the appearance of a single Web page, this is the way to go.

To embed a style sheet with any number of rules, simply add a <STYLE></STYLE> pair of tags between the lead <HTML> and <BODY> tags of your HTML document. All the style sheet rules go within the <STYLE> tag. Here's an example:

```
<HTML>
 <STYLE TYPE="text/css">
 <!--
  BODY  { background: white;
          font-family: helvetica }
  H1    { font-weight: bold;
          font-size: 24pt;
          color: blue }
  H2    { font-weight: bold;
          font-size: 18pt;
          color: green }
  P, LI { font-size: 14pt }
  -->
 </STYLE>
<HEAD>
 <TITLE>Style Sheets Are Here!</TITLE>
</HEAD>
<BODY>
 <DIV ALIGN=center>
 <H1>Welcome to the Wonderful World<BR>of <I>Style Sheets!</I></H1>
 <DIV ALIGN=left>
 Making rules is easy, and embedding is easy:
 <OL>
  <LI>Create the rules.
  <LI>Stick them in a STYLE tag in your HTML.
  <LI>And experiment!
 </OL>
 <H2>How to Create the Rules</H2>
 First, buy this book...
```

```
</BODY>
</HTML>
```

Figure 2.4 shows what this looks like in the browser. You can see how each style rule carries through and changes the displayed text. Finally we're getting some serious control over what our Web pages look like!

Figure 2.4

A Web page with embedded style sheet.

You may have noticed the TYPE="text/css" attribute that appears in the <STYLE> tag. This specifies the MIME type so that browsers that do not support the "text/css" type can ignore style sheets altogether. If you're not familiar with MIME types, don't worry about it. Include TYPE="text/css" and you should be fine.

Tip

Hide style sheet tags from older browsers! Some browsers that don't support style sheets will treat your style rules as text and display the rules themselves. (These browsers will ignore the <STYLE> tags, but not the rules themselves, because they're not surrounded by brackets.) That can get ugly (see Figure 2.5).

continues

Figure 2.5

Unless you take precautions, some non-style-sheet browsers (such as Internet Explorer 2.0) will display the rules themselves.

To avoid this problem, put your style definitions within comments as shown in the previous code, beginning with `<!--` and ending with `-->`. Browsers that support style sheets will pay attention to the style rules, whereas older browsers will ignore this "commented out" code.

Linking to an External Style Sheet

Linking to an external style sheet is best if you want multiple pages to share the same basic styles and appearance. If you want to be able to change *one* style sheet document and have it automatically update *many* pages on your site, this is the way to go.

Essentially, you create a text document that consists only of your style sheet and nothing else. Save it with a .css filename extension, and then link to it from however many HTML documents you want, and the result will be multiple Web pages that all get their style from one style sheet.

Let's redo the earlier example with linking. First I create the following text file:

```
BODY  { background: white;
        font-family: helvetica }
H1    { font-weight: bold;
        font-size: 24pt;
        color: blue }
H2    { font-weight: bold;
        font-size: 18pt;
        color: green }
P, LI { font-size: 14pt }
```

I save it as style1.css (or whatever) and upload it to my server like I would any HTML file.

Now I create a standard HTML file, making sure to insert one additional line within the <HEAD> tag:

```
<HTML>
<HEAD>
 <TITLE>Style Sheets Are Here!</TITLE>
 <LINK REL=stylesheet HREF="style1.css" TYPE="text/css">
</HEAD>
<BODY>
 <DIV ALIGN=center>
 <H1>Welcome to the Wonderful World<BR>of <I>Style Sheets!</I></H1>
 <DIV ALIGN=left>
 Making rules is easy, and linking is easy:
 <OL>
  <LI>Create the rules.
  <LI>Save them in a separate text document.
  <LI>Link to the style sheet document from your HTML document.
  <LI>And give many pages style all at once!
 </OL>
 <H2>How to Create the Rules</H2>
 First, buy this book...
</BODY>
</HTML>
```

The <LINK> tag calls up the separate style sheet file and uses its contents as instructions for displaying the page (see Figure 2.6). Note that you can link to a style sheet file using a relative path (such as HREF="../styles/style1.css") or a complete URL (HREF="http://www.mulder.com/style1.css").

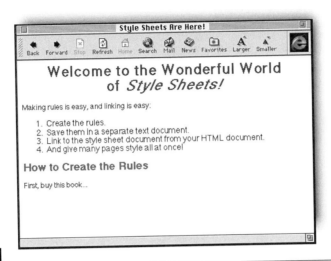

The final Web page, with linked style sheet controlling the appearance of text.

Notice that you don't have to comment out the style sheet link in this situation (see the previous Tip), because non-style-sheet browsers will simply ignore the <LINK> tag when they come across it and don't understand it.

Netscape
Navigator

It's important that you use TYPE="text/css" with your <LINK> tag, because otherwise Navigator might give you an error.

Now you have a style sheet ready to use for any Web page.

As you might have guessed, there is a slight performance penalty for using linked style sheets. After all, now visitors must load two different documents to view this one Web page. But on the other hand, if you're using this linked style sheet over multiple pages, the penalty diminishes, because like any other document, the style sheet is cached the first time it's loaded.

Note that you can also link to more than one style sheet simultaneously. Just add another <LINK> line within <HEAD>.

Navigator 4 does not support links to multiple style sheets. If you link to more than one .css file from your HTML file, Navigator will use only the first one.

Explorer 3 on the Mac supports multiple linked style sheets, but the Windows 95 version does not. In the latter browser, only the last .css document linked to will be used.

In Explorer 4, this problem is fixed; multiple linked style sheets are supported.

The beauty of linking to a style sheet is that if you want to change something such as the font across your entire site later, all you have to do is change that *one* style sheet file and upload it again. Instantly, all your Web pages change, and you can sigh in gratitude and put your feet up for the rest of the day.

Importing an External Style Sheet

This method works similarly to the previous method, and is thus good for styling multiple Web pages simultaneously. The difference here is that style sheets that are *imported* are pulled in from within another style sheet, whereas style sheets that are *linked* must be pulled in from the HTML document itself. In other words, you can import a style sheet by referring to it within another style sheet (for example, I could import style3.css into style1.css, which in turn could be linked to my HTML file).

Importing is accomplished through @import, which appears in the .css file as follows:

```
BODY   { background: white;
         font-family: helvetica }
H1     { font-weight: bold;
         font-size: 24pt;
         color: blue }
P, LI { font-size: 14pt }
@import url(style4.css)
```

Of course, you still need to link to this "container" .css file from your HTML document, as described in the previous section. Theoretically, you can import multiple style sheets in this fashion, simply by adding other @import lines.

Internet explorer

Internet Explorer 3 or 4 does not support importing external style sheets.

Netscape
Navigator

Navigator 4 doesn't support importing external style sheets either. Maybe in the next version…

Imported style sheets can also be templates created by an outside source, not by you. That is, you can also link to outside style sheets. As style sheets catch on, we'll being seeing huge repositories of pre-made style sheets that Web designers can simply refer to in their own HTML to use easily. If you ever used the memo template that comes with Microsoft Word, you know what I'm talking about here. I can imagine a HotWired-style .css file that is made available for public use so that everyone can make Web sites that are hip, happenin', and only semi-legible. Already, Microsoft has made available a collection of ready-to-use style sheets that anyone can download (`http://www.microsoft.com/gallery/files/styles/`).

Note

The legalities of using someone else's style sheets without their knowledge are rather uncertain. All of us have copied HTML or other code from other pages. Is copying style sheets okay too? Be careful! When in doubt, ask.

Adding Styles Inline

This last method of adding styles to Web pages is for changing the appearance of a single tag or group of tags on one page, and not for changing the whole page. If you're going to be changing a style on multiple pages, don't use the inline method—use the linking method instead. Adding styles inline doesn't get you the full power of style sheets, since you have to restyle text one item at a time. But you might find uses for it, so let's dive in.

Style rules for inline styles look a bit different. For example, to make a level-one heading gray and give it a margin, you would use this HTML:

```
<HTML>
<HEAD>
 <TITLE>Style Sheets Are Here!</TITLE>
</HEAD>
<BODY>
<H1 STYLE="color: gray; margin-left: 0.7in; margin-right: 0.5in">
Add styles inline for local effects
</H1>
<H1>Or don't if you don't want to.</H1>
</BODY>
</HTML>
```

The STYLE *attribute* enables you to insert any legal declarations right next to the HTML tag they will affect. There's no code that you need to put above the <BODY> tag to make inline styles work. In Figure 2.7, you can see that the first line is styled, but the second line isn't, because the style applies just to the first <H1>.

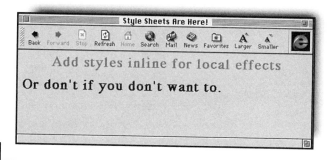

Figure 2.7

Inline styles applied with the STYLE *attribute.*

You can also use inline styles to change the appearance of an entire section of an HTML page. Use the <DIV> tag like so:

```
<HTML>
<HEAD>
 <TITLE>Style Sheets Are Here!</TITLE>
</HEAD>
<BODY>
<DIV STYLE="color: blue; margin-left: 0.7in; font-family: helvetica">
<H1>Add styles inline for local effects</H1>
<CODE>Or don't if you don't want to.</CODE>
<P>It's up to you.</P>
</DIV>
<P>Free at last from sylistic restraint!</P>
</BODY>
</HTML>
```

As you can see (in Figure 2.8), everything within the <DIV> section, no matter what the tag, is constrained to the font, margin, and color specified. After the end of the section (</DIV>), the browser reverts to its default display.

Figure 2.8

Use STYLE *within* <DIV> *to affect a section of a page.*

Inline styles can make HTML messy and make revisions more laborious. Use them carefully!

Classes and Other Options

Style sheets is an evolving specification, but its designers have already added features that make its use easier and more flexible. You can create classes (variations for a single HTML tag), IDs, selectors that act differently depending on their context, and other special effects involving links, drop caps, and more. Read on for the details.

Classes

Let's say you want your main body text to appear in three different fonts and colors on different parts of the page, for whatever reason. Instead of resorting to inline styles, which can make later revisions more difficult, you can create three different *classes* of <P>:

```
<STYLE TYPE="text/css">
 <!--
   P.cour  { color: blue;
            font-family: courier }
   P.chi   { color: red;
            font-family: chicago }
   P.arial { color: gray;
            font-family: arial }
 -->
</STYLE>
```

You can name the classes anything you want. From then on, when you want to use the various styles on the page, you simply activate them within the HTML like this:

```
<P CLASS=cour>This line is styled in Courier, in a blue color.</P>
<P CLASS=chi>This line is styled in Chicago, in a red color.</P>
<P CLASS=arial>This line is styled in Arial, in a gray color.</P>
<P>And this line ain't styled at all.</P>
```

The CLASS attribute tells the browser which variant of <P> to use. Figure 2.9 shows these classes in action.

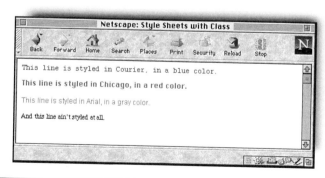

Figure 2.9

Three classes of <P> mean three different appearances of body text.

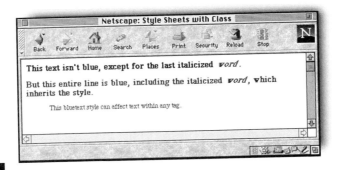

Netscape
Navigator

Navigator doesn't like it when you use numbers as class names (it ignores those classes entirely). Stick to letters.

You can also define a class a bit more generally and have it affect multiple tags. Take the following style sheet:

```
<STYLE TYPE="text/css">
 <!--
   .bluetext  { color: blue }
 -->
</STYLE>
```

By omitting the tag name (but keeping the period), you open up the possibility of making any text (within any tag) blue simply by using the CLASS attribute with that tag. Scan the following code and check out Figure 2.10.

```
<H3>
This text isn't blue, except for the last italicized <I
CLASS=bluetext>word</I>.
</H3>
<H3 CLASS=bluetext>
But this entire line is blue, including the italicized <I>word</I>,
which inherits the style.
</H3>
<BLOCKQUOTE CLASS=bluetext>
This bluetext style can affect text within any tag.
</BLOCKQUOTE>
```

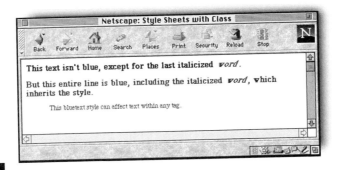

Figure 2.10

You can make classes more flexible by omitting the tag name.

A few final notes about classes:

➡ You can use the classes in any order or amount within the Web page after you've defined them.

➡ Each selector can have only one class. So you can't have a class called `H1.arial.bluetext`, for example.

➡ In the HTML, you can't use the `CLASS` attribute twice for the same tag. If your code looks something like `<H3 CLASS=bluetext CLASS=arial>`, then only one of those classes will actually be used. (Navigator uses the first class you define, whereas Explorer uses the last class defined.)

➡ The normal inheritance rules (see the section earlier in this chapter) will apply to classes. They inherit styles from their "parent" tags.

➡ Classes will work with embedded, linked, or imported style sheets.

IDs

`ID` is an attribute that HTML 3 introduced and can be used to hold a unique value for the length of a document. So you could use it as a style sheet selector, functioning like a class does.

For example, if you set up this rule within your `<STYLE>` tags...

```
#r174p { color: maroon }
```

...then you could refer to it later in the HTML (with the `ID` attribute) to make any bit of text maroon:

```
<H3 ID=r174p>Behold maroon text!</H3>
<P>And one more maroon word right <B ID=r174p>here</B>.</P>
```

By using `ID` as a selector, you can activate styles on individual text elements. This feels like a lot of work to me, but, if you've got a need for it, use it.

Contextual Selectors

The style sheets spec also enables you to set up selectors that are applied only in the context of other specific selectors. For example, the following rule…

```
BLOCKQUOTE I { color: green }
```

…will dictate that all italicized text within a blockquote will be green, but that other italicized text won't, and other blockquoted text won't either. The text goes green only if it is blockquoted *and* it is italicized within that blockquote.

Contextual selectors, as you can see above, are separated by a space in the rule, and there can be any number of them in a single rule.

This can get a little more complicated with some rules:

```
UL LI    { color: red }
UL UL LI { color: blue }
```

Okay, in this example, a list item is turned red only if it occurs in an unordered list (<UL>). But if that unordered list is also part of *another* unordered list (if there's a <UL> within a <UL>), then the list item is colored blue. This apparent conflict of rules is resolved because the second selector is more specific (see the next chapter on the cascading nature of style sheets).

Netscape
Navigator

> For some reason, Navigator can sometimes behave a bit differently from Explorer when parsing more than two contextual selectors, especially if you're using the same tags more than once. Test often!

Contextual selectors can work with traditional HTML tags, of course, but they can also work with classes, IDs, or any combination thereof:

```
P.textblue EM { color: blue }
#s771u H2    { color: red;
               font-family: garamond }
DIV P B      { margin-left: 0.5in }
.gar H1      { font-size: large;
               font-family: arial }
```

These rules can be translated in order as follows:

➡ All emphasized text within <P> tags (if <P> is of the textblue class) will be colored blue.

➡ All text within <H2> tags will be red and Garamond only if there is a tag (like a <DIV>) that is a parent of the <H2> that is attributed with an ID of s771u.

➡ Text will have a half-inch left margin only if it is bold text that is within a normal paragraph that is in turn within a <DIV> tag. If the <DIV> occurs *after* the <P>, then the text in bold *won't* be styled with a margin. The tags must appear in the exact parent-child order specified in the rule.

➡ Text will be in a large-size Arial if it occurs within an <H1> tag that has a parent with the class gar. So if <H1> occurs after a <DIV CLASS=gar> tag, for example, the text is affected.

Obviously this can get complicated. The best way to understand these machinations is to experiment with contextual selectors for yourself.

By the way, you can also group contextual selectors, just like normal selectors.

```
DIV P I { font-family: arial }
UL LI   { font-family: arial }
H2 EM   { font-family: arial }
```

The following rule is the equivalent of the preceding three:

```
DIV P I, UL LI, H2 EM { font-family: arial }
```

Link Effects

A common effect used on Web pages is to change the color of text links from the defaults (using the HTML `<BODY>` attributes `LINK`, `ALINK`, and `VLINK`). The creators of style sheets wisely expanded upon this feature in the style sheets spec, so now you can globally change link color, font, and other characteristics over many Web documents.

Essentially, style sheets have three predefined classes (the official spec calls them "pseudo-classes") for the `<A>` tag:

➡ `A:link`—for unvisited links (before clicking)

➡ `A:visited`—for visited links (after clicking)

➡ `A:active`—for active links (during clicking)

Explorer 3 doesn't support the `A:active` class. However, anything that you set for the `A:link` class will be inherited by both `A:active` and `A:visited`. So if you set links to red and don't specify a color for visited links, then both active links and visited links will also be red.

Explorer 4 does support `A:active`. With 4.0, clicking on a link will cause Explorer to immediately reformat the text of the link to what you have specified for `A:active`.

Strangely, Explorer 3 for Macintosh supports `A:visited`, but the Windows 95 version doesn't seem to, but instead simply inherits the characteristics of `A:link`.

This bug is corrected in Version 4.0.

Navigator 4 doesn't support link effects.

You can use these classes to set any font or text formatting options you like, including color, font-size, font-weight, and text-decoration (see details on all of these in later chapters).

```
<HTML>
 <STYLE TYPE="text/css">
 <!--
   A:link    { background: gray;
               font-size: 16pt;
               font-weight: bold;
               color: blue;
               font-family: arial }
   A:visited { background: blue;
               font-size: 14pt;
               font-weight: bold;
               color: green;
               font-family: times }
   A:active  { background: white;
               font-size: 16pt;
               font-weight: bold;
               color: gray;
               font-family: geneva }
 -->
 </STYLE>
<HEAD>
 <TITLE>Playing with Link Effects</TITLE>
</HEAD>
<BODY>
 Here's a line with a <A HREF="test1.html">normal link</A> in it.
 <P></P>
 Here's a line with a <A HREF="02wss04.html">visited link</A> in it.
 <P></P>
 Here's a line with an <A HREF="test3.html">active link</A> in it.
</BODY>
</HTML>
```

You don't have to use a CLASS attribute, because the browser will track what is unvisited, active, or visited, just like it's always done. Check out the results (see Figure 2.11) and you'll see that in Explorer 3, things don't work entirely like they should in theory. According to the rules, the font of the link in our example should change immediately from Arial to Geneva when you click on it.

But the style sheets spec recognizes that a browser can't necessarily reformat the entire page when you click on a link. (Version 4, however, does exactly this, and it's pretty cool.) But be careful not to go too crazy with the options at your disposal.

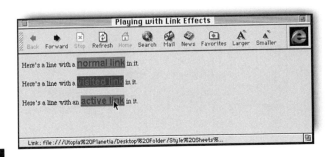

Figure 2.11

Adding effects to text links through the link classes.

Explorer 3 won't dynamically reformat the page when you specify link classes that should change immediately upon user action. And even normal visited links won't change entirely like they should; as you can see in the figure, the visited link text should be Times, but it's still Arial. But at least the colors changed as they should.

Explorer 4, as I mentioned already, *will* dynamically reformat the page to what you specify with the link classes.

Here's an effect that will make many Web designers happy: you can now remove the underlining from links! By setting `text-decoration` to `none` in a link class, you can finally get rid of that pesky, ugly line:

```
A:link { text-decoration: none }
```

Figure 2.12 shows what happens when we add `text-decoration: none` to each of the link classes in our previous example.

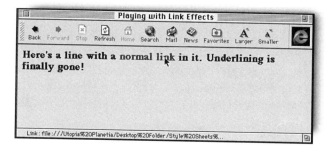

Figure 2.12

Free at last of ugly link underlining!

These link classes can also be used as contextual selectors, which means you can set the border color of linked images like so:

```
A:link     { color: red }
A:link IMG { border: blue }
```

These rules will tell the browser to display text links in red, but give a blue border to images used as links.

Also, you can use link classes in combination with normal classes. The rule might look like this:

```
A.class3:link { color: red }
```

The HTML would then look like this:

```
<A CLASS=class3 HREF="test.html">Here's a link displayed in red that
also gets the characteristics of class3</A>
```

When used as part of contextual selectors, link classes are allowed only in the last simple selector:

```
BLOCKQUOTE A:link { color: red }
```

In this scenario, only unvisited links within blockquotes would be colored red.

Drop Caps and Initial Letter Effects

Here's a typographical effect that you can't currently do with HTML, but now can do with style sheets: drop caps. Using the `first-letter` element, you can specify a larger initial letter around which other text can wrap.

Unfortunately, Explorer 3 and 4 don't support the `first-letter` element.

Navigator 4 does not support the `first-letter` element either.

The code for a drop cap looks like this:

```
<HTML>
 <STYLE TYPE="text/css">
 <!--
   P              { font-family: arial;
                    font-size: 14pt;
                    line-height: 16pt }
   P:first-letter { font-size: 200%;
                    float: left }
 -->
 </STYLE>
<HEAD>
 <TITLE>Playing with Drop Caps</TITLE>
</HEAD>
<BODY>
 <P>
Finally drop caps are possible using the life-savers we call style
sheets! What on earth did we ever do without them? This flexibility
they give us is simply amazing...
 </P>
</BODY>
</HTML>
```

The first letter specified within <P> will be used as the drop cap. In this example, I've specified 200% as the font size, so the drop cap will span about two normal text lines in height. Floating it left makes sure the text wraps around it to the right (see Chapter 7 for more on floating).

Unfortunately, the current style sheet spec allows little control over how large drop-capped characters actually align with the rest of the text. Watch for this element to evolve over time.

Of course, you can do more than just drop caps with first-letter. You can set it to simply display that first character as a different color, or a different font, or whatever. Experiment!

The first-letter element can be used only with a block–level element like <P>, <H1>, or <BODY>.

The browser decides if other characters that are not letters (such as quotation marks, parenthesis, and mathematical symbols) are or are not included as part of the initial letter.

Similarly to link classes, first-letter elements are allowed only as the last selector when used in contextual selectors:

```
BODY H1:first-letter { font-size: 200%;
                       color: green;
                       float: left }
```

Also similarly to link classes, you can combine first-letter with other classes:

```
P.class3:first-letter { color: purple }
```

First Line Effects

Not only can you define effects for initial letters, you can also define the appearance of the entire first line, through the first-line element. Here's the code:

```
<HTML>
 <STYLE TYPE="text/css">
 <!--
  P            { font-family: arial;
                 font-size: 12pt }
  P:first-line { font-family: garamond;
                 font-size: 16pt }
 -->
 </STYLE>
<HEAD>
 <TITLE>Playing with First Lines</TITLE>
</HEAD>
<BODY>
 <P>
Magazines often use this effect to draw readers into a story, and now
we can too on the Web using style sheets. It even reformats if you
change the size of the browser window...
 </P>
</BODY>
</HTML>
```

Wherever the browser wraps the first line, that's where the special formatting instructions end. So, the result is different depending on the width of the browser window.

Unfortunately, Explorer 3 and 4 don't support the `first-line` element at all.

And, you guessed it, Navigator doesn't support it either. Maybe someday.

Just like link classes and `first-letter` elements, `first-line` elements are allowed only as the last selector when used in contextual selectors. They can also be combined with other classes.

Comments

Just a final note about comments. Just like in HTML or C, you can add comments to your style sheet code to explain what things are for (and to help you remember what's what when you go in to make revisions). Comments can be used on any line:

```
H1:first-letter { font-size: 300%; /* first letter spans 3 lines */
                  color: green;
                  float: left }    /* wrap around right side */
```

CHAPTER 3

The Cascade

In the previous chapter, we covered all the basic parts of style sheet rules and how they appear within the HTML document. But the true power of style sheets is the act of *combining* various rules and entire style sheets. In Chapter 1 I talked about the example of using a company style sheet to establish every page's background color and fonts and a department style sheet to fine-tune text colors and margins used. And maybe even more specific than that is a personalized style sheet so that my personal home page pulls its look and feel from the company and department style sheets, yet also fine-tunes details such as link colors that I want to look unique for my page.

With all these style sheets and rules affecting a single page, conflicts are inevitable. Let's look at an incredibly messy example:

```
<HTML>
 <STYLE TYPE="text/css">
 <!--
  BODY { color: yellow;
         font-family: arial }
  H1   { color: red;
         font-family: geneva }
  CODE { color: maroon;
         font-family: courier }
  I    { color: purple;
         font-family: times }
 -->
 </STYLE>
<HEAD>
```

```
<TITLE>When Styles and Rules Collide</TITLE>
<LINK REL=stylesheet HREF="style1.css" TYPE="text/css">
</HEAD>
<BODY>
<H1>
<CODE>
<FONT FACE="palatino">
<I STYLE="color: green; font-family: impact">
What am I?
</I>
</FONT>
</CODE>
</H1>
</BODY>
</HTML>
```

The file style1.css, which is linked from this HTML file, looks like this:

```
I { color: blue;
    font-family: symbol }
```

What does the browser do in this situation? It's faced with no less than *seven* instructions for how to display the italicized text, and each one is different:

➡ The embedded style sheet tells the browser to display everything within the <BODY> (including the italicized text) as yellow Arial.

➡ It says to display everything within <H1> (including the italicized text) as red Geneva.

➡ It also says that everything within <CODE> (including our text) should be maroon Courier.

➡ It says that everything within <I> should be purple Times.

➡ This file also links to a style sheet that defines everything within <I> as blue Symbol font.

→ The HTML tag `<FONT FACE>` (not a style sheet rule at all) orders the browser to use Palatino.

→ Finally, an inline style sheet defines the text as green Impact.

Faced with such an internal conflict, the browser would crash, right? Or at least go schizophrenic? Thank goodness, it does neither.

When faced with conflicts, either between entire style sheets or between individual rules within a style sheet, the browser has to decide which rule is most important and follow it. It does this by following a *cascading order of rules*. Inherent in the style sheets spec and the browser support for the spec is a list of instructions that tells the browser exactly what rules to follow to decide which style sheet rule wins out in a conflict.

In our nightmarish example, the winner is green Impact (see Figure 3.1). The inline style is the most important here. The rest of this chapter covers all the rules of this elegant cascade, and discusses what happens when styles collide with styles, when rules collide with rules, and when rules collide with HTML.

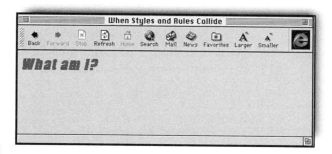

Figure 3.1

The inline style wins out in this case of rule conflict.

When Style Sheets Collide

Let's take a quick look at how many style sheets there could actually be affecting one Web page:

➡ Default browser style sheet: All browsers already have their own default settings for displaying a page. Netscape Navigator, for example, displays gray backgrounds and blue links by default. That's the default style sheet of that browser.

➡ Reader style sheet: Theoretically, users should be able to specify their own style sheets for how they want to view pages, regardless of what the page's author might have specified. Users could in fact already do this (at least a little bit) before style sheets, by going into the browser preferences and changing the font used, for example. In doing so, they would be overriding the browser's default style sheet.

Note

Internet Explorer and Netscape Navigator don't support reader style sheets at this time.

➡ Imported style sheet: These external style sheets are imported by the author from within another style sheet document (see Chapter 2 for more details on this type of style sheet and the next three).

➡ Linked style sheet: These external style sheet files are linked to from within the HTML document.

➡ Embedded style sheet: These rules are embedded within the HTML document using the <STYLE> tag.

➡ Inline style sheet: These rules are applied individually to the HTML elements via the STYLE attribute.

The ideal browser (Explorer comes closer than Navigator for this) treats these style sheets in reverse order of importance. Here is the order of precedence:

1. Inline

2. Embedded

3. Linked

4. Imported

5. Reader

6. Browser default

In an ideal world, inline styles will always be more important embedded styles, which will take precedence over linked styles, and so on. Now you can see why we got the result in our first example. Inline styles always win out. (Well, not always. Read on.)

Navigator 4.0 treats linked styles as more important than embedded styles. We can only pray that Netscape fixes this soon, because it could play havoc with Web pages that use multiple style sheets.

Explorer for Mac rates things correctly, but the Windows 95 versions (3.0 and 4.0) act like Navigator and give more importance to linked styles than to embedded styles. Bizarre.

The bottom line: For now, there's one best strategy if you want to be safe in both browsers. *Use all embedded styles or all linked styles, but don't mix and match.* Because Navigator and Explorer for Windows 95 reverse what should be more important, results will be wacko if you don't follow this advice. Yes, this means that to support both browsers and both platforms, you have to sacrifice the most powerful part of style sheets: combining them. But I guess for now we're at the mercy of the browsers. As always. Sigh…

Adding Importance

There's one thing you can do to override these rules. Using the important element, you can add weight to a declaration so that it becomes more important than any other declaration that's not labeled important.

Take this example:

```
<HTML>
 <STYLE TYPE="text/css">
 <!--
  BODY { color: yellow;
         font-family: impact }
  P    { color: red ! important;
         font-family: arial ! important }
  CODE { color: maroon;
         font-family: courier }
  -->
 </STYLE>
<HEAD>
 <TITLE>When Styles and Rules Collide</TITLE>
</HEAD>
<BODY>
 <P>
 <CODE>
 <I STYLE="color: green; font-family: times">
 What am I?
 </I>
 </CODE>
 </P>
</BODY>
</HTML>
```

Note that ! important must follow each and every declaration that you want to give importance. The ideal browser displays "What am I?" in red Arial. By the strict cascading rules, the inline <I> style and the embedded <CODE> style are more important. But the important elements upset the traditional order and make the <P> style most important.

Navigator does not support the important element yet.

Explorer 3 or 4 do not support the important element yet.

If multiple items are declared important, then the traditional cascading order takes effect. So if the <CODE> style was also labeled important in our example, then <CODE> would win out (because its rule appears after the rule for <I>—more on that evaluation later) and our text would be maroon Courier.

In the future, page visitors could use important to make their own reader style sheets more important than the Web page author's, and thus override the author's display preferences (which are normally more important in the cascade). Of course Web authors can do the same thing: If they use important for all of their rules, then there's no way readers can override them. So I guess we Web designers have the final say…

When Rules Collide

So now we know what happens when rules come from different style sheets. They're judged and ordered in importance depending on what type of style sheet they come from. But what about rules that conflict that originate from the *same* style sheet?

The style sheet specification is very clear about how to resolve rule conflicts. It specifies things that a browser should check when evaluating how to display text:

➡ Follow all specific declarations or, if none, inherited values.

➡ Sort the declarations by importance (the important element).

➡ Sort by specificity of selector. More specific selectors override more general ones.

➡ Sort by order specified in the code.

Let's look at each of these individually.

Follow Declarations or Inherited Values

This first rule is clear; we already talked about it in Chapter 2. If the selector exactly matches the element in question, then that selector should be used, even if the element has a parent element with a different style rule.

```
<HTML>
 <STYLE TYPE="text/css">
 <!--
  P { font-family: courier;
      color: green }
  I { font-family: arial;
      color: purple }
 -->
 </STYLE>
<HEAD>
 <TITLE>When Rules Collide</TITLE>
</HEAD>
<BODY>
 <P>What am I? Green Courier.</P>
 <P><I>What am I? Purple Arial.</I></P>
 <P>What am I? Green Courier.</P>
</BODY>
</HTML>
```

Here, the italicized text has its own style rule, so it follows that rule even though it has a parent <P> with a different rule (see Figure 3.2).

Figure 3.2

<I> *has a rule, so it is followed.*

However, if there is no declaration that matches exactly, then inheritance comes into play:

```
<HTML>
 <STYLE TYPE="text/css">
 <!--
  P { font-family: courier;
      color: green }
 -->
 </STYLE>
<HEAD>
 <TITLE>When Rules Collide</TITLE>
</HEAD>
<BODY>
 <P>What am I? Green Courier.</P>
 <P><I>What am I? Green Courier.</I></P>
 <P>What am I? Green Courier.</P>
</BODY>
</HTML>
```

Now there is no style rule for <I>, so everything within <I> inherits the style rule for <P>. After the <I>, the text continues to be green Courier, although now it's also in italics (see Figure 3.3).

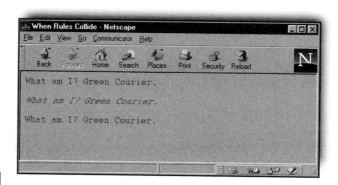

Figure 3.3

When there's no matching selector, inheritance rules.

Sort Declarations by Importance

We talked about this in the section called "Adding Importance" earlier in this chapter. If you declare a rule important, it takes on more weight.

```
<HTML>
 <STYLE TYPE="text/css">
 <!--
  P { font-family: courier ! important;
      color: green ! important }
  I { font-family: arial;
      color: purple }
 -->
 </STYLE>
<HEAD>
 <TITLE>When Rules Collide</TITLE>
</HEAD>
<BODY>
 <P>What am I? Green Courier.</P>
 <P><I>What am I? Green Courier.</I></P>
 <P>What am I? Green Courier.</P>
</BODY>
</HTML>
```

Normally in this situation the italicized text would be in purple Arial, but because I labeled the <P> style important, that rule takes precedence in the ideal browser. (I'd show you a figure, but because neither Navigator nor Explorer supports important at this time, I can't.)

Sort Declarations by Specificity

Now things start to get interesting. More *specific* selectors always override more *general* ones, when they are otherwise of equal weight. The style sheets spec defines *specificity* in a unique way. To find the specificity:

➡ Count the number of ID attributes in the selector

➡ Count the number of class attributes in the selector

➡ Count the number of tag names (if it's a contextual selector)

➡ Concatenate the three numbers (for example, the numbers 1, 4, and 7 would give you a final number of 147)

Pseudo-classes (such as A:link and A:active) and pseudo-elements (such as H1:first-letter and P:first-line) count as normal classes and elements, respectively.

Before you get too deeply into this, know that Navigator ignores specificity entirely.

So do Explorer 3 and 4, alas. Someday I hope the browsers will support specificity, but for now you might want to skip to the next section, unless you're curious to know more.

This is a bit complicated; examples help to make it clearer. The following table shows some example rules and the specificity of each.

Selector(s)	ID Attributes	Class Attributes	Tag Names	Specificity
P	0	0	1	**1**
P I	0	0	2	**2**
P CODE I	0	0	3	**3**
P.red	0	1	1	**11**
P CODE I.red	0	1	3	**13**
P.red first-letter	0	2	1	**21**
#r41t	1	0	0	**100**

Note

A rule with multiple selectors counts as multiple rules for the purposes of specificity. That is, the following rule...

```
H2 B, P.red { color: green;
              font-family: arial }
```

...counts as two rules for calculating specificity: H2 B translates to a value of 2, and P.red is worth 11.

Let's look at a real-world example:

```
<HTML>
 <STYLE TYPE="text/css">
 <!--
  H2 B { color: green;
         font-family: arial }
  I    { color: purple;
         font-family: times }
  -->
 </STYLE>
<HEAD>
 <TITLE>When Rules Collide</TITLE>
</HEAD>
<BODY>
 <H2>
 <B>
 <I>
 What am I? Green Arial.
 </I>
 </B>
 </H2>
</BODY>
</HTML>
```

Without the specificity rule, the browser wouldn't know what to do in this situation. <B> and <I> are both equal parents for the text that appears. Both rules appear as embedded styles, and neither is labeled important. They're equally weighted so far.

Except for specificity. The H2 B rule has two tags (giving it a specificity of 2), whereas I has only itself (specificity 1). For that reason alone, the former rule wins and the text appears in green Arial.

How about this one:

```
<HTML>
 <STYLE TYPE="text/css">
 <!--
  P:first-letter H1.red I   { color: red;
                              font-family: garamond }
  CODE B, BLOCKQUOTE, UL LI { color: yellow;
                              font-family: arial }
```

```
   BODY                        { color: blue;
                                font-size: 16pt }
  -->
  </STYLE>
 <HEAD>
  <TITLE>When Rules Collide</TITLE>
 </HEAD>
 <BODY>
  <P>
  <H1 CLASS=red>
  <CODE>
  <B>
  <I>
 What am I? Red Garamond, 16 point.
  </I>
  </B>
  </CODE>
  </H1>
  </P>
 </BODY>
 </HTML>
```

Again, the rules feel equal except for specificity. The first rule has a specificity of 23 (two classes, three tags). The second rule gets treated as three rules for the purposes of specificity: CODE B, the only relevant rule here, gets 2 points (two tags). The third rule gets 1 (one tag). So red Garamond wins out. But note that the text also inherits the font-size from the <BODY> rule, since no other rule specified a font-size.

Okay, one more:

```
<HTML>
 <STYLE TYPE="text/css">
 <!--
  H1.yel, CODE  { color: yellow;
                  font-family: garamond }
  B BLOCKQUOTE  { color: green;
                  font-family: arial }
  BODY          { color: blue }
  -->
 </STYLE>
<HEAD>
```

```
<TITLE>When Rules Collide</TITLE>
</HEAD>
<BODY>
<H1 CLASS=yellow>
<B>
<P>
What am I? Look carefully.
</P>
</B>
</H1>
</BODY>
</HTML>
```

Trick question! At first glance it looks like it should be yellow
Garamond, since the first rule is more specific. But look carefully
at the HTML. The `<H1>` has a `CLASS=yellow` attribute, but that
doesn't match the class listed in the first rule (`yel`). So the first rule
doesn't even apply to the text at all. The only rules that do are the
second and third. So it must be the second rule, right? Because it's
more specific than the third. Wrong! The second rule contains a
contextual selector; the rule is applied only if text appears within
blockquotes that in turn appear within `<B>`. But there are no
blockquotes in the HTML. And so that leaves rule number three
as the winner. The text displays in blue in the default browser
font.

Sort Declarations by Order

If the rules are still weighted equally after trying all the other tests,
then the browser sorts them using the order they appear in the
HTML document. Of two equal rules, the *latter* rule has more
weight than the rule coming before it.

```
<HTML>
 <STYLE TYPE="text/css">
 <!--
  B { color: green;
      font-family: arial }
  I { color: purple;
      font-family: times }
  -->
```

```
 </STYLE>
<HEAD>
 <TITLE>When Rules Collide</TITLE>
</HEAD>
<BODY>
 <H1>
 <I>
 <B>
 <CODE>
 What am I? Depends on if you want theory or reality.
 </CODE>
 </B>
 </I>
 </H1>
</BODY>
</HTML>
```

In this example, everything's equal, including specificity, between these two rules. So the ideal browser goes with the latter of the two rules declared: The text should appear in purple Times.

Okay, now for *reality*. In real life, both Navigator and Explorer go by the order of the *tags*, not the order of the *rules*. That means that in this example, even though the I rule comes last and should take precedence, it's the <B> that appears closer to the actual text in the HTML itself. So in the browsers, the text appears as green Arial (see Figure 3.4). Go figure!

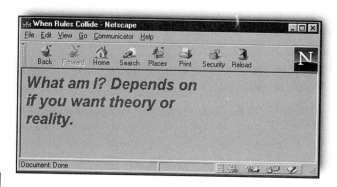

Figure 3.4

The last styled tag before the text is <B>, so <B>'s style wins.

Here's the thing to remember: In Navigator and Explorer, if everything is equally weighted, display is decided by the styled HTML tag that most closely precedes the text being displayed.

A Loophole: ID

If you remember, inline styles get more weight than embedded styles. If there were an inline style in the previous example, I wouldn't have to compare specificities and orders, because the inline style would rule over everything.

Well, almost. A rule with an ID in its selector is worth 100 specificity points, according to the rules listed earlier. That in fact is enough to make it equal in weight to any rule declared inline in a STYLE attribute.

```
<HTML>
 <STYLE TYPE="text/css">
 <!--
  B      { color: green;
           font-family: arial }

  #r554g { color: blue;
           font-family: impact }
 -->
 </STYLE>
<HEAD>
 <TITLE>When Rules Collide</TITLE>
</HEAD>
<BODY>
 <I>
 <B>
 <P ID=r554g STYLE="color: red; font-family: times">
 What am I? Red Times.
 </P>
 </B>
 </I>
</BODY>
</HTML>
```

So, the rules for blue Impact and red Times have equal specificity in this situation. But red Garamond wins out, because the inline rule is declared after the ID-based rule in the HTML. But there might be situations in which you'd want to use the capability of the ID to override an inline style.

When Styles Collide with HTML Tags

Okay, we've seen what happens when style sheets collide and when rules collide with each other. But what about when styles run into HTML tags that also try to influence style? How do browsers rank tags and attributes like ALIGN, <FONT FACE>, and <BIG>?

Essentially, the ideal browser "translates" the tag to a corresponding style sheets rule and gives it a specificity of 1. It then places that imaginary rule at the start of the author style sheet, where of course it can be overridden by other style rules. So in effect, it makes HTML style tags inferior to bona fide style sheet tags.

Ready for an example? I thought so.

```
<HTML>
 <STYLE TYPE="text/css">
 <!--
  H1 { font-family: arial }
 -->
 </STYLE>
<HEAD>
 <TITLE>When Styles and HTML Collide</TITLE>
</HEAD>
<BODY>
 <H1>
 <FONT FACE="courier">
 What am I? Arial.
 </FONT>
 </H1>
 </BODY>
</HTML>
```

In this scenario, the ideal browser sees the <FONT FACE> tag and turns it into an imaginary rule at the top of the style sheet. For all intents and purposes, the style sheet now looks like this:

```
H1 { font-family: courier }
H1 { font-family: arial }
```

These two rules are of equal weight in all regards, including specificity (these imaginary rules always get a specificity of 1), so that means they are sorted by order. The latter rule wins, and the text is displayed in Arial (see Figure 3.5).

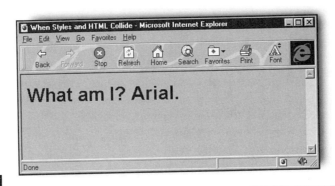

Figure 3.5

HTML style tags get no respect when put up against bona fide style sheets.

Navigator, however, has a mind of its own. It treats HTML tags as more important than style sheets, so in displaying the same example, Navigator would go with Courier.

Internet Explorer 3 correctly displays Arial, because style sheets take precedence over HTML.

But Explorer 4 does the opposite: HTML tags take precedence over style, and thus Courier is displayed. Argh!

Welcome to the Real World

We've seen how individual styles, rules, and tags fight it out over which is more important. The best way to see this all come together is through your own experimentation. But for quick reference, here's a final list of what the browsers support right now, and what order they use for giving style sheet rules importance:

Rank of Importance	IE3 (Mac)	IE3 (Win 95)	IE4 (Win 95)	NN4 (Mac & Win 95)
1	Embedded styles with IDs	Embedded styles with IDs	HTML styles	HTML styles
2	Inline styles	Inline styles	Embedded styles with IDs	Inline Styles
3	Embedded styles	Linked styles	Inline styles	Linked Styles
4	Linked styles	Embedded styles	Linked styles	Embedded Styles
5	HTML styles	HTML styles	Embedded styles	

Will you end up frustrated with the browsers' implementation (or lack thereof) of all the rules? Oh yes. Just like we did (and still do) with the seemingly random and often proprietary ways HTML is implemented in browsers. But the hope is that just as with HTML, the core functionality of style sheets will become more and more reliable and consistent as browsers gain new version numbers. That's why I'm including information even about features that don't work yet, because I believe that soon they will.

Concentrate on the style sheet rules and options that work cross-platform now, and then pray for a brighter future, because if style sheets mature the way they should, the future should definitely be great.

Designing Styled Pages that Degrade Well

There's one other important topic to cover here: How do you get style sheets and HTML to work well together so that your styled pages look good even in non-style-sheet browsers? How do you create pages that degrade well, that look good in other, less-current browsers?

This is a familiar challenge. For decades (well, okay, months—but it certainly feels like decades) our greatest struggle has been to create one set of pages that looks spectacular in Navigator and yet still looks fine in clunky, older browsers like AOL's 2.7 browser and the original Mosaic.

With style sheets, this problem isn't quite as nasty, because as I've said before, if you comment out your style rules, older browsers ignore them. But the problem doesn't go away entirely. There are certain tricks you can use to make your styled pages look even better; let's look at each one.

Use Styles on Similar HTML Tags

Our first trick is easy: If you want to style an element italic, why not use the <I> tag to do it? Here's how it might play out:

```
I { font-size: 12px;
    text-align: center;
    font-style: italic;
    font-family: arial, sans-serif }
```

```
<I>If you wish to contact the author, you can do so through his
<A HREF="http://www.mcp.com/people/mulder">Web site</A> or via email
to <A HREF="mailto:smulder@iquest.net">smulder@iquest.net</A></I>
```

This code is directly from the home page for this book, which we'll use as an example page for this section (see Figure 3.6). As you can see, the very bottom bit of text is centered, in italics, and in the Arial font. All of this is taken care of with the style sheet rule above. But notice that because I use the <I> tag to set the style, the text is guaranteed to be in italics even in non-style-sheet browsers (see Figure 3.7). True, the text won't be centered and in Arial, but there are other ways of taking care of that (see the next section). This is an easy trick; use it when you can.

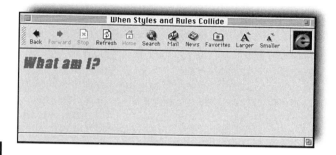

Figure 3.6

The home page for this book, located at `http://www.hayden.com/internet/style/`.

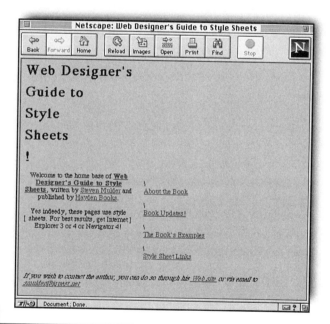

Figure 3.7

In Navigator 3, the page isn't gorgeous, but yes, the text at the bottom is in italics like we want it.

Double Up Styles with HTML Tags

Trick #2 is a natural extension of the first one. If you can't use identically functional HTML tags to set your styles, use other HTML tags to "back up" your intentions. So, if I want the text we looked at earlier to be centered and in Arial, I simply add the familiar HTML tags to make it so:

```
<CENTER><FONT FACE=arial>
<I>If you wish to contact the author, you can do so through his
<A HREF="http://www.mcp.com/people/mulder">Web site</A> or via email
to <A HREF="mailto:smulder@iquest.net">smulder@iquest.net</A></I>
</FONT></CENTER>
```

Nothing changes in the style sheet rules. As we saw earlier in this chapter, good browsers will give more importance to style sheet rules than to these HTML tags, so the styles will always win out in browsers that support them. But for non-style-sheet browsers, you're guaranteed a similar look and feel to what you want (see Figure 3.8).

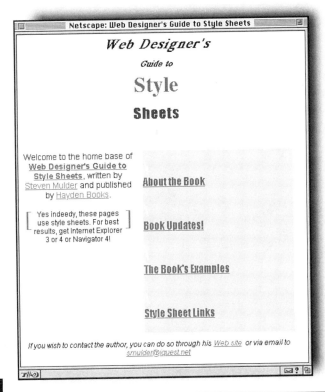

Figure 3.8

In Navigator 3 we can get things to look more like we want by using HTML tags such as <FONT> and <CENTER> to imitate what the style sheets are doing in newer browsers.

Similarly, you can back up your body background-image style with the <BODY BACKGROUND> tag, your A:link color style with the <BODY LINK> tag, your font-size style with the <FONT SIZE> tag, and so on. Double up!

N Netscape
Navigator

Unfortunately, there's a problem with this trick. Navigator 4 has a bug that makes this trick problematic. As we discussed earlier in the section "When Styles Collide with HTML Tags," browsers are *supposed* to treat styles as more important than HTML tags. However, Navigator 4 reverses this rule, and treats HTML tags as more important than style sheets. Because of this, a Web page that uses "backup" HTML tags like I talk about here will get messed up by Navigator 4, since Navigator 4 likes tags better than styles. Navigator 4 will end up displaying some of the tags and some of the styles, and the result will never be what you want (see Figure 3.9).

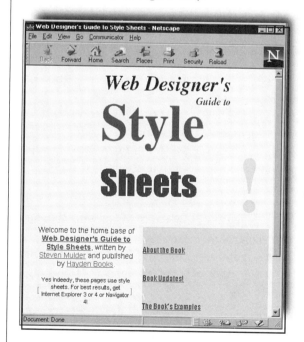

Figure 3.9

The same page as in Figure 3.8, only viewed in Navigator 4. The trick doesn't work because of a bug in Navigator, so the page doesn't look like it should with styles.

continues

In other words, if you want to use style sheets effectively *and* display in Navigator 4, this particular trick is useless for now. Maybe the next release…

Internet explorer

Explorer 4 has the same problem, and for the same reason: it treats HTML tags as more important than style sheets. But for Version 3 this trick works fine.

Make Unwanted Elements "Invisible"

The final trick might come in handy when the first two tricks just don't do quite enough. For example, in Figure 3.8, even though the page doesn't look bad, the brackets in the lower left just aren't working. I can't make them big enough using mere HTML tags (<FONT SIZE>), and they look awkward.

So I think I'll make them "invisible."

```
<P CLASS=brack><FONT SIZE=7 COLOR=white>[</FONT></P>
```

All I did was change gray to white, and now the bracket is the same color as the background, thus rendering it invisible. The page looks the same as ever in browsers that support style sheets, but a bit better in non–style-sheet browsers (see Figure 3.10).

Netscape **Navigator**

Guess what? For the same reason I mentioned earlier, this trick won't work in Navigator 4 either. Even though the styles tell Navigator to display the brackets in gray, Navigator pays more attention to the HTML tags, thus undoing your hard style sheet work.

Internet explorer

Explorer 4 has the same problem. But Version 3 doesn't.

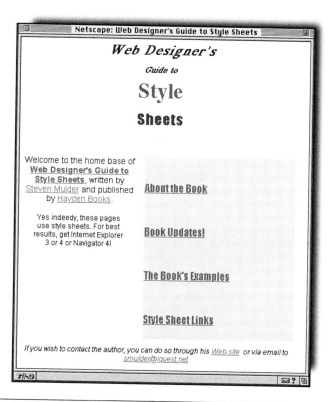

Figure 3.10

Match foreground color to background color, and the unwanted elements disappear!

As an extension of this trick, you could make an entire section of a page invisible, but then make something else visible instead for older browsers. To make something visible in older browsers but invisible in style-sheet-aware browsers, try the visibility property (see Chapter 8 for details).

Make Your Pages Degrade as Well as You Can

I can't shout this loud enough. When you start doing really far-out special effects with style sheets, it takes as much work to make those pages look good in older browsers as it does to create the styles in the first place. If you don't take the time to make sure your pages degrade properly, you'll end up alienating many visitors. Look at it this way: If your visitors don't have a browser plug-in that they need to view a movie on your site, at least they can still read the text on your page. But if you use style sheets poorly, visitors might be greeted by an unreadable, dumb-looking mess (see Figure 3.11). Not good.

Of course, there's only so much you can do. For example, in Figure 3.10, there's nothing more I can do to make the page look better in Navigator 3 (or another such non-style-sheet browser). I can't close up the vertical spacing between the right-hand links simply using HTML (without wrecking the style sheet effect, that is). After you've done all you can to make the page degrade well, take a deep breath of contentment. You done good.

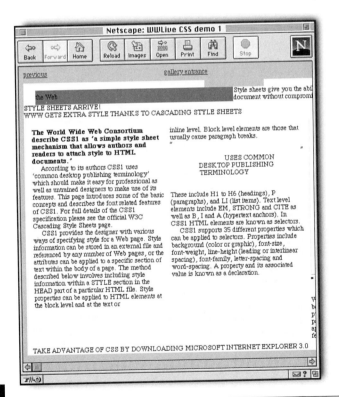

Figure 3.11

This page looks terrific in Navigator 4. Really! (See the third example in Chapter 10.) But in Navigator 3, it's totally worthless. No gentle degrading. Bad design.

In the case of this book's home page, I'm willing to live with the page as I've improved it. That's largely because I know who my site's visitors will be: readers of this book, and thus people who are interested in style sheets and thus most certainly using a style-sheet-capable browser. Aren't you?

As always, design for your audience, and you can't go wrong.

CHAPTER 4

Fonts

Once upon a time, Web designers had absolutely no control over what fonts were used to display their Web pages. Well, that's not quite true: We could always control which text appeared in a monospaced font (via HTML tags such as `<CODE>`) and which in a "normal" font. But we could never define exactly which monospaced or normal fonts those were.

Fortunately, the four major browsers (I call them four because each of them acts independently: Netscape Navigator for Windows, Netscape Navigator for Macintosh, Internet Explorer for Windows, and Internet Explorer for Macintosh) come with a normal font and a monospaced font already defined. On the Mac, Navigator uses 12-point Times and 10-point Courier, respectively, and Explorer uses Times and Monaco. On Windows 95, both Navigator and Explorer use 12-point Times New Roman and 10-point Courier New.

Note

> Something else to keep in mind: 12-point on a Mac does *not* equal 12-point on a Windows machine. Fonts on a PC monitor are generally larger than on a Mac monitor. You can see that in Figures 4.1 and 4.2, which show the same text and graphic on Mac versus Windows.
>
> *continues*

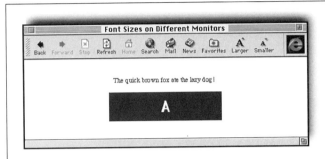

Figure 4.1

12-point Times next to a graphic on a Mac monitor.

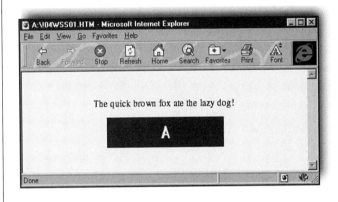

Figure 4.2

The same stuff on a PC monitor. The text is larger relative to the graphic.

But let's face it: even if these browsers used the same exact versions of the same two fonts, there's just not a lot you can do with only two fonts at your disposal. Things get boring pretty quickly. After all, it seems ridiculous that I have 30 or so fonts on my machine, and yet Web pages can contain only two.

The Cascading Style Sheets, level 1 specification is the first definitive step in changing all that. Style sheets enables Web authors to finally specify particular fonts by name, and at the same time define things we've long been waiting for, such as point size, italics style, small caps, and different weights of bold. It's about time.

But you might already be saying, "Wait, we already have this kind of control via the <FONT> tag. We can control font face, size, and so on." It's true that Netscape's proprietary tags have enabled some limited control over fonts, but that control is neither flexible enough nor open enough. <FONT SIZE>, for example, enables you to specify text size from a value of 1 through 7. But with style sheets, you can specify absolutely *any* size you want—either smaller or larger than is possible through traditional HTML. Also, you can adjust size using a variety of units (such as points, pixels, and ems) that weren't possible to use before. Netscape might have introduced some font control through HTML tags, but style sheets gives you more complete control that ever before possible.

A Painful Detour: Calling Fonts by Name

If you've worked in desktop publishing or design, you know that the world of fonts is a messy world. For one thing, there's more than one type of font format, though PostScript Type 1 fonts and TrueType fonts now dominate. But what's even more problematic is that the actual names of fonts (and their associated variants, such as Bold, Oblique, Heavy, and so on) are not at all consistent, especially as you cross platforms between Mac and Windows. There's simply no universally accepted taxonomy for naming fonts and their variations and classifying them in a coherent way. It's a mess.

Note

For a refresher on the elements of fonts and typography, the artistry of using type, and the technology of applying them across platforms, I recommend Sean Cavanaugh's *Digital Type Design Guide* (Hayden Books).

Obviously this inconsistent naming creates some problems with specifying fonts in Web pages. Courier on the Mac, for example, is called Courier New on Windows machines. So if I build a page on my Mac and specify the main body text in Courier, will Windows users see it in Courier New, or will the browser not know what "Courier" is and thus use its default font, Times New Roman? What if a font has an "italic" variant on my machine, but on other machines it's called "oblique" or "slanted" or "cursive"? Is a font such as Garamond Bold the same or different from normal Garamond with bold applied? Argh! These are the kinds of questions that can drive one batty. And these kinds of issues make calling fonts by name no easy task.

The style sheets spec attacks all these issues head-on with its own rules for matching properties to font faces. This algorithm (created by the style sheets gurus at the World Wide Web Consortium) presents the process that a Web browser should follow when trying to interpret font instructions:

1. The Web browser creates a database that contains all the fonts and their relevant style sheet properties that the browser is aware of. These consist of fonts that came with the system, fonts installed from disk, and fonts downloaded from the Web. If the browser finds two fonts with exactly the same name, it ignores one of them.

2. When it comes across an element in an HTML document, the browser gathers all the possible font properties applicable to that element. It takes the font families one at a time and tests them against the declared style sheet rule, according to the matching criteria described with each property:

    a. The browser tries `font-style` first. (These properties will be fully dissected in upcoming sections.) `italic` will be confirmed only if there is a font in the Web browser's database that is labeled with the word "italic" (or, as a second choice, "oblique"). Otherwise the values must match exactly, or the `font-style` test will fail.

    b. Next, `font-variant` is tried. `normal` matches a font only if it is labeled with "normal." `small-caps` is approved in any one of three situations: 1) a small-caps font, 2) a synthesized small-caps font (reducing and widening the uppercase letters of a normal font, for example), or 3) the use of uppercase letters as replacements for lowercase letters.

c. Next comes `font-weight`. This match never fails; see the section "`font-weight`" later in this chapter.

d. However, `font-size` must be matched within a certain margin of tolerance as defined by the Web browser. It's typical for browsers to round scaleable fonts to the nearest whole pixel; the tolerance for bitmap fonts could be as high as 20%.

If the browser finds matches for all these properties for a given font family, then it decides that this one must be the correct font face for this element.

3. If the browser can't find a match for `font-family` in step 2, and if there is an alternative `font-family` listed in the style sheet, the browser repeats step 2 with this "second choice" font.

4. If there is a matching font face, but it lacks a glyph (character) for a particular character specified on the Web page, the browser repeats step 2 with any alternative `font-family` that's listed.

5. If the browser simply can't find a match among any of the alternatives, it uses its own default font to display the element.

Note

Okay, so that's what *should* happen in an ideal browser. To see what *actually* happens in Navigator and Explorer, watch for details throughout this chapter.

Reading rather complicated rules is one thing; looking at examples is quite another, and is my favorite way to see exactly how all this works.

Example 1

Let's say I have a Web page with a style sheet that I set to use the font Goudy Sans Bold. I set Arial as a second choice. Let's see the previously listed steps in action:

1. Internet Explorer creates a list of all the fonts installed on my Mac system. Goudy Sans (with Bold, Italic, and Bold Italic variants) is on the list.

2. In my style sheet I've used the font Goudy Sans Bold, and Explorer confirms that not only is Goudy Sans on my system, but so is Goudy Sans Bold.

3. There are no other style sheet font instructions to match, so Explorer displays my text in the font chosen (see Figure 4.3).

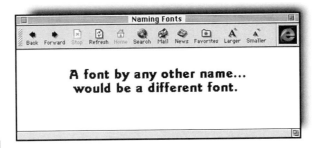

Figure 4.3

Internet Explorer (Mac) recognizes Goudy Sans Bold, which I have on my system.

Note   Remember that every Web page and example of style sheets discussed in this book is online at the book's Web site, which is located at `http://www.hayden.com/internet/style/`. You'll also find book updates there.

Example 2

If I simply take the same Web page onto my Windows 95 system, and try Navigator 4, I get different results:

1. Navigator creates a list of all the fonts installed on my Windows 95 system. Goudy Sans Bold is *not* on the list.

2. Navigator sees that my style sheet's first choice is Goudy Sans Bold. It can't find this font on my system; the match fails.

3. Navigator moves on to my second choice, Arial, and finds that this font is indeed on my system.

4. The font is displayed appropriately in the browser window (see Figure 4.4).

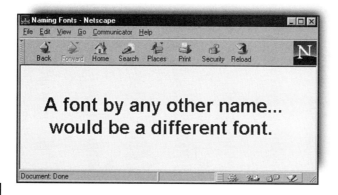

Figure 4.4

Navigator (Windows 95) can't find Goudy Sans Bold, so it uses my second choice, Arial.

Example 3

What if my style sheet lists a font face whose name is close to but not an exact match? For example, what if I want Impact Italic?

1. The browser creates a list of all the fonts installed on my system. Impact is on the list, but Impact Italic is *not*.

2. The browser sees that my style sheet's first choice is Impact Italic. It can't find this exact font name on my system; the match fails. And unfortunately, neither browser is "smart enough" yet to know it should instead use regular Impact.

3. Instead, the browser moves on to my second choice, Arial, and finds that this font is indeed on my system.

4. The font is displayed (see Figure 4.5).

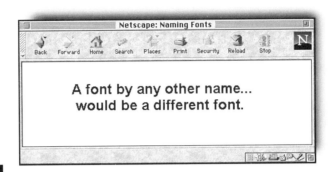

Figure 4.5

If the browser can find the exact font name (Impact Italic), it moves on to the next choice (Arial).

Example 4

Finally, what if my system does not have a single font that's listed among the choices in my style sheet?

1. The browser creates a list of all the fonts installed on my system. Neither Impact Italic nor Arial is on that list.

2. The browser sees that my style sheet's first choice is Impact Italic. It can't find this exact font name on my system; the match fails.

3. Instead, the browser moves on to my second choice, Arial, but finds that this font is also not on my system. This match also fails.

4. The browser sees no more choices specified in the style sheet, and so falls back on its own default display font, Times.

5. The font is displayed (see Figure 4.6).

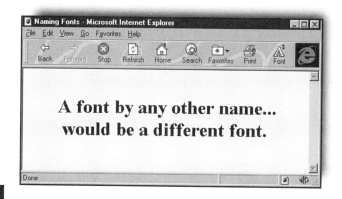

Figure 4.6

If there are no font matches, the browser reverts to its default font.

Okay, enough of the background info on naming fonts. It's time to get to the actual syntax and usage rules of all these style sheet properties.

Note

For a reminder of how to interpret the syntax and notation of each of the properties that follow, refer back to the "Using this Book" section that precedes Chapter 1.

font-family

Syntax:

```
[[<family-name> ¦ <generic-family>],]* [<family-name> ¦ <generic-family>]
```

Default value: Defined by Web browser
Applies to: All elements
Inherited: Yes
Percentage values: N/A

Examples:

```
H1 { font-family: garamond }
```

```
H1 { font-family: futura, sans-serif }

H1 { font-family: caslon, bookman, serif }

<H1 STYLE="font-family: courier, monospace">
```

Defining a font means using `font-family` to make a prioritized list of font family names and/or generic family names.

Note that all the font names in the examples are lowercase. The style sheets spec recommends this spelling, and the browsers prefer it, so it's probably best to use it. However, if you're ever having problems getting a lowercase font to work, try a mixed-case spelling.

Note

A font will work on someone's screen only if she has that exact font installed on her system. So how do you know what font faces most people are likely to have installed? How do you know which font faces are safer to use? It's a tough question, but there are some helpful strategies. Operating systems ship with certain fonts, for example, and so do commonly used applications.

For full details, see Appendix B, "Online Resources," for lists of recommended fonts to use. There I talk about specific fonts and what's likely to be on the average Mac and PC.

Tip

In general, when you're establishing multiple style rules, always use `font-family` *last*. That is, when you have a style rule that looks something like this…

```
H1 { font-family: chantilly, bookman, times, serif;
   font-size: 30pt;
   color: red;
   background: white;
   margin-top: 50px }
```

> ...you're better off rearranging the order to this:
>
> ```
> H1 { font-size: 30pt;
>    color: red;
>    background: white;
>    margin-top: 50px;
>    font-family: chantilly, bookman, times, serif }
> ```
>
> The reason for this is some reports of odd problems in Internet Explorer 3. Occasionally, if font-family occurs anywhere but last in the list, the entire style sheet rule will fail. Better to play it safe and always put font-family last.

Family Names and Generic Families

A *family name* is the name of a specific font family, as we're used to talking about fonts. Examples include Garamond, Palatino, Arial, Helvetica, and Symbol.

A *generic family* is a more general category of font, not a particular font family. Generic font families include:

- serif (such as Times)

- sans-serif (such as Arial)

- cursive (such as Comic Sans, Zapf Chancery)

- fantasy (such as Ransom)

- monospace (such as Courier, Monaco)

With any font-family rule, the Web browser will use the first font listed as the preferred font, and use any alternatives listed if necessary. Note that each font name is separated by a comma (unlike most other style sheet properties).

Internet explorer

Regrettably, Explorer 3 and 4 for Windows 95 do not support alternative font lists. They will recognize only the first font listed, and otherwise use the default font. (The Mac version works fine.)

```
H1 { font-family: caslon, bookman, serif }
```

In this example, the browser will display all <H1> text in Caslon if this font is installed on the computer. If it isn't, the browser looks for Bookman and uses that. If that isn't available on the system either, the browser uses the more generic "serif" font.

Always include a generic family as the final alternative value in the font-family property. That way you can ensure that even if visitors don't have any of the specific fonts you list, at least they'll see something that comes close to what you intend. If it's a matter of me choosing the default font or the browser choosing it, guess what I'll pick? The more control I can get over page appearance, the better.

Just so you know, here are the default fonts each browser uses for the generic families:

Generic Family	NN4 (Windows 95)	NN4 (Mac)	IE4 (Windows 95)	IE3 (Windows 95)	IE3 (Mac)
serif	Times New Roman	Times	Times New Roman	Times New Roman	Times
sans-serif	Arial	Times	Arial	Arial	Times
cursive	Times New Roman	Times	Comic Sans MS	Comic Sans MS	Times
fantasy	Arial	Times	Ransom	Ransom	Times
monospace	Courier New	Times	Courier New	Courier New	Monaco

Results may vary depending on the machine and the fonts installed.

Obviously the only browser that has it together in this department is Internet Explorer for Windows 95. Kudos to Microsoft!

Watch what happens in Figures 4.7 through 4.9 when the following HTML document is displayed on different computers:

```
<HTML>
 <STYLE TYPE="text/css">
 <!--
  H1 { font-family: gradl, chantilly, serif }
 -->
 </STYLE>
<HEAD>
 <TITLE>Specifying Fonts and Alternatives</TITLE>
</HEAD>
<BODY>
 <H1>
 Egad, what font am I?
 </H1>
</BODY>
</HTML>
```

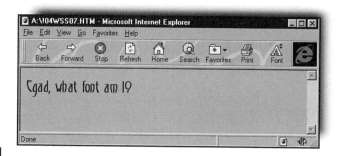

Figure 4.7

On this Windows 95 system, Internet Explorer finds the font called Gradl on the system.

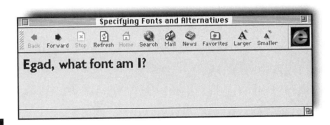

On this Mac system, Gradl isn't installed, so Explorer uses the second choice, Chantilly.

On this different Mac system, there's no Gradl or Chantilly, so Explorer uses its default serif font, Times.

Fonts with Long Names

One important note about font-family, which you might have already noticed: font names containing more than one word should appear in *quotes*:

```
H1 { font-family: "gill sans", "times new roman", sans-serif }

<H1 STYLE="font-family: 'new baskerville', serif">
```

Embedded style rules get double quotes, and inline styles get single quotes. If you forget these, the Web browser ignores any spaces before or after the font name. Also, multiple spaces within the font name are converted to a single space.

 **Internet** explorer

If you have trouble viewing a particular font in Explorer (especially on the Windows side), try adding a semicolon after font names enclosed in quotes, even if the font name is the last property in a group. Example:

```
H1 { font-family: "comic sans ms"; }
```

If you forget the semicolon, Explorer might possibly ignore *all* other style sheet elements that follow. Then again, sometimes a font works only if you *leave out* the semicolon. In other words, test thoroughly when using fonts.

 Internet explorer

Also, Explorer 3.0 for Windows 95 doesn't recognize multiple-word font names if used in *inline* styles. The following code won't work, even if you add a semicolon:

```
<H1 STYLE="font-family: 'comic sans ms'">
```

The 4 version does support multiple-word font names inline. And so does the Mac 3 version.

 Netscape Navigator

Navigator 4 bucks the system. Multiple-word font names will work only if you don't use quote marks. Don't use quote marks for fonts for Navigator 4.

Bold/Italic Fonts versus Bold/Italic Styles

What if you want to specify a bold or italic font? Well, you have to be careful. If you want to use the font Goudy Sans Bold, for example, your rule would look like this:

```
H1 { font-family: "goudy sans bold", sans-serif }
```

But here's the trick: If visitors have Goudy Sans installed on their machines but *not* Goudy Sans Bold, the Web browser will not display Goudy Sans at all, but instead will display its default sans serif font. In other words, the browser won't automatically use normal Goudy Sans and apply a bold style. The whole name you use must *exactly* match what the visitor has installed, or there won't be a match. So, if you think it's more likely that users have Goudy Sans than Goudy Sans Bold on their machines, use this instead:

```
H1 { font-weight: bold;
     font-family: "goudy sans", sans-serif }
```

With this rule, the browser will use Goudy Sans, then apply bold to it via the `font-weight` property (discussed later in this chapter). So this rule will work for those who have Goudy Sans but might not have Goudy Sans Bold. Goudy Sans Bold is an exact font name; Goudy Sans bold is a font with an applied style of bold. Remember the difference! (It's also important to note that Goudy Sans Bold and Goudy Sans bold actually look different onscreen, though not much.)

Tip

An even better solution might be this: *use both kinds of rules*. That is:

```
H1 { font-weight: bold;
   font-family: "goudy sans bold", "goudy sans", sans-serif }
```

In this scenario, the browser will use Goudy Sans Bold if it's available, and otherwise use Goudy Sans. It will apply bold to either one. For some fonts, the result will be identical, since making a Bold bold has essentially no effect. For other fonts, though (Goudy Sans happens to be among these), applying bold creates something even bolder than Goudy Sans Bold is already (see Figure 4.10). Isn't this fun?

Figure 4.10

On the top is Goudy Sans Bold, and on the bottom is Goudy Sans Bold with bold applied. But not all fonts will display a difference. Experiment!

Other Problems and Tricks with Font Names

As I discovered in my experiments with the `font-family` property, some fonts will simply give you a hard time and not display when they should. I suspect this happens for some fonts because the name *we* associate with the font is not the same as the name the system and/or the browser associates with the font. In many cases, you can simply try alternative spellings for the value of `font-family`, and soon you'll find the one that works.

For example, to call up a font such as Snap, you need to use its complete name, Snap ITC. Same thing goes for a font such as Brush Script MT (though why you would want to throw those hideous letterforms on your Web page, I have no idea).

Also, keep in mind that the fonts at your disposal are not necessarily all the fonts you see in your Fonts folder or directory. You might have a file for something called Lucida Fax Demibold, for example, but in fact that font name used as-is won't work. You have to use just Lucida Fax, then control its weight with `font-weight`.

On the Windows side, you can pretty much trust that if a font is listed in the Font pull-down menu of Microsoft Word, then it's available in style sheets using that exact same spelling.

On the Mac side, that's not a reliable rule of thumb. For example, Arbitrary Bold is a font Microsoft Word for the Mac has access to, but Internet Explorer doesn't display it. Instead, I have to spell it `arbitrarybold`, as one word, in my style sheet; then it works. And if I look at the screen font file in the System Folder, that's how it's actually spelled: one word, as ArbitraryBold. When I test various other fonts, I get the same results, which leads to this rule of thumb for the Mac: don't trust the font spelling as it appears in an application; instead, use the spelling as it appears in the screen font file (the font file within the Suitcase icon) in the System Folder.

And then there are those fonts that make the browsers behave strangely. When playing with Comic Sans MS, for example, I ran into strange results when I varied the font name spelling and the use of a semicolon. Sometimes it worked, sometimes it didn't, depending on the browser and situation. The moral of the story: test your pages constantly!

font-size

Syntax:

`<absolute-size> ¦ <relative-size> ¦ <length> ¦ <percentage>`

Default value: Defined by Web browser
Applies to: All elements
Inherited: Yes
Percentage values: Relative to parent element's font size

Examples:

`H1 { font-size: 14pt }`

`H1 { font-size: small }`

`H1 { font-size: larger }`

`H1 { font-size: 125% }`

```
H1 { font-size: 1.5em }

<H1 STYLE="font-size: 12pt">
```

There are, to the delight of Web designers everywhere, a number of different ways to define the size of text:

➡ Points

➡ Absolute keywords

➡ Relative keywords

➡ Length units

➡ Percentage units

(For more details on some of these units, see Appendix A, "Units.") Let's look at them one at a time.

Points

This is the easy one, the one you're used to in print design. And now it's at your disposal on the Web. Just use pt after your number.

Point size refers to an imaginary box that extends from the descender line (the bottom of the "p," for example) to the ascender line (the top of the "d," for example). The actual sizes of the characters can vary quite a bit within this box. That's why two fonts that are technically the same point size don't necessarily "look" like they're the same size onscreen.

Point sizes in style sheets must be specified as whole units. Something like 12.5pt won't work; the Web browser will round it down to something it understands.

Figures 4.11 through 4.13 show what various point sizes look like in the browsers. (The browsers are using their default font face: Times New Roman on Windows 95 and Times on the Mac.) This test document contains the following:

➡ One line of normal, unaffected `<P>` text

➡ Ten lines of `<P>` text that have been sized from 2 points up through 24.7 points (which the browser rounds down to 24 points)

➡ Two lines of `<H1>` sized at 8 points and 18 points

➡ One final line of `<P>` text sized at −4 points, just to see what happens

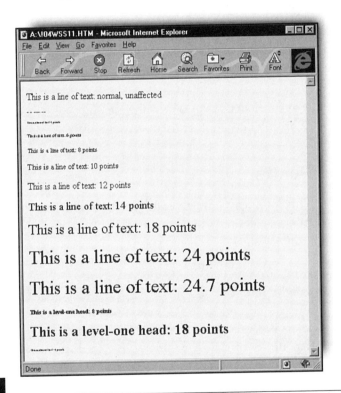

Explorer 3 for Windows 95 sizes text nicely. Notice that the first line (unaffected, default text) is the same size as the line of 12-point text, as you would expect.

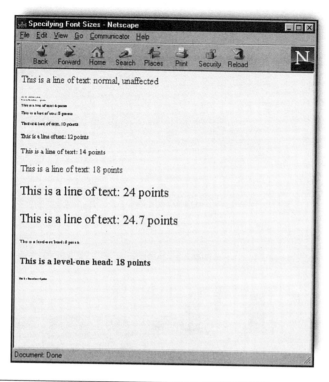

Figure 4.12

Navigator 4 for Windows 95 sizes text a bit differently. Notice how much smaller it is! We know that Navigator default text is 12-point, but here it looks more like 18-point. Something strange is going on here.

 Last Minute note

A later beta corrected this bug.

Note that all these browser windows are exactly the same size. You can see by comparing Explorer screens that fonts are generally larger on a PC monitor than on a Mac, as I pointed out previously.

What's particularly strange in these tests is how much smaller Navigator for Windows 95 defines font sizes compared to Explorer. Definitely something to be aware of when sizing text.

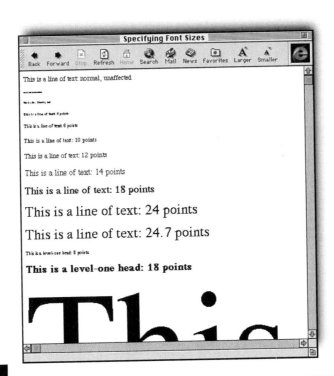

Figure 4.13

Explorer 3 for Macintosh looks fine. Check out how big that negatively sized text is.

In addition to points, you can also set absolute text size using inches (`in`), centimeters (`cm`), or pixels (`px`). See Appendix A for details.

Absolute Keywords

Absolute keywords still specify particular font sizes, but let the browser make more of the decisions about what exact display size is best. Your choices include:

➡ `xx-small`

➡ `x-small`

➡ `small`

➡ `medium`

➡ `large`

➡ `x-large`

➡ `xx-large`

Note

> By the way, these seven values correspond to the seven numerical values (1–7) you can use to specify font size for Netscape Navigator via HTML tags like `<FONT SIZE="3">` and `<FONT SIZE="+2">`.

The Web browser decides what point size each of these values becomes. The style sheets spec recommends that each value is 150% of the value smaller than itself. So if `large` is 18 points, `x-large` is 27 points and `medium` is 12 points. These values could vary depending on the font family used—at the Web browser's discretion. In the future, the browser might be able to recognize different display media (other than a standard monitor), and so adjust point sizes based on which medium is present.

Of course, the browser manufacturers like to make up their own minds about what they should or shouldn't do. The following table shows what point sizes Netscape Navigator and Internet Explorer use for each of the absolute keywords for the appropriate default fonts, Times New Roman (for Windows 95) and Times (for Mac).

Absolute Keyword	NN4	NN4 (Mac)	IE4	IE3	IE3 (Mac)
xx-small	12-point	12-point	8-point	6-point	9-point
x-small	12-point	12-point	10-point	8-point	10-point
small	12-point	12-point	12-point	10-point	12-point
medium	12-point	12-point	14-point	12-point	14-point
large	12-point	12-point	18-point	14-point	18-point
x-large	12-point	12-point	24-point	18-point	24-point
xx-large	12-point	12-point	36-point	24-point	36-point

Check out the interesting differences between the Windows and Mac versions of Explorer (see Figures 4.14 and 4.15). The 4 Windows version is like the 3 Mac version, so it looks like Microsoft is heading toward consistency.

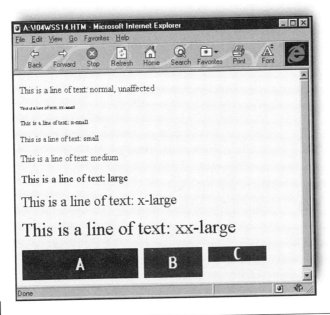

Figure 4.14

Explorer 3 for Windows 95 displays keyword-sized text.

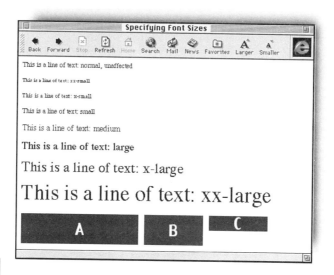

Figure 4.15

Explorer 3 for Macintosh uses the same keyword values. Note this time that, relative to identical graphics, the Mac text is bigger than the Windows text, as the previous table testifies.

As you can see in the previous table, the Windows 95 version of Navigator recognizes most of the keywords, but the Mac version doesn't. I suspect this will be fixed by the final release.

Relative Keywords

Relative keywords are relative to the size of their parent element. Your choices are:

➡ smaller

➡ larger

A value of smaller will adjust the size of the font down one "notch" on the scale of absolute keywords listed in the previous section; larger will move it up a "notch." Check out this example:

```
<HTML>
 <STYLE TYPE="text/css">
 <!--
   H1     { font-family: arial, sans-serif;
            font-size: 24pt }
   B      { font-size: smaller }
   H2     { font-family: garamond, serif;
            font-size: medium }
  STRONG { font-size: larger }
 -->
 </STYLE>
<HEAD>
 <TITLE>Specifying Font Sizes by Relative Keywords</TITLE>
 </HEAD>
<BODY>
 <H1>
 Now I'm 24 points, and <B>now I'm 16 points</B>.
 </H1>
 <H2>
 Now I'm medium size, and <STRONG>now I'm large</STRONG>.
 </H2>
 </BODY>
 </HTML>
```

As you can see, these relative keywords can work with absolute keywords as well as specific point sizes. When 24-point <H1> text is ordered down a notch by the keyword smaller, the browser uses the 150% scaling to make the text 16 points. And when the relative keyword larger is applied to absolute keyword medium, the text gets bumped up to large size (see Figure 4.16).

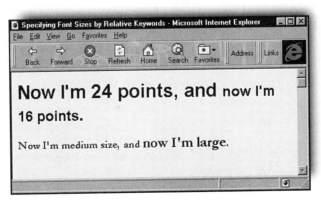

Figure 4.16

smaller *and* larger *make text, well,* smaller *and* larger.

Internet explorer

At least that's how it's supposed to work. At this time, Explorer 3 doesn't support `smaller` or `larger` at all. But 4 does.

Netscape Navigator

Navigator 4 for Windows 95 supports `smaller` and `larger` and I'm sure the Mac version will too, although it doesn't in early beta.

What happens if text that is `xx-large` is made `larger`? The good browser will extrapolate new values based on the values it already has for the other keywords. That is, it simply increases the value by another 150%.

Length Units

Length values, less commonly used for `font-size`, include the following:

➡ `em`

(An em is a unit of distance equal to the point size of a font. In 14-point type, an em is 14 points wide. See Appendix A.)

➡ `ex`

(X–height refers to the height of the lowercase letters [not including ascenders or descenders, such as "h" or "p" have] of a font. See Appendix A.)

When used with the `font-size` property, `em` and `ex` units refer to the font size of the *parent* element (on other properties, they refer to the size of the current element).

```
<HTML>
 <STYLE TYPE="text/css">
 <!--
  P { font-size: 20pt }
  B { font-size: 1.5em }
 -->
```

```
</STYLE>
<HEAD>
<TITLE>Specifying Font Sizes by Length Units</TITLE>
</HEAD>
<BODY>
<P>
Now I'm 20 points.
<B>
But look! Now I'm 1.5 ems of what I was before: 30 points.
</B>
</P>
</BODY>
</HTML>
```

In the ideal browser, text within <B> gets displayed at 30 points, which is 1.5 ems of the inherited size of 20 points. Essentially, the text is displayed at one-and-a-half times the size of its parent.

Explorer handles em a bit differently. On the Mac side, it always uses the default font size as its base, and ignores inheritance in this instance. That is, Explorer treats 1 em <P> text as always 12-point, its default. 1.5 em text would always be 18-point, regardless of any other font size it inherits. So in the previous example the text would be 18-point, not 30-point. Obviously this removes any uniqueness or value in using em for font-size.

Explorer for Macintosh treats ex exactly the same way.

On the Windows side, em and ex values are treated like they're *point* size values! 2em equals 2-point text, and so on. Yuck.

Navigator doesn't support em or ex.

Length units calculate inherited font sizes totally independent of the keyword values we talked about earlier.

Percentage Units

Percentage values also work through inheritance. Values include any whole number.

```
<HTML>
 <STYLE TYPE="text/css">
 <!--
  P { font-size: 15pt }
  B { font-size: 300% }
  -->
 </STYLE>
<HEAD>
 <TITLE>Specifying Font Sizes by Percentage</TITLE>
</HEAD>
<BODY>
 <P>
 Now I'm 15 points, and <B>now I'm 45 points!</B>
 </P>
</BODY>
</HTML>
```

The Web browser takes the size of the <H1> text and makes the bold text 300% of that size. Pretty straightforward.

Explorer 3 uses the percentage of the default font size, not any other size. That is, in the example, the text would be 36 point (because the default <P> size is 12 point in Explorer 3), not 45 point.

Navigator doesn't support percentage values. In fact, if you use percentage values on the Windows 95 version, it treats them as *point* sizes (300% equals 300-point text, for example), so results can be surprising!

Last Minute note

> Beta 3 does support percentages.

font-style

Syntax:

```
normal ¦ italic ¦ oblique
```

Default value: `normal`
Applies to: All elements
Inherited: Yes
Percentage values: N/A

Examples:

```
H1 { font-style: italic }

H1 { font-style: normal }

<H1 STYLE="font-style: oblique">
```

With the `font-style` property, you can choose between normal (Roman) text, italic text, or oblique text.

➡ `normal` selects a font that is classified as "normal" in the Web browser's font database.

➡ `italic` specifies a font from the font database that is labeled "italic." If the browser finds no font labeled "italic," it should theoretically use a font labeled "oblique" if one is available. Unfortunately, no browser currently does this; instead, the match fails entirely, and the text is displayed in its normal form.

➡ `oblique`, not surprisingly, specifies a font that is labeled "oblique."

Internet explorer

Explorer 3 supports `italic`, but not `normal` or `oblique`. (Version 4, however, does support `normal` and `oblique`.) A page on the Microsoft Web site claims that you can also use `small-caps` as a value for `font-style`, but I couldn't confirm this.

Keep in mind that by styling a font `italic` or `oblique`, you might possibly be instructing the computer to create an artificial font by forcing the normal font into a slant. If a certain font (such as Monotype Corsiva) has no italic or oblique version at all, the computer will "invent it" on the spot and display the normal version slanted even further than it is already. This unnatural italics might not be what you want (see Figure 4.17).

Figure 4.17

Monotype Corsiva normal and artificially italicized.

Perfect Web browsers will treat any fonts with "Italic," "Cursive," or "Kursiv" in their names as `italic`. Similarly, they classify any fonts with "Oblique," "Slanted," or "Incline" in their names as `oblique`. Unfortunately, Navigator and Explorer are not perfect, and so they don't do this. Match the font name *exactly*, or the match will fail.

By the way, the `normal` value can come in handy:

```
<HTML>
<STYLE TYPE="text/css">
<!--
  H1   { font-style: italic;
         font-family: arial }
  H1 I { font-style: normal }
-->
```

```
</STYLE>
<HEAD>
 <TITLE>Specifying Font Styles</TITLE>
</HEAD>
<BODY>
 <H1>
 Now I'm italicized, but <I>now I'm not</I>.
 </H1>
</BODY>
</HTML>
```

By using a contextual selector to set <I> only when its parent is <H1>, I've specified that all italicized text within a level-1 head should *not* be italicized (see Figure 4.18)! Weird, but in some cases useful.

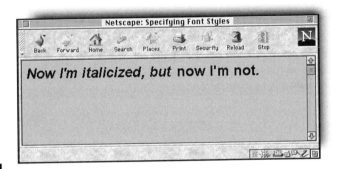

Figure 4.18

Using normal *can guarantee no italics—even within* <I>!

font-weight

Syntax:

```
normal ¦ bold ¦ bolder ¦ lighter ¦ 100 ¦ 200 ¦ 300 ¦ 400 ¦ 500 ¦ 600
¦ 700 ¦ 800 ¦ 900
```

Default value: normal
Applies to: All elements
Inherited: Yes
Percentage values: N/A

Examples:

```
H1 { font-weight: bold }
```

```
H1 { font-weight: 200 }
```

```
<H1 STYLE="font-weight: lighter">
```

If you thought `<B>` was fun, wait till you get a load of `font-weight`. This property enables you to adjust the boldness or weight of the font. The basic way to do this is through the values of `normal` and `bold`, as we saw with `italic` in the previous section.

> Explorer 3 supports `bold`, but not `normal`. Version 4 supports both.
>
> Instead, Microsoft gave Explorer its own range of keywords, which include `extra-light`, `light`, `demi-light`, `medium`, `demi-bold`, `bold`, and `extra-bold`.

> Navigator for Windows 95 supports both `bold` and `normal`.
>
> Navigator for Macintosh, however, supports neither.

But wait, there's more! Let's look at the numerical and relative weight values allowed.

Numerical Weight Values

For even more flexibility, you can use numbered values, from `100` through `900`. Each of these numbers corresponds to a certain weight value; each one represents a weight that is at least as bold as the one below it. The `normal` value is the same as `400`, and `bold` is normally `700`. So `500` might be characterized as "a little bold," `600` as "somewhat bold," and `800` as "extremely bold." `300` would be "a bit light," `200` "quite light," and `100` "very light." You get the idea. These are relative measurements, for the Web browser to decide based upon the font at hand.

Internet explorer

> Internet Explorer 3 doesn't recognize these numerical values, on a Mac or on Windows. But version 4 does (sort of; keep reading).

 Netscape **Navigator**

> Navigator 4 does support numerical values, so read on!

Unfortunately, it's not quite this simple. If you've worked with fonts for a while, you know that they don't just come in "Normal" and "Bold" versions. There's "Regular," "Book," "Medium," "SemiBold," "DemiBold," "Heavy," "Black," and probably many more. And—no surprise—there is no agreed-upon standard of what these names mean in precise terms. So Chantilly Bold might not be as bold as the normal version of Impact, for example. These terms are used to distinguish fonts within the same family; they're almost useless for distinguishing fonts *between* families.

That's why the creators of style sheets chose to make 400 the "normal" value for any given font. Depending on the font, 400 can correspond to "Normal," "Regular," "Book," "Roman," and sometimes "Medium."

But for the other numerical values, the Web browser has to assign one to each variant of the font. The following rules determine what arbitrary term gets associated with which numerical value:

➡ If the font at hand uses a numerical scale with nine values in it, then font weights can correspond easily to those values. OpenType fonts will work this way (see Appendix B).

➡ If the font has a variant named "Medium," but also one named "Book," "Regular," "Roman," or "Normal," the "Medium" variant is the one that gets a value of 500.

➡ Most often, the font variant named "Bold" will get the value of 700, as I said earlier.

➡ If there are fewer than nine weights that come with a font family, then things get a little complicated. The browser needs to "fill in the holes" (assign the other numerical values) as follows:

➡ If the value of 500 isn't assigned to any font variant, it will get the same variant as 400.

➡ If either 600, 700, 800, or 900 remains unassigned, they are each assigned to the same variant as the next darker assigned keyword, if any, or the next lighter one otherwise. So if there's a "Black" face that gets a value of 900, and a "Bold" face that gets 700, then 800 gets assigned to "Black," and 600 to "Bold."

➡ Finally, if 100, 200, or 300 are still not assigned, each gets assigned to the next lighter assigned keyword, if any, or otherwise the next darker keyword. So if there's a "Medium" (500) but nothing lighter, then 100 through 300 all get assigned to "Medium" too.

Let's see how this works with two font families that are on my Mac right now: Chantilly and New Baskerville.

Font Variant	Value	Assigned Value
Chantilly Light	200	100, 300
Chantilly Regular	400	500
Chantilly Bold	700	600
Chantilly Heavy	800	
Chantilly Ultra Bold	900	

Font Variant	Value	Assigned Value
New Baskerville Regular	400	100, 200, 300, 500
New Baskerville SemiBold	600	
New Baskerville Bold	700	800, 900

Here's Eras from my PC:

Font Variant	Value	Assigned Value
Eras Light	200	100, 300
Eras Medium	400	500
Eras Demi	600	
Eras Bold	700	
Eras Ultra	900	800

If we try this one out on a Web page using Navigator, we can see it in action. The following HTML document defines classes for each numerical value of Eras, and Figure 4.19 shows the result.

```
<HTML>
 <STYLE TYPE="text/css">
 <!--
  BODY { background: white }
  P    { font-size: 24pt;
         font-family: eras }
  .a   { font-weight: 100 }
  .b   { font-weight: 200 }
  .c   { font-weight: 300 }
  .d   { font-weight: 400 }
  .e   { font-weight: 500 }
  .f   { font-weight: 600 }
  .g   { font-weight: 700 }
  .h   { font-weight: 800 }
  .i   { font-weight: 900 }
 -->
 </STYLE>
<HEAD>
 <TITLE>Specifying Font Weights</TITLE>
</HEAD>
<BODY>
 <P CLASS=a>Hi, I'm a line of text: value of 100</P>
 <P CLASS=b>Hi, I'm a line of text: value of 200</P>
 <P CLASS=c>Hi, I'm a line of text: value of 300</P>
 <P CLASS=d>Hi, I'm a line of text: value of 400</P>
```

```
<P CLASS=e>Hi, I'm a line of text: value of 500</P>
<P CLASS=f>Hi, I'm a line of text: value of 600</P>
<P CLASS=g>Hi, I'm a line of text: value of 700</P>
<P CLASS=h>Hi, I'm a line of text: value of 800</P>
<P CLASS=i>Hi, I'm a line of text: value of 900</P>
</BODY>
</HTML>
```

The page doesn't quite match what we'd expect, but it's close. The lines with values of 100–300 are indeed Eras Light, and 400 is Medium. 500 doesn't show up, however, 600 and 700 are not different enough. Finally, while 800 and 900 are Eras Ultra, it's strange that 800 looks more condensed.

Explorer 4 only partially supports these number values. It displays the same page slightly differently: lines 100–500 are Medium, 600–800 are Bold, and 900 is Ultra. Explorer 4 seems to display every font this way.

Navigator 4 for Mac handles things similarly. 100–600 are normal, and 700–900 are bold.

The lesson is that fonts will rarely behave exactly as they're supposed to. If I try the same experiment with Arial, I find that the browser decides to use Arial Narrow as well as regular Arial as it assigns font variants. Like I said at the beginning of this chapter, the world of fonts is a messy world.

Relative Weight Values

Finally, you can also use the values lighter and bolder to specify font weights that are relative to some inherited value. (Child elements inherit the resultant weight, not the relative value of lighter or bolder.)

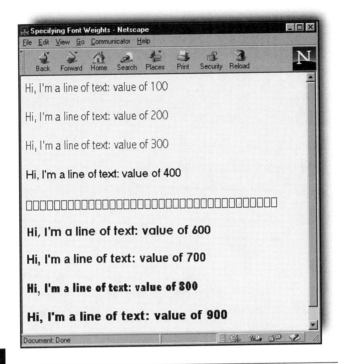

Figure 4.19

Numerical weight values in action, getting their assignments based on the font variants available.

These relative values enable you to adjust the font weight within a font family. So, declaring something `bolder` doesn't mean the browser simply adds `100` "points" to its numerical value. Instead, the browser takes the font weight to the next variant.

For example, if we start with Eras with a bold value of `400` (Eras Medium), and then give a child element a `font-weight` value of `lighter`, then we'll end up with Eras Light. If another child element has a value of `bolder`, it will be displayed as Eras Demi. Look at it as a simple ladder that values can climb up and down via `bolder` (up a step) and `lighter` (down a step).

Internet explorer

Internet Explorer 3 doesn't support either `bolder` or `lighter`, though the Microsoft Web site claims it does.

Explorer 4, however, does support both `bolder` and `lighter`.

Netscape Navigator

Netscape Navigator supports neither.

If there is no heavier font face to find, then the browser adds `100` to the value, but displays the font unchanged. For example, if a child element inherited New Baskerville Bold (numerical value: `700`) from a parent element, and if a style sheet rule told that child element to be `bolder` yet, the browser would increase its value to `800`, but still display it as Bold (since there is no variant of New Baskerville that is bolder than Bold).

By the way, numerical values cannot exceed `900`. So if you tried to make a font face `bolder` than something like Chantilly Ultra Bold, all you would get is an identical Chantilly Ultra Bold.

The `lighter` value works the same way, only in reverse, so I won't go into the same kinds of details here. In this case, numerical values cannot go lower than `100`.

font-variant

Syntax:

`normal ¦ small-caps`

Default value: `normal`
Applies to: All elements
Inherited: Yes
Percentage values: N/A

Examples:

```
H1 { font-variant: small-caps }

<H1 STYLE="font-variant: normal">
```

This is an easy one. You can control the display of small caps through font-variant, which comes with only two values. In small caps, the lowercase letters look similar to the uppercase letters, but they're slightly smaller and with different proportions.

In an ideal situation, there will be a small caps variant of the font being used. In that case, the browser will display those characters. But often, the font has no pre-established small caps characters. In this situation, the characters are "created" by reducing and widening the uppercase characters. If that doesn't work, the browser will simply use the uppercase characters as is. The best advice: When in doubt, test, test, test.

 Internet explorer

Unfortunately, Explorer 3 does not support small caps via font-variant.

Version 4, however, does! It supports small-caps, but not normal. It small-caps *everything*, including capitalized letters. All characters end up with exactly the same height (see Figure 4.20).

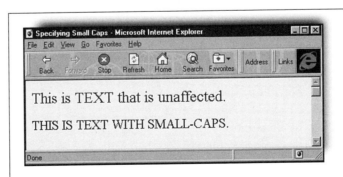

Figure 4.20

All small-caps characters, even if they're capitalized, are the same size in Explorer 4.

Netscape Navigator

Navigator doesn't support font-variant.

Remember, if there is a font called Bergamo Small Caps or something similar, chances are you can still use it by including its complete name under font-family.

As the official style sheets spec recognizes, there's definitely room for other values of font-variant in the future. After all, some fonts have expanded or condensed variants, and "old style" variants, and funky old style numerals, and so on. Keep an eye out as this property expands to include new values.

text-transform

Syntax:

```
capitalize ¦ uppercase ¦ lowercase ¦ none
```

Default value: none
Applies to: All elements
Inherited: Yes
Percentage values: N/A

Examples:

```
H1 { text-transform: uppercase }
```

```
<H1 STYLE="text-transform: none">
```

There might be a situation in which you want a style rule to lowercase all text, or to capitalize the first letter of every word. In that case, text-transform is your answer.

Your choices are:

→ `capitalize` if you want the first character in every word capitalized, but the rest of the characters left alone

→ `uppercase` if you want every single character capitalized

→ `lowercase` if you want none of the characters capitalized

→ `none` if you want to negate any inherited value which might impact capitalization

Internet explorer

We'll here's a switch: This time Explorer 3 doesn't support any of `text-transform`, but Navigator supports it all.

Explorer 4, just out in beta as I write this, does in fact support `text-transform` and all of its values.

Let's play:

```
<HTML>
 <STYLE TYPE="text/css">
 <!--
  BODY  { font-size: 20pt }
  SPAN  { text-transform: none }
  P.cap { text-transform: capitalize }
  P.up  { text-transform: uppercase }
  P.low { text-transform: lowercase }
 -->
 </STYLE>
<HEAD>
 <TITLE>Specifying Uppercase and Lowercase</TITLE>
 </HEAD>
<BODY>
 <P>Here I am, Great Text to be played with.
 </P>
 <P CLASS=cap>Here I am, Great Text to be played with.<BR>
```

```
<SPAN>Here I am, Great Text to be played with.</SPAN>
</P>
<P CLASS=up>Here I am, Great Text to be played with.<BR>
<SPAN>Here I am, Great Text to be played with.</SPAN>
</P>
<P CLASS=low>Here I am, Great Text to be played with.<BR>
<SPAN>Here I am, Great Text to be played with.</SPAN>
</P>
</BODY>
</HTML>
```

Check out what the tags do to each pair of lines after the first normal line (see Figure 4.21). Note that `<SPAN>` automatically negates the rule and tells the browser to go back to the initial text display.

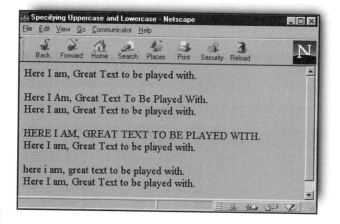

Figure 4.21

Playing with case via `text-transform`.

A slight bug in Explorer 4: The first letter of the text line ("H") appears in lowercase when `capitalize` is used.

text-decoration

Syntax:

`none ¦ [ underline ¦ overline ¦ line-through ¦ blink ] +`

Default value: `none`
Applies to: All elements
Inherited: No (see below)
Percentage values: N/A

Examples:

`H1 { text-decoration: underline }`

`H1 { text-decoration: line-through }`

`<H1 STYLE="text-decoration: blink">`

This property represents a kind of "miscellaneous" section, which perhaps could jokingly be known as "other things you can do to display text to make it less readable."

The choices are pretty clear:

➡ `underline` imparts an underline to the text

➡ `overline` adds a line above the text

➡ `line-through` gives a strike-through appearance

➡ `blink` is all too familiar

➡ `none` neutralizes any inherited settings and brings things back to normal

Explorer 3 doesn't support `overline` and `blink`, much to my delight. Explorer 4 does support `overline`, but not `blink`.

Netscape
Navigator Everything works in Navigator except `overline`, which causes underlining instead of overlining.

Undoubtedly the makers of Web browsers will add to this list, and the number of options will increase. I can't even imagine what hokey horrors will result...

As I mentioned in Chapter 2, a great use of `text-decoration` is to remove the ugly underlines that browsers give to linked text. You can use the pseudo-classes `A:link`, `A:visited`, and `A:active` to do so:

```
A:link, A:visited, A:active { text-decoration: none }
```

Note See Chapter 2 for details on how the browsers support or don't support this effect.

The `text-decoration` property is not inherited, but you should make sure elements match their parent(s). If all `<H1>` text is underlined, all `<B>` text within that level-1 heading should be underlined too. Otherwise it looks weird.

By the way, you can try to apply these "decorations" to non-text elements such as images, but they will have no effect.

font

Syntax:

```
<font-size> [/ <line-height> ]? <font-family>
```

Default value: Not defined
Applies to: All elements
Inherited: Yes
Percentage values: On `<font-size>` and `<line-height>` only

Examples:

```
H1 { font: 14pt/16pt arial }

H1 { font: large times }

H1 { font: 2em "new baskerville", serif }

<H1 STYLE="font: 80%/120% garamond">
```

The `font` property is different from the others in that it is essentially a shorthand method for specifying up to three font properties simultaneously. Most of the time, all we want to set is font family, size, and leading—so why can't there be a shortcut for doing just this, so we won't have to type the full rules every time? Well, here it is.

With the `font` property, you specify font size, leading (`line-height`), and font family, in that order. You must always specify at least size and family; leading is optional. Each value is separated by a space (although separating `font-family` names requires a comma, as usual).

Note

For more detailed information on the `line-height` property, which defines leading (the vertical space between lines of text), see the next chapter.

Netscape Navigator

Navigator supports the `font` property only so far as it supports the individual components. Tread softly.

Any value that you can normally use for these properties can also be used here. As you can see in the previous example rules, `font-size` can be specified in points, keywords, percentages, ems, and so on. The same guidelines apply.

For the purposes of cascading order, using a `font` rule is the same as declaring separate rules at the same point in a style sheet.

CHAPTER 5

Typography

In the previous chapter, we looked at all the details for specifying fonts and changing the appearance of type. This chapter is a continuation of that discussion, but here we'll be talking about the *alignment* and *spacing* of type and sections of type, not about the appearance of the type itself.

word-spacing

Syntax:

```
normal ¦ <length>
```

Default value: normal
Applies to: All elements
Inherited: Yes
Percentage values: N/A

Examples:

```
H1 { word-spacing: 0.3em }
```

```
H1 { word-spacing: 4mm }
```

```
<H1 STYLE="word-spacing: 0.5em">
```

The horizontal space between words is now under your control via the word-spacing property. The value you use will be *added* to the default space that occurs between words; it won't simply replace the default. So in the first example on the preceding page, the space between each word would be 0.3 ems more than what the browser would normally display.

Before you get too excited, you should know that Versions 3 and 4 of Internet Explorer don't support word-spacing.

Netscape
Navigator

And neither does Navigator 4, unfortunately. If you have a moment, email both companies and demand that they get to work!

Word spacing enables typographical control that is difficult in HTML (you have to resort to invisible GIFs or some such "hack"). Adjusting word spacing can create some elegant typographical effects, particularly for headlines and small amounts of text. However, playing too much with this capability for large amounts of text can hurt readability.

For the ideal browser, you can define word-spacing using any of these length units:

➡ Inches (in)

➡ Centimeters (cm)

➡ Millimeters (mm)

➡ Points (pt)

➡ Picas (pc)

➡ Em (em)

➡ X–Height (ex)

➡ Pixels (px)

For more information on these units of measurement, see Appendix A.

You can also set `word-spacing` to `normal`, which will guarantee that the default word spacing is used instead of any inherited value.

How spacing actually appears depends on the browser, so test everything thoroughly. In particular, word spacing can be affected if you justify text (see `text-align` later in this chapter).

You might also be able to use negative values for `word-spacing` and get some very interesting results: overlapping text. See Chapter 7 for more details on how to overlap elements.

letter-spacing

Syntax:

```
normal ¦ <length>
```

Default value: `normal`
Applies to: All elements
Inherited: Yes
Percentage values: N/A

Examples:

```
H1 { letter-spacing: 0.1em }

H1 { letter-spacing: 2mm }

<H1 STYLE="letter-spacing: 0.2em">
```

Adjusting the space between individual characters, which is also known as *kerning*, is possible through the `letter-spacing` property. This one works similarly to `word-spacing` in that the value is added to the default spacing used by the browser.

Here's an example of `letter-spacing` at work:

```
<HTML>
 <STYLE TYPE="text/css">
 <!--
  H1.a { letter-spacing: 10px }
```

```
     H1.b { letter-spacing: .3in }
     -->
     </STYLE>
    <HEAD>
     <TITLE>Specifying Letter Spacing</TITLE>
    </HEAD>
    <BODY>
     <H1>
     Look ma! I can adjust the space between letters!
     </H1>
     <H1 CLASS=a>
     Look ma! I can adjust the space between letters!
     </H1>
     <H1 CLASS=b>
     Look ma! I can adjust the space between letters!
     </H1>
    </BODY>
    </HTML>
```

As Figure 5.1 shows, the first paragraph is normal text, the second has a `letter-spacing` of 10 pixels, and the third three-tenths of an inch.

It seems as though it's all the rage these days to increase the kerning in standard mixed-case text. Although this effect can look cool in certain situations, it can also slow down readability. It's much more effective to limit kerning adjustments to large text, headlines, short phrases, and so on.

Explorer 3 does not recognize `letter-spacing`.

But Explorer 4 does!

Navigator 4 does not recognize `letter-spacing`.

You can use the same length units as for `word-spacing`, so I won't list them again here.

You can also use negative values to achieve overlapping characters, but use this capability wisely. Effective uses of this might be tight kerning for prominent text and artificially created ligatures (since ligatures aren't possible in normal HTML). See both in Figure 5.2.

Figure 5.1

Give letter-spacing *a value and instantly adjust kerning.*

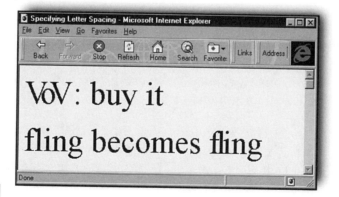

Figure 5.2

Negative letter-spacing *creates the "VoV" effect and the ligature in "fling."*

If you justify text with `text-align` (discussed later), the Web browser is usually free to adjust the kerning to make the justification happen. But if you want, you can override this by setting `letter-spacing` to zero:

```
P { letter-spacing: 0 }
```

With that rule set, the browser can achieve justified text by adjusting word spacing, but not by adjusting kerning.

line-height

Syntax:

```
<number> | <length> | <percentage>
```

Default value: Depends on the browser
Applies to: All elements except replaced elements (see Note)
Inherited: Yes
Percentage values: Relative to the font size of the element itself

Examples:

```
H1 { line-height: 2 }
```

```
H1 { line-height: 1.4em }
```

```
<H1 STYLE="line-height: 120%">
```

You've been waiting for this one, right? At long last, it's easy to adjust the space between lines of text, or the *leading*. Specifically, this property adjusts the distance between the baselines of two adjacent lines of text.

The `line-height` property gives the total height of a line of text, which includes space above and below the line. There is of course a default `line-height` used by the browser, but this property enables you to override those built-in settings. If you have 12-point text and specify a `line-height` of 16 points, then 4 points are added to the overall height, 2 above the line and 2 below the line.

Navigator actually adds all the `line-height` spacing *before* the text line, and none after.

Explorer does exactly the same thing. So, your first line of leaded text will always get bumped down a bit.

Leading actually refers to the difference between the height of the text and the `line-height`. Leading for the 12-point/16-point example technically is 4 points. *Half-leading* is just what's added above or below the text line (2 points, for example). (Keep in mind that many people refer to leading and line height as the same thing.) When all is said and done, the total area of text and leading makes up a *line box* (see Figure 5.3). The total height of the box is equal to `line-height`.

Figure 5.3

Anatomy of a line box.

If you ever have a line of text with two different `line-height` values, then those two sections also have different half–leading values. In that case, the line box extends from the top of the highest section to the bottom of the lowest section. Thus, the browser uses the larger of the `line-height` values for determining how it will display the elements.

The only elements that don't always have `line-height` in style sheets are *replaced elements*, which are any elements that are replaced by other content. For example, the `<IMG>` tag is replaced by an actual image, so <IMG> is a replaced element. Images and graphics can't technically have line-height, according to the style sheets spec.

Netscape
Navigator

One workaround for this in Navigator is to place the <IMG> within another tag that *can* have a line-height. So, if you surround the image like so...

```
<SPAN><IMG SRC="logo.gif"></SPAN>
```

...and add this style sheet rule at the top...

```
SPAN { line-height: 200% }
```

...then you can adjust the "leading" of the image by adjusting the line-height of SPAN. It's a cheat, but it works in Navigator (and Explorer).

Internet
explorer

Actually, Explorer *does* allow you to add line-height directly to <IMG> tags. Rules such as this one work fine to space out images vertically:

```
IMG { line-height: 200% }
```

That completes the background information you need to know before using line-height. Now for the details. You can specify line-height in any of three ways:

➡ Number

➡ Length

➡ Percentage

Leading by Number

When you specify line-height by a number, the browser figures out the actual line height by multiplying the font size of the current element by the number you specify:

```
<HTML>
 <STYLE TYPE="text/css">
 <!--
  H1 { font-size: 20pt;
       line-height: 1.2 }
  H2 { font-size: 20pt;
       line-height: 2 }
  H3 { font-size: 20pt;
       line-height: 5 }
 -->
 </STYLE>
<HEAD>
 <TITLE>Specifying Leading with Numbers</TITLE>
 </HEAD>
<BODY>
 <H1>Adjusting leading with numbers involves multiplying the number
 by the font size of the element in question.</H1>
 <H2>Adjusting leading with numbers involves multiplying the number
 by the font size of the element in question.</H2>
 <H3>Adjusting leading with numbers involves multiplying the number
 by the font size of the element in question.</H3>
 </BODY>
 </HTML>
```

In this example, the line height calculated by the browser for each of the blocks of text is 24, 40, and 100, respectively (see Figure 5.4).

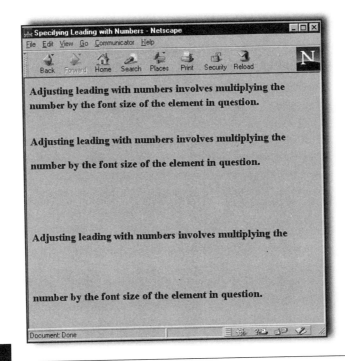

Figure 5.4

Leading defined by number.

Internet explorer

Navigator does this just fine, but Internet Explorer 3 (Mac and Windows) uses absolute `line-height` numbers differently. Check out Figure 5.5.

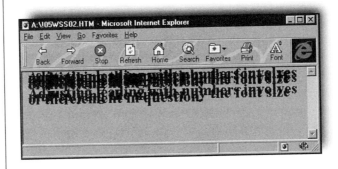

Figure 5.5

The same Web page viewed in Explorer 3.

Yes, it is indeed an ungodly mess. In Explorer 3, `line-height` number matches point-size number in default text display. So, `line-height` for 20-point text is 20 unless set differently (whereas it should be 1 according to the official style sheet rules). If you go too much less than that, text lines start to overlap in Explorer 3, as you can see. (This can be useful; see the section coming up on overlapping text and images.)

This is not a problem in Explorer 4. Version 4 works correctly, as Navigator does.

But the fact that Explorer 3 and Navigator handle `line-height` differently when using absolute values means that you should avoid using numbers for now. Try length or percentage values instead (see the next sections).

For the purposes of inheritance, when you use a number, child elements will inherit the calculated line height, not the actual `line-height` number. Check this out:

```
<HTML>
 <STYLE TYPE="text/css">
 <!--
  H1 { font-size: 12pt;
       line-height: 1.5 }
  B  { font-size: 24pt }
 -->
 </STYLE>
<HEAD>
 <TITLE>Messing with Leading Inheritance</TITLE>
 </HEAD>
<BODY>
 <H1>
 Spring has finally arrived, and the brown lawns across this great
 land are finally turning green again. This paragraph is the parent.
 </H1>
 <H1><B>
 Spring has finally arrived, and the brown lawns across this great
 land are finally turning green again. This paragraph is the child.
 </B></H1>
</BODY>
</HTML>
```

Line height is calculated for the first paragraph of text as 18 points. For the second paragraph, instead of recalculating the line height, the browser stays with the original. So the line height remains 18 points instead of being recalculated to 36 points (see Figure 5.6).

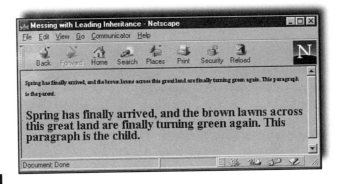

Figure 5.6

Inherited number line-height *stays the same value even when text size changes.*

Internet explorer

> Explorer 4 doesn't handle inheritance correctly. The 4.0 browser *does* in fact recalculate the line height. The second paragraph is displayed with a line height of 36 points instead of 18 points.

Leading by Length Value

You can also specify line-height using any of the length units we talked about previously for word-spacing and letter-spacing. The point (pt) is a common unit for line height, as is em:

```
H1 { font-size: 10pt;
     line-height: 1.4em }
```

An em is a unit of distance equal to the point size of a font. So this rule would define the line height as 14 points. (In Navigator, a numerical value of 1.4 would result in the same line-height value.)

As Appendix A discusses, Explorer for Windows 95 doesn't like em values, but it does work fine with point values. Explorer for Macintosh supports both. So using pt values to define line-height will work fine across browsers and across platforms.

The Mac version of Explorer does something weird with line-height: It adds line height to the last line of text that appears *before* the leaded text. In Figure 5.7, the second paragraph has a line-height style, but the first and second don't at all. But as you can see, Explorer for some reason adds line-height to the last line of the first paragraph, whether you use length values or percentage values (see next section). A definite bug in the Mac version only.

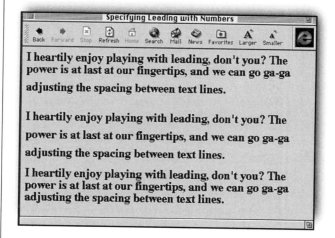

Figure 5.7

A bug in the Mac version of Explorer adds leading where it shouldn't.

The Windows 95 version of Explorer 3 has its own unique problem. When you add line-height to a paragraph, Explorer 3 adds a good bit of vertical space above the paragraph—more than it should. Why? I have no idea. See Figure 5.8, which is the same Web page displayed in Figure 5.7.

continues

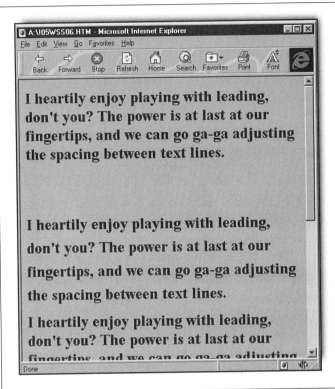

The Windows 95 version has its own problems: It adds extra space above leaded paragraphs.

Explorer 4 does not share this bug.

Just as with number values, length values are inherited directly. There is no recalculation or change based on any change in text size. 18-point line height remains 18-point line height, even if a child element's font size is different.

Leading by Percentage Value

Finally, you can adjust line-height through a percentage value. The value you specify is relative to the font size of the element at hand:

```
H1 { font-size: 10pt;
     line-height: 140% }
```

Like the previous example, the result here would be a line height of 14 points, or 140% of 10 points.

For inheritance, it's the same rule we saw earlier. Child elements inherit the calculated value; the browser doesn't recalculate the line height based on any new text size.

Overlapping Text and Images

For `line-height`, negative values are not allowed. But that doesn't mean you can't overlap text:

```
H1 { font-size: 24pt;
       line-height: 50% }
```

In this scenario, `line-height` is defined as half of the point size of the text, or 12 points. The leading in this case, based on the official definition mentioned earlier, is –12 points. The result is overlapping text (see Figure 5.9).

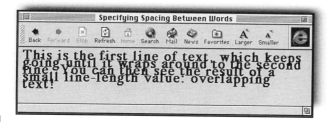

Figure 5.9

To overlap text, `line-height` *must be positive and leading negative.*

Overlapping elements can get ugly, of course, but this capability can also be very useful for special effects (see Figure 5.10).

Figure 5.10

Overlapping text can enable some interesting typography.

Remember that you can also add `line-height` to images and graphics, and thus overlap them with each other and with text (see Figure 5.11).

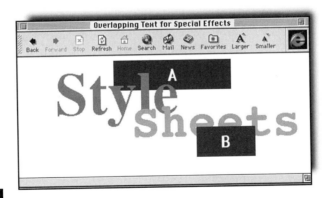

Figure 5.11

You can even overlap text and images for some layering effects.

Note | `line-height` isn't necessarily the best property to use for over-lapping and layering. We'll look more closely at these capabilities in Chapters 7 and 8.

text-align

Syntax:

```
left ¦ right ¦ center ¦ justify
```

Default value: left
Applies to: Block-level and replaced elements
Inherited: Yes
Percentage values: N/A

Examples:

```
H1 { text-align: center }
```

```
<H1 STYLE="text-align: right">
```

Want to align a block of text or justify it? text-align is the tool. This property works only on block-level elements—that is, elements that on their own define a new paragraph, such as <P>, <H1>-<H6>, <BLOCKQUOTE>, and <UL>. It also works for aligning "replaced elements" such as images and applets.

Note that text is aligned relative to the edges of the element, not necessarily to the edge of the browser window. For example, right-aligning text in <BLOCKQUOTE> will still result in a right margin, since most browsers display text in this tag with a right and left margin (see Figure 5.12).

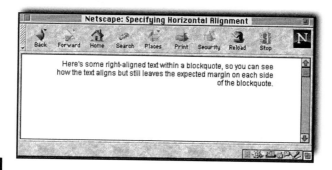

Figure 5.12

Text right-aligned within a blockquote.

Explorer 3 doesn't always restrict alignment to the edge of the element. Right-aligned blockquote text, for example, gets aligned all the way to the edge of the browser window.

How justification is handled depends on the browser. Each browser has its own algorithm for determining the actual display of justified text. A browser is free to adjust the word spacing and/or letter spacing. Netscape Navigator adjusts word spacing only (see Figure 5.13). No matter how you resize the browser window, the text will rewrap so that it's justified.

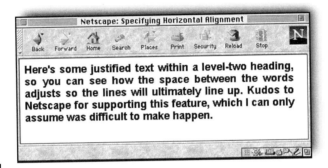

Figure 5.13

Justification in Navigator 4—the space between the words is adjusted as necessary.

Browsers that don't support justified text are supposed to display the text in some replacement format—typically left-aligned.

Explorer 3 and 4 don't support `justify`. They display justified text as left-aligned.

vertical-align

Syntax:

```
baseline ¦ sub ¦ super ¦ top ¦ text-top ¦ middle ¦ bottom ¦ text-
bottom ¦ <percentage>
```

Default value: `baseline`
Applies to: Inline and replaced elements
Inherited: No
Percentage values: Refer to the line-height of the element itself

Examples:

```
H1 { vertical-align: top }
```

```
H1 { vertical-align: 40% }
```

```
<H1 STYLE="vertical-align: text-bottom">
```

This property enables you to control the vertical alignment of inline text as well as images. Some of these values correspond to what the HTML attribute ALIGN accomplishes.

Don't get too excited. Explorer 3 doesn't recognize `vertical-align` at all.

Explorer 4 recognizes the `sub` and `super` values of `vertical-align`, but that's it.

Netscape Navigator

Navigator 4 doesn't support `vertical-align` at all.

Most of the keyword values you can use are relative to the parent of the element in question:

➡ `baseline` ensures that the baseline of the element is aligned with the baseline of the parent.

➡ `sub` puts the element in subscript.

➡ `super` puts the element in superscript.

➡ `text-top` aligns the top of the element with the top of the font of the parent element.

➡ `middle` places the vertical midpoint of the element aligned with the baseline of the parent plus half the x–height (x–height refers to the height of the lowercase letters of a font). `middle` is often used for aligning images.

➡ `text-bottom` aligns the bottom of the element with the bottom of the font of the parent element.

There are also two other keyword values you can use for `vertical-align` that are relative not to the parent, but instead to the formatted line that the element is part of:

➡ `top` aligns the top of the element with the tallest element on the line.

➡ `bottom` aligns the bottom of the element with the lowest element on the line.

Finally, you can also use percentage values to specify `vertical-align`. Percentage values refer to the `line-height` of the element itself:

```
SPAN { vertical-align: 20% }

SPAN { vertical-align: -50% }

SPAN { vertical-align: -100% }
```

In these examples, the positive value raises the baseline 20% of the distance from baseline to baseline of text lines. A negative value lowers the baseline appropriately. A value of –100% actually places the baseline of the element exactly the same place as the baseline of the text line underneath. Yes, in the future this might be another way to overlap elements.

text-indent

Syntax:

```
<length> ¦ <percentage>
```

Default value: 0
Applies to: Block-level elements
Inherited: Yes
Percentage values: Refer to the width of the parent element

Examples:

```
H1 { text-indent: 2em }
```

```
H1 { text-indent: 10% }
```

```
<H1 STYLE="text-indent: 1in">
```

The last property we'll discuss in this chapter deals with indentation. Define the amount of text-indent, and the first formatted line of a block element will be indented that much.

You can specify `text-indent` using any of length units that you can use for `word-spacing` (see the beginning of this chapter, and also Appendix A). You can also specify a percentage value. In the second example above, the first line of <H1> text would be indented 10% of the width that <H1> would otherwise have (this isn't always the entire browser window width). So if <H1> occurred within a table that took up half the window width, then the indent would be 10% of that, or 5% of the browser window. Any indents also respect margins you've specified, and thus are indented from the edge of the margin.

Figure 5.14 shows various paragraphs with the following `text-indents` defined:

➡ <P> text indented half an inch

➡ <P> text indented 2 ems

➡ <P> text indented 10%

➡ <BLOCKQUOTE> text indented 10%

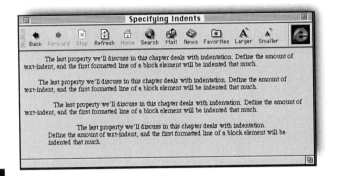

Figure 5.14 _____

Various text-indent settings.

_____

  Indents are not used in the middle of an element that is
                      broken by another element. So if a <BR> is inserted within a
                      <P></P>, the next line will not be indented.

If you want a so-called "hanging indent," you can set text-indent
to a negative value (see Figure 5.15):

```
<HTML>
 <STYLE TYPE="text/css">
 <!--
  H1          { text-indent: -.4in }
  BLOCKQUOTE { text-indent: -5% }
 -->
 </STYLE>
<HEAD>
 <TITLE>Specifying Negative Indents</TITLE>
</HEAD>
<BODY>
 <H1>
 Behold the wonders of text-indent, which can be specified with a
 negative value so the result is a cool hanging indent. Style sheets
 are wondrous, are they not? I bow before them and give thanks.
 </H1>
 <BLOCKQUOTE>
 Yes, they certainly are, even for us lowly blockquote tags, which
 can also enjoy the treats that style sheets have to offer. The mak
 ers of HTML would be proud to see their language grow thusly.
```

```
</BLOCKQUOTE>
</BODY>
</HTML>
```

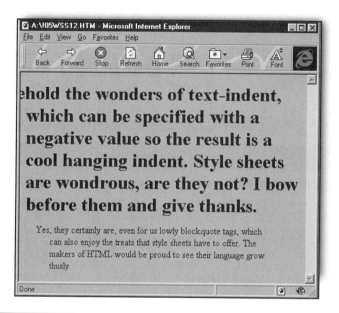

Figure 5.15

Negative `text-indent` *gives you a hanging indent.*

Of course, the big danger with using hanging indents is that words can get cut off, as you can see in the figure.

Netscape **Navigator**

Navigator ignores hanging indents if any words will get cut off, but otherwise it supports them.

What do all of these typographical properties mean? We finally have serious control over the layout of our pages, from leading all the way down to specific indents. This isn't quite PageMaker yet: There are many inconsistencies and bugs, and the control isn't as precise as we'd like it. But it's a lot better than anything before style sheets.

6

Colors and Backgrounds

This chapter consists of some powerful style sheet properties, most of which enable us to do things we've never been able to do before. With the color property, we can control an element's color in a variety of ways. With the related background properties, we can apply background colors and images behind elements— and even control the exact positioning and behavior of those background images.

color

Syntax:

```
<color>
```

Default value: Depends on the browser; usually black
Applies to: All elements
Inherited: Yes
Percentage values: N/A

Examples:

```
H1 { color: aqua }
H1 { color: rgb(51,204,0) }
<H1 STYLE="color: #ff0000">
```

Defining the color of a text element is straightforward via the color property. In essence, you're specifying the "foreground" color of elements.

If you're used to dealing with color values in HTML (via the <FONT COLOR> tag, for example), then color values in style sheets will seem familiar. A color is defined by any of the following:

➡ Color name

➡ Hexadecimal number

➡ RGB value

Color Names

The color names recommended by the style sheets specification include the following:

➡ aqua

➡ black

➡ blue

➡ fuchsia

➡ gray

➡ green

➡ lime

➡ maroon

➡ navy

➡ olive

➡ purple

➡ red

➡ silver

➡ teal

➡ white

➡ yellow

> Make sure to spell gray with an "a," not an "e." grey makes Explorer display black, and Navigator a weird minty green.

These 16 colors all come from the Windows VGA palette and are also part of the official HTML 3.2 spec. They are all "browser-safe colors," meaning that they come from the 216-color palette that Netscape Navigator uses to display graphics. These colors are guaranteed not to dither across platforms or in Internet Explorer. In other words, they're safe bets.

Lucky for us, Netscape and Microsoft have added hundreds of other color names to that list, which include such creative concoctions as moccasin, lawngreen, and lightskyblue3. The best site I've found for seeing all these colors firsthand is HYPE's Color Specifier, located at http://www.users.interport.net/~giant/COLOR/ 1ColorSpecifier.html (see Figure 6.1). As well as showing the colors, this helpful page gives the correct color names, hexadecimal equivalents, and even RGB values for each. (In case you ever have trouble getting through, a decent alternative site is http:// www.nps.navy.mil/internal/tutorial/colortbl.htm.)

Note

> It's important to note that these hundreds of colors are mostly *not* in the browser-safe family. That is, there's a good chance they will dither and not look great across platforms.
>
> For more detailed information on the important issues of browser color palettes and Web color optimization, see David Siegel's *Creating Killer Web Sites* (Hayden Books) or Lynda Weinman's *Coloring Web Graphics* (New Riders)—both unparalleled books. Or for starters, visit their respective Web sites at http://www.killersites.com and http://www.lynda.com.

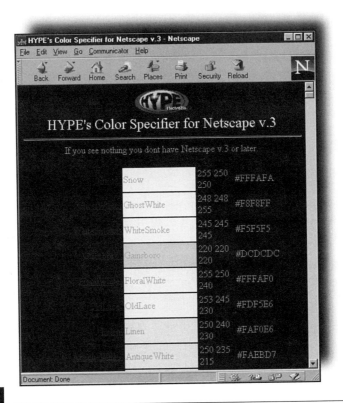

Figure 6.1

HYPE's Color Specifier shows all the color names you can use.

Be careful with grays/greys. `darkgray` is a correct spelling, but so is `lightgrey`. Somebody somewhere messed up. But that's the way it is.

In style sheet rules, color names are used as follows:

```
BODY { color: teal }
H1   { color: red }
```

Using color names is always an act of approximating color. It's not like using a specific numerical value that always gives a result that you expect. Different browsers treat color names differently; a `teal` on one browser might not match `teal` on another. In other words, using hexadecimal numbers gives you more control.

Hexadecimal Numbers

A hex on Netscape for originally forcing us to define colors in hex! But it's out there, so we have to live with it. As in HTML, you can define colors in style sheets by hexadecimal values. This is far more flexible than using color names, because there are far more possible colors at your disposal (over 16 million, in fact).

Of course this means that the vast majority of colors you can use via hexadecimal do not belong to the browser-safe color palette. Fortunately, there's an easy way to know if your hex color is a "safe" color. A hex number consists of three pairs of "numbers"; each number starts at 0 (zero), goes to 9, then continues with a through f (it's called "hexadecimal" because it's a 16-base number system, so you need to use letters in addition to numbers). Anyway, you know you have a safe color if every pair of numbers comes from this list: 00, 33, 66, 99, cc, ff. By that rule, these are safe colors: 00ff66, cc0000, 66ff99. But these aren't: 01ffc2, 1ff56c, 0ffcc0.

Okay, here's how hex looks in style sheet rules:

```
BODY { color: #33cc00 }   /* teal */
H1   { color: #ff0000 }   /* red */
```

(Navigator and Explorer will both render the colors even if you leave out the # character, but it's still best to include it.) As you can see by the comments, the first rule defines a teal color, and the second rule defines red. Both of these colors are browser-safe.

Style sheets also support a shorthand for hex values. You can use a three-digit format, which the browser will translate to the six-digit form. The following code specifies the same colors as the code we just looked at:

```
BODY { color: #3c0 }   /* teal */
H1   { color: #f00 }   /* red */
```

RGB Values

Hex values actually correspond to RGB (Red, Green, Blue) values traditionally used in graphics applications such as Photoshop. In HTML, we always had to convert RGB values to hex in order to get the solid background or text colors into our Web document (for example, teal is `51,204,0` in RGB and `#33cc00` in hex). But style sheets gloriously support RGB values themselves.

This means we can specify color like so:

```
BODY { color: rgb(51,204,0) }   /* teal */
H1   { color: rgb(255,0,0) }    /* red */
```

These colors match what we specified earlier, only now the values are in RGB. Values must fall in the range of 0–255.

> Explorer 3 does not support colors specified in this `rgb()` format.
>
> Version 4, however, does support `rgb()`.

> Navigator 4 doesn't support the `rgb()` format (and when it sometimes seems to, it in fact displays the wrong color!).

> Beta 3 does in fact support the `rgb()` format.

But wait, there's more! You can also define colors by a *percentage* of RGB value. Our same example would now look like this:

```
BODY { color: rgb(20%, 80%, 0%) }   /* teal */
H1   { color: rgb(100%, 0%, 0%) }   /* red */
```

Values can range from `0.0%` to `100.0%`.

A few general notes about defining color:

➡ Can methods be combined? You bet. In the same style sheet, you can have rules that define color by name, hex value, and RGB file. The browser should translate them all just fine.

➡ What happens when there's a number outside of the possible range? Theoretically, the browser should translate it to the nearest valid value. If you specify an RGB value of `300,95,256`, for example, the browser should treat it as `255,95,255`.

But in reality, Navigator 4 and Explorer 3 actually revert back to the element's default color instead of translating your incorrect value. In most cases, this means displaying black. (Explorer 4 handles this situation correctly, as described in the previous paragraph.)

Netscape Navigator

> If you give Navigator an invalid color name, it arbitrarily picks a color for you. For example, if you spell `darkgray` incorrectly as `darkgrey`, Navigator displays magenta for your viewing pleasure. Weird.

➡ Are you getting different colors when you look at your pages on different monitors? Welcome to the world of Web design. Monitors are calibrated differently and have different gamma settings; in particular, colors on a Windows monitor often display much darker than they do on a Mac screen. Your only choice is to accept your fate and make sure you always test on different browsers and platforms! (And you might check out PNG, a new graphics format that corrects for these problems. Go to a bookstore and ask about *Web Designer's Guide to PNG, GIF, and JPEG*.)

background-color

Syntax:

`transparent ¦ <color>`

Default value: `transparent`

Applies to: All elements
Inherited: No
Percentage values: N/A

Examples:

```
H1 { background-color: blue }
```

```
H1 { background-color: transparent }
```

```
H1 { background-color: #ff0000 }
```

```
<H1 STYLE="background-color: lawngreen">
```

Previously, HTML has enabled us to define a background color for an entire page, and even specify various background colors on a page using table backgrounds. Style sheets takes this concept to a whole new level via the `background-color` property (and other properties that follow). Now, without resorting to awkward tables, we can specify the background color of any given text element or group.

This is important: Explorer 3 does support background colors, but *only* if you use the "shorthand" version of the property: `background` (see the last section in this chapter for details). Instead of using `background-color` as the property, you have to use `background`, or it won't work.

Why? Because Internet Explorer 3 came out while the Cascading Style Sheets spec was still evolving, and at that time there was just one broad `background` property proposed; it wasn't yet split into various properties (such as `background-color` and `background-image`). Essentially, Explorer 3 supports an older version of the spec. Fortunately, it will still work, as long as you use `background` for all background-related styles.

Explorer 4 works fine with either `background-color` or `background`.

Note

> Because an element's background is transparent by default,
> there's no need for a parent's background to inherit. It will
> show through automatically.

Transparent Backgrounds

Defining an element as transparent simply means there is no
background. Whatever would normally show through behind the
text will.

```
BODY { background-color: white }
H1   { background-color: lightblue }
I    { background-color: transparent }
```

These rules define the entire page with a white background. All
<H1> text is on a light blue background (see the next section), but
all italic text that occurs within <H1> is set to be on a transparent
background, so instead of seeing another light blue background,
the white underneath shows through (see Figure 6.2).

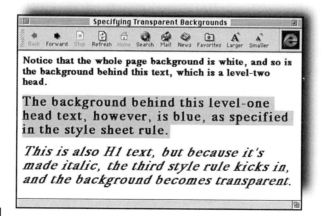

Figure 6.2

A transparent *setting lets whatever is underneath show through.*

> Navigator 4 doesn't support the `transparent` setting. In our example, Navigator decides to display the third paragraph with a dark blue background; I'm not sure why.

Color Backgrounds

Defining backgrounds as solid colors is much more common. You can use any unit of color that we discussed in the previous `color` section, including color name, hexadecimal number, and RGB value.

As you saw in Figure 6.2, defining different color backgrounds for different sections of text results in rectangles of different colors:

```
<HTML>
 <STYLE TYPE="text/css">
 <!--
  BODY       { background-color: white }
  H1         { background-color: orange }
  BLOCKQUOTE { background-color: blue }
  B          { background-color: lime }
  I          { background-color: yellow }
 -->
 </STYLE>
<HEAD>
 <TITLE>Specifying Background Colors</TITLE>
 </HEAD>
<BODY>
 <H1>Hi, I'm a level-one heading with
 <B>a few words of bold</B> and
 <I>a few words of italics</I>.</H1>
 <P>New paragraph here. Let's insert just a little
 <B>bold</B> and <I>italics</I>.</P>
 <BLOCKQUOTE>A blockquote here. Let's insert just a little
 <B>bold</B> and <I>italics</I>.</BLOCKQUOTE>
 </BODY>
 </HTML>
```

The result is rather odd-looking (see Figure 6.3). If anything, this tells me to be careful of using too many background colors on one page.

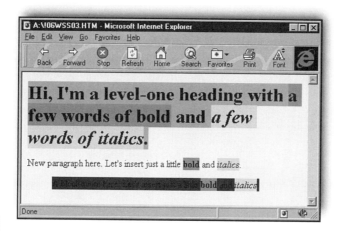

Figure 6.3

Watching the background colors fight it out.

Navigator sometimes goes loopy (for lack of a better word when you change styles in the middle of a paragraph, as I mentioned in Chapter 2. And all the background properties are susceptible to this problem. Figure 6.4 shows how Navigator breaks to a new line every time the background color changes. The text is also not styled as you'd expect: the <H1> text isn't larger and bold, the <I> text isn't italicized, and so on. The effect is, to say the least, not what was intended!

As you can see in the figures, in Explorer 3 and Navigator 4 background color doesn't mean the whole paragraph is enveloped in a single colored rectangle that goes all the way to the browser window. The color appears only where it's actually behind text; the result is a "ragged right" of rows of background color.

Explorer 4, however, handles this differently: the background color extends to the edge of the element's possible display area, forming a large rectangle for each block-level element (see Figure 6.5).

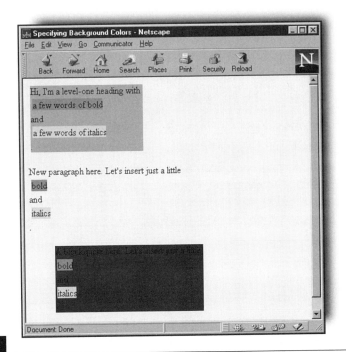

Figure 6.4

Navigator displays the same page—but adds line breaks.

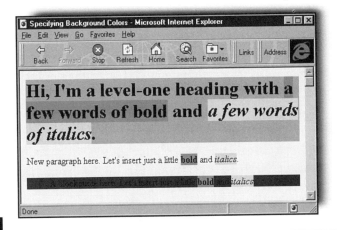

Figure 6.5

Explorer 4 extends background color as it should.

Vertically, the color extends from the exact bottom of descenders (such as the "g" in "heading" in Figure 6.3) to a bit *above* the top of ascenders. Notice how the orange background extends beyond the top of the "Hi" in the same figure.

If you increase the line-height of text with a background color, the color *doesn't* expand with the new leading. Instead, you get strips of white between each line (see Figure 6.6).

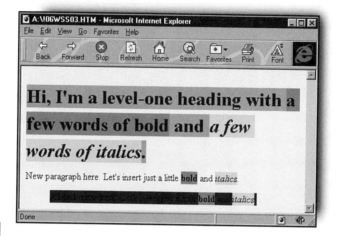

Figure 6.6

Background colors don't expand when you increase line-height.

Once again, Explorer 4 emerges as slightly more sophisticated. It expands the background colors to "fill in" the vertical space (see Figure 6.7).

continues

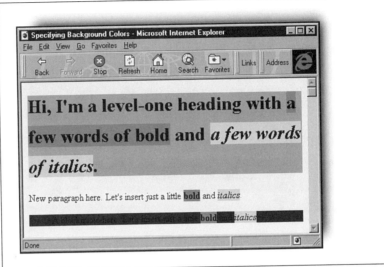

Explorer 4 expands background colors to fit changed leadings.

Furthermore, when you decrease line-height, background colors still maintain their original dimensions. You just get odd–looking overlaps (see Figure 6.8).

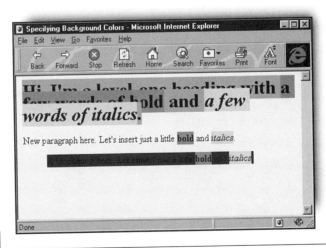

Background colors don't shrink when you decrease line-height.

Explorer 4 makes sure the text doesn't get covered. The effect is odd, but probably better than what we saw in the previous figure (see Figure 6.9).

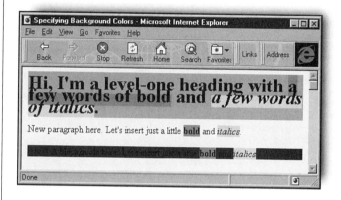

Figure 6.9

Explorer 4 shrinks background colors to fit decreased leading.

Background colors handle inheritance the traditional way. They also fight out the cascading order the expected way:

```
<HTML>
 <STYLE TYPE="text/css">
 <!--
  BODY { background-color: white }
  DIV  { background-color: blue }
  H1   { background-color: yellow }
  B    { background-color: lime }
 -->
 </STYLE>
<HEAD>
 <TITLE>Specifying Background Colors</TITLE>
</HEAD>
<BODY>
 <DIV><H1><B>This is text on a lime background</B></H1></DIV>
</BODY>
</HTML>
```

The B style rule is most relevant, so it wins out, and the text gets a lime-colored background (see Figure 6.10).

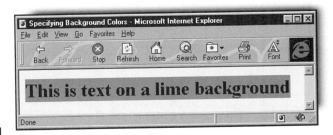

Figure 6.10

The appropriate rule wins the cascading order battle, and the background is lime.

Netscape
Navigator

Navigator handles this a bit differently, as the somewhat shocking Figure 6.11 shows.

Figure 6.11

Navigator incorrectly displays all the colors, not just the lime.

As you can see, Navigator adds frames of color around the final text. The background color is inherited properly, because the ultimate background is lime. But we can also see the yellow of the <H1> and the blue of the <DIV>. I suspect this results from the way Navigator handles the formatting model (see the next chapter); it apparently adds a padding, border, or margin around each tag, even if that tag contains nothing.

Explorer 3 has bugs of its own. Normally, child elements are supposed to be transparent when it comes to backgrounds, so that the background of their parent elements can shine through. If <BODY> is the parent, all is well. But if another element is the parent, things can go awry:

```
DIV { background: red }
P   ( color: white }
...
<DIV>
<P>This is a test. I'm supposed to have a red background.</P>
</DIV>
```

In this scenario, <P> text is *supposed* to let the background color of <DIV> shine through. But it doesn't. Instead, we get a default gray background behind the text. Something to be aware of!

This bug is corrected in Explorer 4.

background-image

Syntax:

```
<url> ¦ none
```

Default value: none
Applies to: All elements
Inherited: No
Percentage values: N/A

Examples:

```
H1 { background-image: url(stripes.gif) }
H1 { background-image: none }
H1 { background-image: url(background.gif) white }
<H1 STYLE="background-image: url(woods.jpg)">
```

Pretty much anything you can do with `background-color`, you can also do with `background-image`, though of course here you're using image files as backgrounds instead of solid colors. You specify an image file with a URL, and you can even specify a backup color that "sits" behind the image.

You can also specify `none` for this property, which is useful if you don't want to include a background image behind a child element that would otherwise inherit a background image.

This will sound familiar, because it's true of all the background-related properties: Explorer 3 supports background images, but *only* if you use `background` (not `background-image`). All the values that follow in this section (and the next several) can still be specified through `background` (see the last section).

Explorer 4 supports both `background-image` and `background`.

Using URLs

URLs, or Uniform Resource Locators, are those ever-present Internet addresses that define the location of a file. URLs appear in style sheets like so:

```
H1 { background-image: url(http://www.hayden.com/img/stars.gif) }
```

You can also use relative URLs, which don't specify the full pathname:

```
H1 { background-image: url(../images/stars.gif) }
```

The important thing to note here is that partial URLs such as this one are relative to the location of the *style sheet document*, not the location of the HTML document. So, if you look at the example directory structure in Figure 6.12, you can see that the URL must point from the linked style sheet main-style.css to stars.gif. That means we need to "climb" a directory, then go into the images directory—hence the ../images/stars.gif.

Figure 6.12

Relative URLs always begin from the style sheet location.

 Internet
explorer

Using image URLs works fine with Explorer 3 unless you're using a *linked* style sheet (see Chapter 2). Then it doesn't display the image at all. Make sure to use embedded or inline styles for background images.

Inserting Background Images

Okay, let's throw some background images into a page. Before we start, look at Figure 6.13 to see the actual images we'll be using throughout the rest of this chapter.

Figure 6.13

From left to right: background.gif, stripes.gif, woods.jpg, and face.gif.

N Netscape
  Navigator

> Navigator 4 doesn't always recognize background images when
> they're applied to inline elements. For example, if `<B>` is
> supposed to get a background image, Navigator sometimes
> doesn't display it if the bold text appears mid-paragraph.

```
<HTML>
 <STYLE TYPE="text/css">
 <!--
  BODY       { background-image: url(../graphics/background.gif) }
  H1         { background-image: url(../graphics/face.gif) }
  BLOCKQUOTE { font-size: 25px;
               background-image: url(../graphics/woods.jpg) }
  B          { background-image: url(../graphics/stripes.gif) }
 -->
 </STYLE>
<HEAD>
 <TITLE>Specifying Background Images</TITLE>
</HEAD>
<BODY>
 <H1>This is some sample text; isn't it exciting? This is some
 sample text; isn't it exciting?
 <B>This is some sample text in bold; isn't it exciting? This is
 some sample text in bold; isn't it exciting?</B>
 </H1>
 <H2>New paragraph here. Let's insert just a few <B>bold words</B>.
 </H2>
 <BLOCKQUOTE>This is some sample blockquote text; isn't it exciting?
 This is some sample blockquote text; isn't it exciting?
 <B>This is some sample blockquote text in bold; isn't it exciting?
```

```
  </B></BLOCKQUOTE>
</BODY>
</HTML>
```

Yowsa. Check out Figure 6.14 and say it with me: Yowsa!

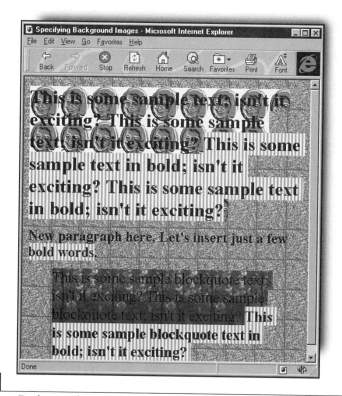

Figure 6.14

Background images: powerful, unless used poorly like this!

Let's look at this page not as an aesthetic success, but as a technical test. As you can see, background images are placed behind text
elements the same way background colors are. Also, background
images applied to <BODY> fill the entire window. And just as we're
used to in HTML backgrounds via the <BODY BACKGROUND> tag, the
images tile across and down the page.

Another thing to notice is that the upper left corner of the styled
element is aligned with the upper left corner of the background
image. This means that the first paragraph begins with the full

face GIF, and the third paragraph begins with the full woods JPEG. This is in fact a coincidence here. Alignment doesn't always happen, on Windows or on the Mac. If we look at the same page on the Mac, we'll see that backgrounds *aren't* aligned based on where the elements start (see Figure 6.15). So the face is cut off both horizontally and vertically, and the third paragraph begins in the middle of the woods image instead of at the top. This can happen on any page, so test carefully.

Last Minute note

> Explorer 4 doesn't support any repeat values in beta 1, but I predict it will in the final release.

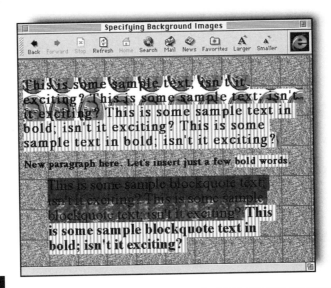

Figure 6.15

The same Web page: background images can align rather haphazardly.

But background images can also enable effects never before possible, or at least ones that are much more bandwidth-friendly. You can overlay text onto images to liven up headlines, and use text over images as callouts pointing to specific areas, for example on a map (see Figure 6.16).

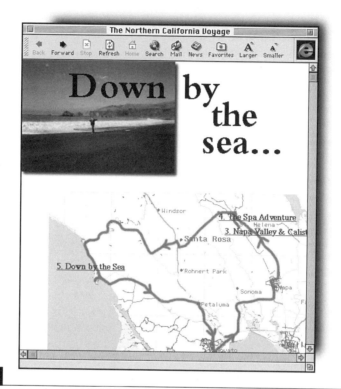

Figure 6.16

Use background images, and suddenly all sorts of creative effects are possible.

By the way, you can use background images in combination with solid color backgrounds.

Adding a Backup Color

It's always a good idea to specify a solid color behind every image that you use. This solid color will be used:

➡ Behind the element while the image loads

➡ To show through any transparent regions of the image

➡ If no URL is specified or if the URL doesn't work

Here's how the code looks:

```
<HTML>
 <STYLE TYPE="text/css">
 <!--
  BODY { background-color: white }
  H1   { color: white;
         background-image: url(../graphics/face2.gif);
         background-color: blue }
  -->
 </STYLE>
<HEAD>
 <TITLE>Specifying Background Images</TITLE>
</HEAD>
<BODY>
 <H1>
 Hi, I'm a level-one heading with a funky background of faces.
 Note that while the background image loads, you see the solid
 color (blue)—otherwise you couldn't read this white text on a
 white background. Notice also that the image has transparent
 areas, and in those areas the blue shines through.
 </H1>
</BODY>
</HTML>
```

Blue serves as the "backup" solid color. It's displayed as the background image face2.gif loads, and also it shows through the transparent areas of the GIF (see Figure 6.17).

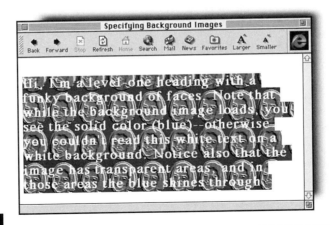

Figure 6.17

A backup color for background images can be very useful.

If you don't specify a backup color for an element (which is certainly an option if you want), then the area will be transparent.

background-repeat

Syntax:

```
repeat ¦ repeat-x ¦ repeat-y ¦ no-repeat
```

Default value: repeat
Applies to: All elements
Inherited: No
Percentage values: N/A

Examples:

```
H1 { background-image: url(stripes.gif);
     background-repeat: repeat-x }
H1 { background-image: url(background.gif) };
     background-repeat: no-repeat }
```

```
<H1 STYLE="background-image: url(woods.jpg); background-repeat: re-
peat">
```

With background-repeat, you can finally control exactly how background images tile or don't tile across an area. To use this property, there has to be a background image defined through background-image or background!

> Reminder: With Explorer 3, you have to use the background property to get these repeat values to work; background-repeat won't work.

We're used to background images repeating. Using the HTML <BODY BACKGROUND> tag, we can use graphics as background images, and they tile across and down the page no matter what we do. Many times this is a good thing, because it enables us to fill an entire background with a texture using a small 20 × 20-pixel graphic. But sometimes this tiling is horrifying, such as when you're using a large image that you don't want to repeat (see Figure 6.18).

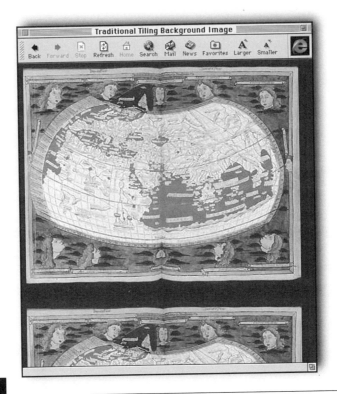

Figure 6.18

On big monitors, the background image on this page repeats when we don't want it to, giving Web designers ulcers.

Don't you just wish you could turn off the tiling?! Guess what? With background-repeat, you can (see Figure 6.19). You can specify whether and how background images tile (repeat).

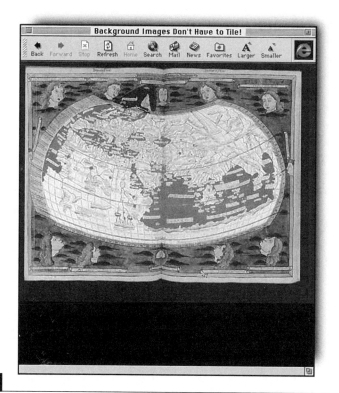

Figure 6.19

Background images no longer have to tile if you don't want them to.

Here are your options:

➡ no-repeat means the background image won't repeat at all, but instead display just once.

➡ repeat causes the background image to repeat (tile) as it normally does (horizontally and vertically) to fill the entire space.

➡ repeat-x makes the background image tile only horizontally.

➡ repeat-y forces the background image to tile only vertically.

Figure 6.20 shows these four options in action.

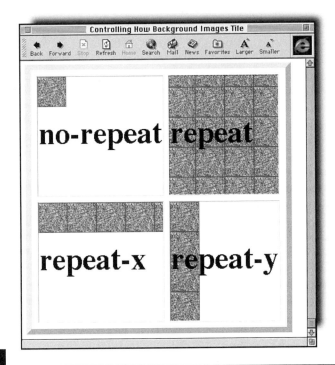

Figure 6.20

Finally we can control (sort of) how or if background images tile.

We noticed earlier that Explorer 3 doesn't align background images with the tops (and left sides) of the elements they're behind. But when you use no-repeat, repeat-x, or repeat-y, it does align the background images, as the figure shows.

If you don't specify a background-repeat value, then a normal repeat is assumed (the image will tile horizontally and vertically).

background-attachment

Syntax:

```
scroll ¦ fixed
```

Default value: scroll
Applies to: All elements
Inherited: No
Percentage values: N/A

Examples:

```
BODY { background-image: url(stripes.gif);
      background-attachment: fixed }
BODY { background-image: url(background.gif) };
      background-attachment: scroll }

<BODY STYLE="background-image: url(woods.jpg); background-attachment:
fixed">
```

The background-attachment property enables you to define whether a background image should be fixed in relation to the browser window, or whether it should "scroll" with the text of the Web page:

➡ scroll means the background image will scroll along with the page's contents. This is what we're used to seeing.

➡ fixed is a new option for Web designers. The background image will not scroll, but remain fixed in place (see Figures 6.21 and 6.22). This is surprising at first!

Using a `fixed` *background-attachment, no matter where you scroll...*

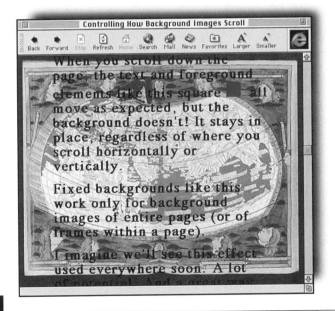

...the background image always remains in place. Text and foreground images (such as the square) move, but not the background.

It's important to note that background-attachment works only on *page* background images—that is, backgrounds that are styled to the <BODY> tag. Backgrounds styled to other elements cannot be declared fixed.

Reminder: With Explorer 3, you have to use the background property to get these values to work; background-attachment won't work. Explorer 4 doesn't yet support this property.

Unfortunately, background-attachment doesn't work in Navigator 4 at all.

If you don't specify either fixed or scroll, then the browser assumes you mean scroll.

background-position

Syntax:

```
[ <percentage> ¦ <length> ] {1,2} ¦ [ top ¦ center ¦ bottom ] ¦¦ [
left ¦ center ¦ right ]
```

Default value: 0% 0%
Applies to: Block-level and replaced elements
Inherited: No
Percentage values: Refer to the size of the element itself

Examples:

```
BODY { background-image: url(stripes.gif);
       background-position: center bottom }
BODY { background-image: url(background.gif) };
       background-position: 50% 100% }

<BODY STYLE="background-image: url(woods.jpg); background-position:
center">
```

Background images can even be positioned exactly where you
want them relative to the elements they're behind. You can define
`background-position` in any of several ways:

➡ Percentage values

➡ Length values

➡ Keyword values

Reminder: With Explorer 3, you have to use the `background`
property to get these values to work; `background-position` won't
work.

Also, in Explorer 3, `background-position` works *only* on background images styled to the `<BODY>` tag. You can't control the
position of an image background behind a `<P>` element, for
example—just the entire page. Explorer 4 does not yet support
`background position`.

Unfortunately, `background-position` doesn't work in Navigator 4
at all.

Background Positioning by Percentage

Percentage values for `background-position` always appear as a pair.
The first value always refers to the horizontal positioning; the
second declares the vertical positioning. Values can range from `0%`
to `100%`.

The best way to see how this works is through several examples:

```
BODY { background-image: url(background.gif);
       background-position: 0% 0% }
```

Using this rule, the browser places the upper left corner of the
background image (background.gif) exactly at the upper left corner of the "box" that surrounds the actual content of `<BODY>` (in

the case of <BODY>, that translates into the entire browser window). This is the default placement we're used to (see Figure 6.23). The image tiles as expected, since I didn't set background-repeat to no-repeat.

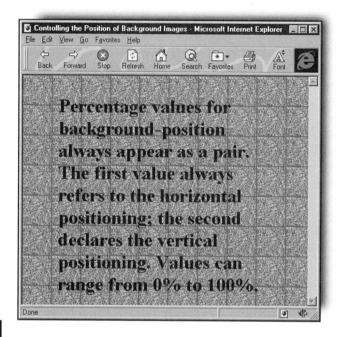

Figure 6.23

The default placement: upper left matches upper left.

Note

Note that for positioning background images, the browser always uses the "box" that immediately surrounds the element. This is the same "line box" we talked about in Chapter 5. That means that it *doesn't* include the box that surrounds the padding, border, or margin of an element (see the next chapter).

Let's try another example:

```
BODY { background-image: url(background.gif);
       background-position: 50% 50% }
```

For this rule, the browser takes the point halfway (50%) over in the background image (the horizontal center, that is) and places it halfway across the <BODY> element (the browser window). In other words, it centers the background image horizontally. Also, it places the vertical middle of the background image halfway down the browser window, thus centering the image vertically. Now that the initial tile is placed, the browser tiles the background image across (to the right) and down the way it normally does (see Figure 6.24).

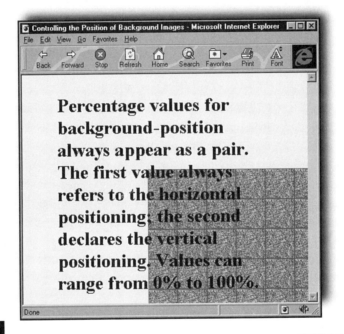

Figure 6.24

The initial background image is aligned in the exact center of the window, then tiled.

Internet explorer

Here's something weird: the Mac version of Explorer 3 doesn't tile the image off-screen the way it should (see Figure 6.25). The initial background image is centered, but notice that the Mac version refuses to display a "tile" of the image unless it can display a *complete* tile. It will no longer bleed the tiles offscreen like it should. Quite disconcerting.

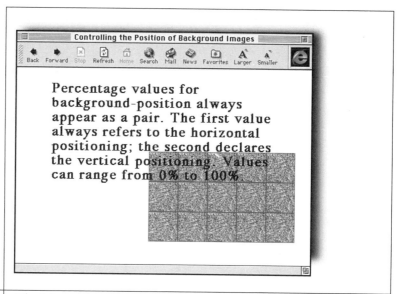

Figure 6.25

The Mac version doesn't tile images correctly off-screen when you use background-position.

A final example:

```
BODY { background-image: url(background.gif);
       background-position: 100% 20% }
```

These percentage values work the same way as the previous example. The point on the GIF that's 100% across from the left edge is placed 100% across the browser window (the right edge of the GIF meets the right edge of the window). The point on the GIF that's 20% down from the top edge is placed 20% down the browser window (see Figure 6.26).

By the way, if the values are identical, such as 35% 35%, you can simply state the value once, and the browser will assume you mean 35% for both horizontal and vertical placement.

A final note about percentage values: As you might have guessed, resizing the browser window will cause the background image to move because the percentages depend on the size of the window.

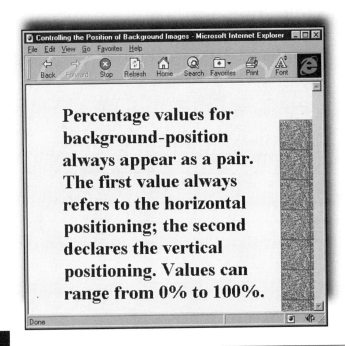

Figure 6.26

The result of `100% 20%` *positioning.*

Background Positioning by Length

Positioning background images by length value works much the same way. The first number declares a horizontal distance from the top left, and the second number a vertical distance from the top left. You can use any of the length units discussed in Appendix A.

```
BODY { background-image: url(face.gif);
       background-position: 1in 6.5cm }
```

In this example, the point one inch across and six and a half centimeters down the GIF is placed the same measurements across and down the browser window.

Explorer 3 does not accept length values for `background-position`. You'll have to make do with the other options.

Just as with percentage values, if the browser finds only one length value specified, then it simply applies that value to both horizontal and vertical offset.

Can you combine percentage values and length units? In the ideal browser, yes. Can you use negative values? No.

Background Positioning by Keyword

Your final option for `background-position` is to use a keyword. Here are all the keywords and their corresponding percentage values:

➡ `top` (`0%`)

➡ `bottom` (`100%`)

➡ `left` (`0%`)

➡ `right` (`100%`)

➡ `center` (`50%`)

As always, the first value specifies horizontal placement, and the second vertical placement.

```
BODY { background-image: url(face.gif);
      background-repeat: repeat-y;
      background-position: top center }
```

In this example, the center of the top of the background image is placed at the center of the top of the window (see Figure 6.27). In other words, `top` is the same as specifying `0%`, and `center` is the

same as 50%. A value of center top would mean exactly the same
thing; order is irrelevant. (Note that for this one I've turned off
horizontal tiling with background-repeat set to repeat-y.)

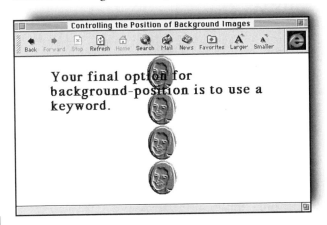

Figure 6.27

The result of top center *positioning.*

center can be used for horizontal or vertical positioning, but the
rest have just one use: top and bottom for vertical offsets, and left
and right for horizontal.

Explorer 3 also supports a value of middle—middle specifies
only vertical positioning, though center can specifies both vertical and horizontal positioning.

If only one position is specified, then the browser will usually
assume the other should be center.

Well, Explorer 3 handles this a bit differently:

➡ Specify only left, and Explorer adds top

➡ Specify only right, and Explorer adds bottom

➡ Specify only top, and Explorer adds left

➡ Specify only `bottom`, and Explorer adds `left`

➡ Specify only `center`, and Explorer adds `center`

➡ Specify only `middle`, and Explorer adds `left`

Are we having fun yet?

Can keyword values for `background-position` be combined with percentage or length values in a rule? No.

A final note about background images: If an image doesn't scroll but is fixed on the browser window (via `fixe`, then any position values are relative to the entire window, not just to the element. The following rule makes the background image centered at the bottom of the window, regardless of how you scroll on the Web page or how you size the window (and Figures 6.28 and 6.29). This unleashes all kinds of interesting opportunities for ever-present logos, content frames, and so on.

```
BODY { background-image: url(face.gif);
      background-repeat: no-repeat;
      background-attachment: fixed;
      background-position: center bottom }
```

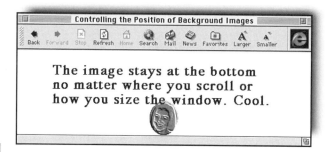

Figure 6.28

Set a no-repeat *background image to* fixed *and get a graphic that never moves...*

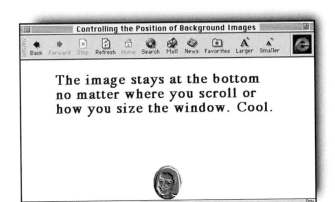

Figure 6.29

...no matter where you scroll or how you resize the window. Cool.

Oh, and yet another final note: If you don't specify a `background-position` value at all for a background image, then the browser assumes you mean `0% 0%`.

background

Syntax:

```
<background-color> ¦¦ <background-image> ¦¦ <background-repeat> ¦¦
<background-attachment> ¦¦ <background-position>
```

Default value: Not defined
Applies to: All elements
Inherited: No
Percentage values: Allowed on `background-position`

Examples:

```
BODY { background: url(stripes.gif) center bottom }
BODY { background: url(background.gif) white repeat-x 50% 100% }
<BODY STYLE="background: url(woods.jpg) no-repeat fixed">
```

The background property is like the font property (see Chapter 4) in that it is a shorthand way of declaring multiple style rules in one rule. With background, you can specify background image, color, repeat, attachment, and/or position all at once.

background is the magic key for Internet Explorer 3. As I mentioned previously, this is the one property that will enable you to do everything with backgrounds that we've been talking about.

Whatever background-related properties and values didn't work in Navigator 4 won't work here either. Sigh.

You can set any number of the allowed values; you don't have to set them all in every rule. Anything you don't set will revert back to its default value.

All the values work the same as described in the previous sections. Here, you simply put them into a slightly different format.

```
BODY { background: url(../graphics/face.gif) white repeat-y fixed 85%
18% }
```

In this example, the rule tells the browser to display the background image (face.gif) thusly:

➡ Use white as the backup solid background color.

➡ Place the initial image 85% across and 18% down the browser window.

➡ Tile the image vertically (down) but not horizontally.

➡ Fix the background so that it doesn't scroll with the page's contents.

And the browser obeys (see Figures 6.30 and 6.31).

Figure 6.30

The page loads with the background images placed precisely…

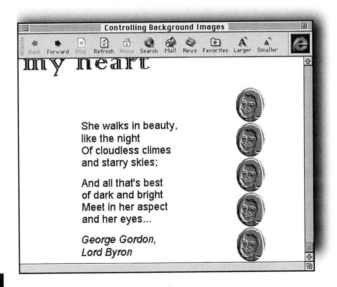

Figure 6.31

…even when you scroll down. Style sheets are cool.

Layout, Part I

In this chapter, we'll dive into what the style sheet specification calls "box properties"—that is, properties that control margins, borders, floating images, and other elegant layout capabilities. I'm positive you'll leave this chapter (and the next, part two of this discussion) wondering how you've lived this long without style sheets.

But first we have to take a detour and explain what "box" and other layout terms mean in the context of style sheets.

The Formatting Model

In style sheets, every single block-level element (tags such as <P> and <H1>, which automatically define their own block or paragraph) has what is called a *box*. The box is the sum of the following parts:

➡ The *element* itself (text, image, animation, or whatever)

➡ The *padding* around the element

➡ The *border* around the padding

➡ The *margin* around the border

Got that? Better yet, see Figure 7.1.

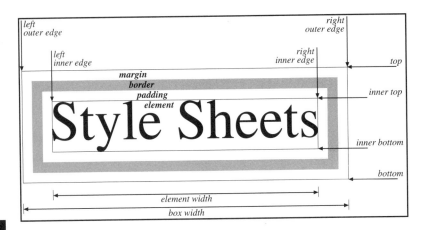

Figure 7.1

The basic formatting model within style sheets.

You set the size of the padding, border, and margin around each element with properties that we'll look at later in this chapter (unsurprisingly, they're named `padding`, `border`, and `margin`). With those same properties, you can also adjust the color and style of the border. The margin, by the way, is always *transparent*; whatever is behind it will always shine through. By the way, each of these properties is optional; you don't necessarily have to define every one.

So, the size of the element's box is the sum of all of these parts, as the figure shows. You also see other terminology introduced:

➡ *top* is the top of the box including any padding, border, and margin.

➡ *inner top* is the top of the actual element, without any padding, border, or margin.

➡ *inner bottom* is the bottom of the actual element.

➡ *bottom* is the bottom of the entire box.

➡ *left outer edge* is the left edge of the entire box, including padding, border, and margin.

➡ *left inner edge* is the left edge of the actual element, without padding, border, or margin.

➡ right inner edge is the right edge of the actual element.

➡ *right outer edge* is the right edge of the entire box.

Also, *width* refers to the width of the element: the distance between the left inner edge and the right inner edge. *Height* is the height of the element: from inner top to inner bottom.

Let's see how these boxes interact in the real world:

```
<HTML>
<HEAD>
 <TITLE>Defining the Box</TITLE>
</HEAD>
<BODY>
 <DIV>
 <P>This line is one paragraph.</P>
 <UL>
 <LI>This is line one.
 <LI>This is line two.
 </UL>
 </DIV>
</BODY>
</HTML>
```

If we view this simple page in a browser, we see some text within a division (<DIV>). Inside the <DIV> are a paragraph and an unordered list. In other words, it's a hierarchy of block elements:

```
<DIV>
  <P>
  <UL>
    <LI>
    <LI>
```

In the formatting model, each of these block elements gets its own box, with padding, border, and margin (see Figure 7.2).

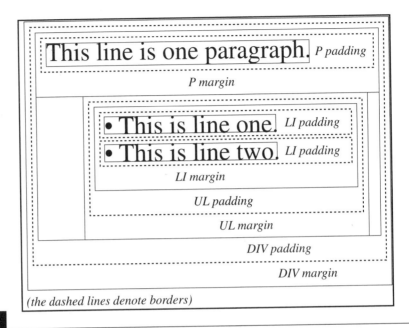

This line is one paragraph. *P padding*

P margin

• This is line one. *LI padding*

• This is line two. *LI padding*

LI margin

UL padding

UL margin

DIV padding

DIV margin

(the dashed lines denote borders)

Figure 7.2

Boxes within boxes: the formatting model in action.

Looks like a mess, right? Well, look at it this way: The more boxes there are, the more control you have to specify exact layout on the canvas. So a mess of boxes is a *good* thing.

Note

In the universe of style sheets, the *canvas* is the drawing surface onto which the Web browser puts documents. For all intents and purposes, the canvas equals the browser window (including any part of the page that you need to scroll to in order to see).

The distance between two elements is controlled by the size of their margins. If you have multiple margins that are adjoined (so there's nothing between them, including content, padding, and border), then those margins are collapsed and the larger of the margin sizes is used. In the previous example, between the first line and the first bulleted text, the <P> margin, <UL> margin, and <LI> margin would be collapsed as long as no borders or padding existed between any of them (refer to Figure 7.2).

> **Note**
>
> At least this is how it's *supposed* to work. To discover what the browsers actually do, read on.

Margins can also be negative, as you'll see later in this chapter. In this situation, for two adjoining margins, the negative margin should be subtracted from the positive margin. (I promise: it will become clearer later in this chapter when we look at some examples.)

With that behind us, let's dive into the actual properties.

margin-top

Syntax:

```
<length> ¦ <percentage> ¦ auto
```

Default value: 0
Applies to: All elements
Inherited: No
Percentage values: Refer to parent element's size

Examples:

```
H1 { margin-top: 20px }
```

```
H1 { margin-top: 10% }
```

```
<H1 STYLE="margin-top: auto">
```

The margin-top property sets the margin above any given element. You can use any length value or percentage value. You can also set it to auto, which we'll look at shortly. By default, margin-top is set to 0, or no extra top margin. (That is, a margin set to 0 doesn't mean that text will begin right at the top of the browser window; it means that text begins where it normally begins, slightly down from the window edge.)

194

Web Designer's Guide to **Style** Sheets

Yes, you can apply margins to images as well as to text. The easiest way is to specify a style to the <IMG> tag. But you can also add margin–related tags to another tag, and then have <IMG> inherit those styles.

 Netscape **Navigator**

With Navigator 4 you have to use this inheritance workaround, because this browser ignores any styles the <IMG> tag itself has.

 Internet explorer

Explorer 4.0, at least in its first beta version, does not support vertical margins at all (top or bottom). (Strangely, it does support negative margins, as described later in this chapter.) I assume this will be fixed before the final release.

Margin by Length

In setting a top margin by a length value, you can use any length unit described in Appendix A. This includes absolute and relative units:

➡ Inches: `in`

➡ Centimeters: `cm`

➡ Millimeters: `mm`

➡ Points: `pt`

➡ Picas: `pc`

➡ Ems: `em`

➡ X-Height: `ex`

➡ Pixels: `px`

Let's look at an example:

```
<HTML>
 <STYLE TYPE="text/css">
 <!--
  SPAN.a { margin-top: 30px;
           font-size: 20pt }
   SPAN.b { margin-top: 1in;
           font-size: 20pt }
   SPAN.c { font-size: 20pt }
  -->
 </STYLE>
<HEAD>
 <TITLE>Specifying a Top Margin</TITLE>
 </HEAD>
<BODY>
 <IMG HEIGHT=10 WIDTH=480 SRC="box-sm.gif"><BR>
 <SPAN CLASS=c>This is text with a 0 margin.
 <IMG ALIGN=top SRC="box-C.gif"></SPAN>
 <P></P>
 <IMG HEIGHT=10 WIDTH=480 SRC="box-sm.gif"><BR>
 <SPAN CLASS=a>This is text with a 30-pixel margin.
 <IMG ALIGN=top SRC="box-C.gif"></SPAN>
 <P></P>
 <IMG HEIGHT=10 WIDTH=480 SRC="box-sm.gif"><BR>
 <SPAN CLASS=b>This is text with a 1-inch margin.
 <IMG ALIGN=top SRC="box-C.gif"></SPAN>
</BODY>
</HTML>
```

As you can see, both the text lines and the rectangles can be moved down from the base solid line using different values for margin-top (see Figure 7.3).

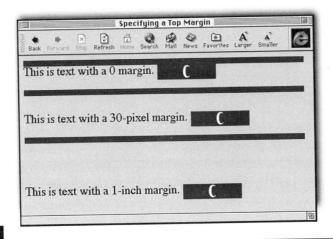

Figure 7.3

Adjust `margin-top` *by a certain length, and you get different top margins. Simple.*

The Windows 95 version of Explorer 3 is sometimes erratic in how it displays the "ruler units" (inches, centimeters, and so on) for `margin-top`. Often it will add a certain amount of extra space to top margins. With other margins, however, the display seems accurate. The Mac version doesn't have this problem at all.

Margin by Percentage

Specifying a top margin by percentage value means that the margin takes its size from the box size of the parent element. `0%` means no top margin.

Here's an example:

```
SPAN.a { margin-top: 5%;
         font-size: 20pt }
SPAN.b { margin-top: 12%;
         font-size: 20pt }
SPAN.c { font-size: 20pt }
```

If we take the previous example and simply change the rules to what you see above, then we can see percentage values at work (see Figure 7.4). The second line of text is displayed 5% of the parent element's box size below the solid horizontal line, and the last text line is 12% below.

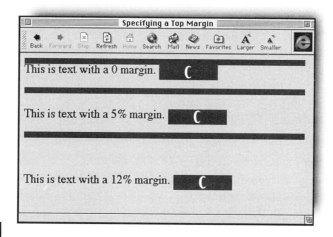

Figure 7.4

Percentage values offer an alternative way to control margins.

Automatic Margins

Your final choice for `margin-top` is a setting of `auto`, which means that the browser automatically calculates the element's top margin so that the sum of it, the top margin, the top border, the top padding, the element's height, the bottom padding, the bottom border, and the bottom margin equals the entire parent element's total box height.

At least that's how it *should* work. Unfortunately, Internet Explorer 3 doesn't support `auto`.

> Neither does Navigator 4.

Negative Margins

Okay, start salivating. Overlapping text and images is easy by simply giving negative values to margin-top.

The proof is in examples:

```
<HTML>
 <STYLE TYPE="text/css">
 <!--
   BODY { background: gray;
          color: white;
          font-size: 30px }
   H1    { color: black;
           font-family: arial }
   P.a   { margin-top: -33px }
   .b    { margin-top: -33px }
 -->
 </STYLE>
<HEAD>
 <TITLE>Specifying a Negative Top Margin</TITLE>
</HEAD>
<BODY>
 <IMG HEIGHT=50 WIDTH=240 SRC="box-med.gif">
 <P CLASS=a>Negative margins! My stars!</P>
 <P></P>
 <IMG HEIGHT=50 WIDTH=240 SRC="box-med.gif">
 <BR><SPAN CLASS=b>Negative margins! My stars!</SPAN>
 <P></P>
 <H1>This is unaffected text.</H1>
 <SPAN class=b>Negative margins! My stars!</SPAN>
</BODY>
</HTML>
```

Figure 7.5 shows the results. A negative margin on the white text line brings it right up into the element above it. But even though all of these lines have the same negative margins (–33 pixels), how much they "invade" the element above them depends on the situation. As you can see, there's a `<P>` between the rectangle and the text in the first example, but only a `<BR>` in the second. So because there would normally be (by browser default) less existing vertical space in the second, the text line overlaps the graphics more than it does in the first.

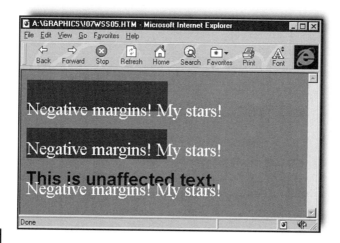

Figure 7.5

Negative `margin-top` *values translate into overlapping elements.*

What would happen if we wanted to overlap even more things on top of the line of text? Just give the elements after the text a negative margin as well:

```
<HTML>
 <STYLE TYPE="text/css">
 <!--
  BODY { background: gray;
        color: white;
        font-size: 30px }
  H1   { margin-top: -33px;
        color: black;
        font-family: arial }
  .a   { margin-top: -33px }
 -->
 </STYLE>
<HEAD>
```

```
<TITLE>Specifying a Negative Top Margin</TITLE>
</HEAD>
<BODY>
<IMG HEIGHT=50 WIDTH=240 SRC="box-med.gif">
<P CLASS=a>Negative margins! My stars!</P>
<H1>And even more overlapping!</H1>
<SPAN CLASS=a>
<IMG HEIGHT=25 WIDTH=70 SRC="box-sm.gif">
</SPAN>
</BODY>
</HTML>
```

The smaller rectangle is on top of the black text, which is on top
of the white text, which is on top of the large rectangle (see Figure 7.6).

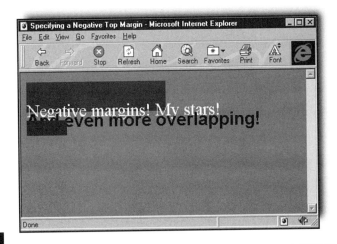

Figure 7.6

More negative margins result in more overlapping elements.

There's a problem with using negative margins to overlap elements. In some situations, the element that you'd think would
appear on "top" gets layered underneath instead. Let's look again
at the example shown in Figure 7.5. Figure 7.7 shows the exact
same page, viewed in another browser/platform combination.

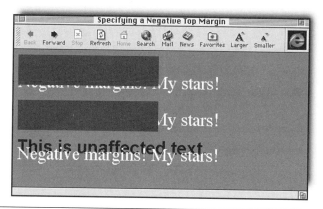

Figure 7.7

The text should be on top of the graphic, but it isn't.

We expect the text to be displayed over the rectangle, but it's not here. Why? From what I can tell, elements that overlap are displayed *in the order that they load* into the browser.

In the code that precedes Figure 7.5, you can see that for the rectangles I specified HEIGHT=50 WIDTH=240. As we all know, specifying height and width for an image enables the browser to load the rest of the page more quickly, because it can "reserve" that many pixels on the page for the graphic, load and flow the rest of the text, and then go back and load the graphic into place. And that's why the text appears *behind* the rectangle: the end result is that even though the image appears first in the HTML, it is actually loaded into the browser window *after* the text.

Let's look at it another way. Suppose I remove the HEIGHT and WIDTH attributes entirely. The result is that the browser no longer goes through the "reserving" process, but instead loads the elements in the order in which they appear in the HTML. The graphic comes first, then the text. Thus, the text appears on top of the graphic (see Figure 7.8). (The graphic is smaller because I'm no longer artificially stretching it with HEIGHT and WIDTH.)

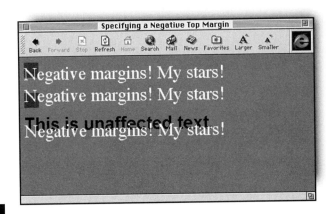

Figure 7.8

With no HEIGHT *or* WIDTH *specified, the loading order is reversed.*

Explorer 3 for the Macintosh works in the way just described: Text is displayed underneath graphics unless you remove any HEIGHT and WIDTH attributes. The 4.0 Windows version works this way as well.

But the Windows 3.0 version is different. On it, elements that appear later in the HTML will *always* be displayed on top of earlier elements. In our example, the text is always over the rectangle.

The bad news is that Navigator 4 (for Windows and Mac places graphics on top no matter what you do. Apparently Navigator *always* loads images after text, so you can never put text on top of images (unless the images are in the background, of course).

Ready for something even weirder? When Internet Explorer displays graphics on top of text (even though it's not supposed to), you can "undo" this effect simply by scrolling down the page, then back up. When the browser redraws the window *this* time, it draws the text on top (see Figure 7.9). Presumably this happens because the graphic is already loaded, so now the browser is free to display everything in the order it appears in the HTML: graphic first, text second.

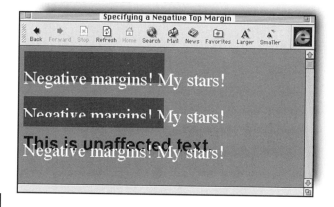

Figure 7.9

Now you can see the text that was out of sight a second ago when I scrolled down the page.

This same "undo" effect occurs whenever the screen is redrawn: after you switch applications, after a dialog box covers the browser window, and so on.

Does this same "undo" effect work in Navigator? Unfortunately, no. Even if you scroll down and come back up a page, images will still cover up text.

The same is true for Explorer 4.0. Images will always cover up text.

So as you can see, overlapping elements can be powerful and enable never-before-seen effects. But it can also be dangerous because of the different ways browsers draw to the screen and handle load order. The bottom line is exactly what we're already used to with HTML: If an effect looks screwy for a good portion of your audience, don't do it! You'll just end up with a page that looks like a mistake.

Oh, by the way, you can also use negative margins to place the element entirely outside the browser window. A negative margin-top on some text would cause the text to start displaying above where you can see it. Not sure why you'd want to use this, but you never know...

 Netscape **Navigator**

> Navigator 4 generally avoids allowing elements to "display" outside the browser window. Usually it will place the element at the very edge of the window instead.

margin-bottom

Syntax:

```
<length> ¦ <percentage> ¦ auto
```

Default value: 0
Applies to: All elements
Inherited: No
Percentage values: Refer to parent element's size

Examples:

```
H1 { margin-bottom: 20px }
```

```
H1 { margin-bottom: 10% }
```

```
<H1 STYLE="margin-bottom: auto">
```

margin-bottom works just like margin-top. It offers the same kinds of values and units, the same negative margins, and the same browser display inconsistencies. So go back and re-read that section if you want details.

Internet
explorer

> Keep in mind that the first beta of Explorer 4 does not support
> top or bottom margins at all.

We do need to examine, however, what happens when an element with a bottom margin appears just above an element with a top margin:

```
<HTML>
 <STYLE TYPE="text/css">
 <!--
   BODY { background: white }
   .a   { margin-bottom: 50px }
   .b   { margin-top: 20px }
 -->
 </STYLE>
<HEAD>
 <TITLE>When Top and Bottom Margins Meet</TITLE>
</HEAD>
<BODY>
 <SPAN CLASS=a>
 <IMG SRC="box-A.gif">
 </SPAN>
 <BR>
 <SPAN CLASS=b>
 <IMG SRC="box-B.gif">
 </SPAN>
</BODY>
</HTML>
```

When two margins meet, the style sheet's spec says that the browser is supposed to collapse the margins and use the greater of the two margins as the total margin. In this case, that would mean the margin between the two rectangles should be 50 pixels.

But it's not, at least in Navigator 4 or Internet Explorer 3. The browsers calculate the total margin between the elements by simply *adding* the two margins together. So the resulting margin in our example is displayed as 70 pixels (see Figure 7.10).

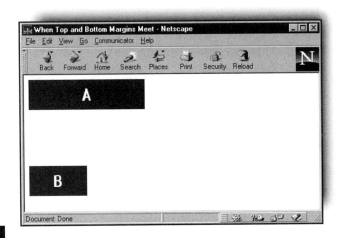

Figure 7.10

Box A has a bottom margin of 50 pixels, and B has a top margin of 20.
The total is 70.

 Internet
            explorer

Okay, this is really strange: Explorer 3 doesn't recognize
`margin-bottom` for every single tag. For example, if you give a
`margin-bottom` to <SPAN> or <BODY>, Explorer ignores it entirely
and won't display a bottom margin (see Figure 7.11). I also
had trouble using `margin-bottom` with classes. But if you give a
`margin-bottom` to a simple <P>, it usually works fine. (Even with
<P>, I ran across problems with the Mac version recognizing
`margin-bottom`.)

For some reason known only to the wizards at Microsoft,
`margin-top` doesn't have this same bug; it seems to work fine
with all HTML tags.

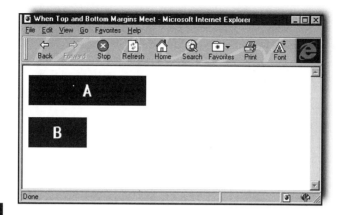

Figure 7.11

Explorer 3 ignores margin-bottom if it's applied to <SPAN> (among other tags), so it displays the same page with a margin of 20 pixels.

If a positive margin meets a negative margin, the negative margin should be subtracted from the positive margin.

```
<HTML>
 <STYLE TYPE="text/css">
 <!--
  BODY { background: white }
  .a   { margin-bottom: 50px }
  .b   { margin-top: -20px }
 -->
 </STYLE>
<HEAD>
 <TITLE>When Top and Bottom Margins Meet</TITLE>
</HEAD>
<BODY>
 <SPAN CLASS=a>
 <IMG SRC="box-A.gif">
 </SPAN>
 <BR>
 <SPAN CLASS=b>
 <IMG SRC="box-B.gif">
 </SPAN>
</BODY>
</HTML>
```

And so it is (see Figure 7.12). The space displayed between rectangle A and B is 30 pixels.

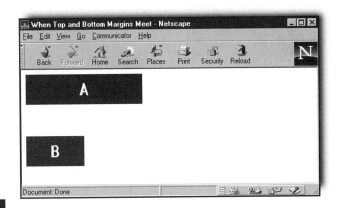

Figure 7.12

Subtract negative from positive for the total margin.

What if both margins were negative? What if the bottom margin in this example were -10px instead of 50px? Well, you might think that the result would be a total of −30 pixels. But actually, the browsers don't add two negative numbers in this case. Instead, they use only the margin-bottom value. So the total in this example would be −20, not −30.

 Internet
explorer

> The Windows version of Explorer 3 will also resort to moving the top element up and "out of the way" of the second element, so to speak, so that there is enough room for the second element to have its required top margin. Keep an eye out for odd results.

margin-right

Syntax:

```
<length> ¦ <percentage> ¦ auto
```

Default value: 0
Applies to: All elements
Inherited: No
Percentage values: Refer to parent element's size

Examples:

```
H1 { margin-right: 20px }
```

```
H1 { margin-right: 10% }
```

```
<H1 STYLE="margin-right: auto">
```

`margin-right` works just like `margin-top` and `margin-bottom`, more or
less. It offers the same kinds of values and units, the same negative
margins, and the same browser display inconsistencies. So no
sense in me restating all that stuff here. But there are differences
and unique problems.

One thing to note is that you can't use `margin-right` to add horizontal space between two replaced elements (images, for example). The browsers ignore any attempt to do so.

Apparently, the only way to adjust the margin horizontally between two elements (text or replaced elements) is if the two elements are in adjoining table cells.

Let's look at what we *can* do with `margin-right`:

```
<HTML>
 <STYLE TYPE="text/css">
 <!--
   BODY { background: white }
   P    { margin-right: 100px }
   I    { margin-right: 100px }
   .a   { margin-right: 100px }
 -->
 </STYLE>
<HEAD>
 <TITLE>Specifying a Right Margin</TITLE>
</HEAD>
<BODY>
```

```
<P>margin-right works just like margin-top and margin-bottom.
It offers the same kinds of values and units, the same negative
margins, and the same browser display inconsistencies. So no
sense in me restating all that stuff here.</P>
<H4>margin-right works just like margin-top and margin-bottom.
<I>It offers the same kinds of values and units, the same negative
margins, and the same browser display inconsistencies. So no
sense in me restating all that stuff here.</I></H4>
<IMG CLASS=a ALIGN=right SRC="box-B.gif">
</BODY>
</HTML>
```

In Figure 7.13 are the results of these three different tests of
margin-right. The first paragraph, which is given a right margin
of 100 pixels, dutifully follows orders. So does the graphic, which
is right-aligned and then given an equal margin as the text. But
the second paragraph is a bit peculiar: the entire paragraph isn't
supposed to have a margin, but most of the text within it is italicized, and <I> *is* supposed to have a margin. The result? The first
line (which contains the non–italicized text) has no margin, but
the rest of the lines do.

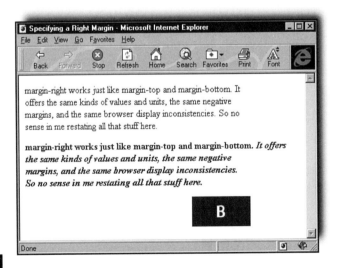

Figure 7.13

Explorer 3.0 supports right margins nicely (and so does 4.0).

Netscape
Navigator

You knew there had to be an exception. Navigator has two problems with `margin-right`.

First, it handles the second paragraph more rudely, so to speak. Where the italicized type begins, Navigator places the text at the beginning of the same line, thus overprinting the earlier text. The result is a mess (see Figure 7.14).

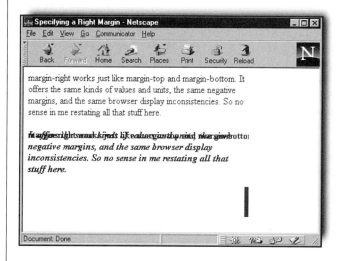

Figure 7.14

Navigator 4 freaks out with horizontal margins on inline elements and graphics.

Second, good grief, what happened to the image? Instead of giving the image a margin of 100 pixels, Navigator *chops off* 100 pixels and displays only what remains! Essentially, the `ALIGN=right` HTML attribute is more powerful than the `margin-right`.

Last Minute note

A later beta fixes this second problem.

> **Tip**
>
> The bottom line about giving margin styles to inline elements? Don't do it. Restrict margins to block-level elements.

An important thing to note about `margin-right` (and also `margin-left`—see the next section) is that horizontal margins are *cumulative*. If you put a 50-pixel right margin on the `<BODY>` tag and a 25-pixel margin on `<H1>`, then all level-one heading text on the page will have a right margin of 75 pixels—the sum of the two applied margins. This is different from normal inheritance; we'd expect the margin on `<H1>` to be just 25 pixels, but it's not.

This is not the case with `margin-top`. A `margin-top` value for `<BODY>` will not "trickle down" to other elements on the page. If the same values were applied to `margin-top` instead of `margin-right`, then all `<H1>` text would get just a 25-pixel top margin, not 75 pixels.

Oh, remember that you can also make elements appear beyond or partway over the edge of the browser window by setting the margin to a negative value.

margin-left

Syntax:

```
<length> ¦ <percentage> ¦ auto
```

Default value: `0`
Applies to: All elements
Inherited: No
Percentage values: Refer to parent element's size

Examples:

```
H1 { margin-left: 20px }
H1 { margin-left: 10% }
<H1 STYLE="margin-left: auto">
```

`margin-left` works just like `margin-right`—same kinds of values and units, same negative margins, and same browser display inconsistencies.

Let's take the same Web page used in the previous section, and turn all the right margins into left margins (see Figure 7.15). What we see is what we expect based on the discussion of `margin-right`.

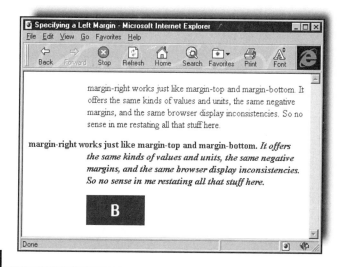

Figure 7.15

Once again, Explorer 3 handles margins (this time `margin-left`) *nicely.*

Netscape
Navigator

The only difference is that here I removed the ALIGN attribute entirely, in the hopes that Navigator would give the image a left margin. No such luck. Navigator appears to ignore left margins when applied to any image.

> One other surprise: Although Explorer 4 gives a right margin to an image, it fails to give a left margin to an image.

Okay, let's also ask the same question we asked regarding top and bottom margins: What happens when `margin-right` and `margin-left` meet?

First of all, the only way to get them to "meet" is by putting elements in adjoining table cells. Positive margins function normally in table cells. If you give a right margin of 50 pixels to text (or images) within a table cell that's 50% of the width of the browser window, the text and images still move over 50 pixels, and the text simply rewraps within the cell (see Figure 7.16).

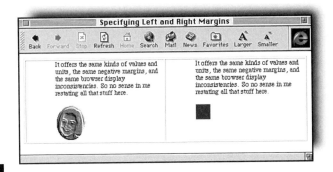

Figure 7.16

Margins work as expected within table cells.

What if we enter the land of negative margins? On the same page, if I give the elements in the right table cell a left margin of –30 pixels instead of 50, things get strange (see Figure 7.17). The elements in the right cell "cross over" the edge of their cell (30 pixels, in fact—just what we'd expect). The graphic in the right cell (the face) doesn't seem affected by this invasion; its left margin remains 50 pixels. But the text on the left side tries to "get out of the way," only fails to do so entirely. Look for unpredictable results.

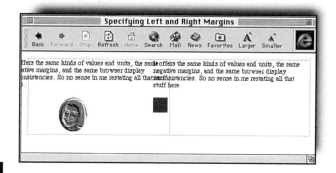

Figure 7.17

Negative horizontal margins can cause a mess.

margin

Syntax:

```
[ <length> ¦ <percentage> ¦ auto ] {1,4}
```

Default value: Not defined
Applies to: All elements
Inherited: No
Percentage values: Refer to parent element's size

Examples:

```
H1 { margin: 20px 10px 20px 40px }
```

```
H1 { margin: 34% 27% }
```

```
<H1 STYLE="margin: auto">
```

Want to assign all four margins in one fell swoop? Use margin, a shorthand property that includes margin-top, margin-bottom, margin-right, and margin-left.

Navigator 4 doesn't support `margin`. You have to use the four individual margin properties instead.

Last Minute note

A later beta does in fact support `margin`.

```
<HTML>
 <STYLE TYPE="text/css">
 <!--
  BODY { background: white }
  H3   { margin: 10% 30% 20% 5% }
 -->
 </STYLE>
<HEAD>
 <TITLE>Specifying All Margins</TITLE>
 </HEAD>
<BODY>
 <H3>I'm giddy with the joy that margins bring. Through margin,
 margin-top, margin-right, margin-bottom, and margin-left, I can
 skip merrily along in my Web design, moving text around like I'm
 using a virtual shovel. It is indeed wondrous.</H3>
 <P>Here's a second paragraph.</P>
 </BODY>
 </HTML>
```

In this example, I've specified values for all four margins. According to the official style sheets spec, they should be interpreted by the browser in this order: `margin-top`, `margin-right`, `margin-bottom`, `margin-left`. Internet Explorer is right on the mark: the paragraph is displayed with a top margin of 10%, a right margin of 30%, a bottom margin of 20%, and a left margin of 5% (see Figure 7.18).

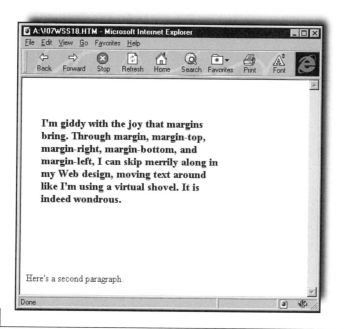

Figure 7.18

Explorer supports percentage values for margin.

You don't have to provide all four values every time:

➡ H3 { margin: 20% }

Listing one value only tells the browser to use that value for every single margin: top, right, bottom, and left.

➡ H3 { margin: 20% 5% }

Providing two values tells the browser to take the first value as the top and bottom margins, and the second value as the right and left margins.

➡ H3 { margin: 20% 5% 12% }

Use three values, and the first will be the top margin, the second will be the right *and* left margins, and the third will be the bottom margin.

Internet
      explorer

> Percentage values work fine for `margin`, but in Explorer 3, other values do not. If you list four different pixel values, for instance, Explorer will ignore all but the *first* value. It will then use that first value to specify all the different margins. So, if you have...
>
> `H3 { margin: 10px 30px 20px 5px }`
>
> ...then Explorer will use 10 pixels for *every* margin, even though there are other values specified.

Just as for the four individual margin properties, you can use negative values for `margin` as well.

padding-top

Syntax:

`<length> ¦ <percentage>`

Default value: `0`
Applies to: All elements
Inherited: No
Percentage values: Refer to parent element's size

Examples:

```
H1 { padding-top: 20px }
H1 { padding-top: 10% }
<H1 STYLE="padding-top: 1.2in">
```

The `padding-top` property sets the padding above any given block-level element or replaced element. The padding, you remember, is the space between the actual element and any border.

Like margin properties, you can use any length value or percentage value for padding properties. By default, `padding-top` is set to `0`, or no extra top padding.

Sorry to disappoint, but Explorer 3 (Mac and Windows) doesn't support *any* kind of padding.

Same thing for Explorer 4: no padding.

In practice, padding works just like margin. You'll run into the same opportunities and the same problems, so refer back to those sections. (So why have both? Because one is inside any border you want around a element, and the other is outside. Stay tuned for the border properties.)

One difference between padding and margin is that padding properties *cannot* be negative. If you want to overlap, stick with margin properties.

padding-bottom

Syntax:

```
<length> ¦ <percentage>
```

Default value: 0
Applies to: All elements
Inherited: No
Percentage values: Refer to parent element's size

Examples:

```
H1 { padding-bottom: 20px }
H1 { padding-bottom: 10% }
<H1 STYLE="padding-bottom: 1.2in">
```

`padding-bottom` sets the padding below a given element. It is similar to `padding-top`, and works similarly to `margin-bottom` (although you can't use negative values). Go re-read those sections.

Padding values interact just like margin values do. When an element with a `padding-bottom` value appears above an element with a `padding-top` value, Navigator adds the two values together to get a total padding value for separating the elements.

By the way, when padding and margins interact, the browsers usually take the grand sum of padding and margin values between them to calculate the distance between the two elements.

padding-right

Syntax:

```
<length> ¦ <percentage>
```

Default value: 0
Applies to: All elements
Inherited: No
Percentage values: Refer to parent element's size

Examples:

```
H1 { padding-right: 20px }
H1 { padding-right: 10% }
<H1 STYLE="padding-right: 1.2in">
```

This property sets the padding to the right of a given element. It works similarly, of course, to `margin-right`.

A few things to keep in mind:

➡ Once again, you can't use negative values.

➡ You can't adjust the horizontal padding between two adjacent elements (unless they're in different table cells).

➡ Navigator exhibits the same weird behavior that it does for `margin-right`. That is, it overprints text if you ever give padding to inline tags, and it doesn't allow padding to be applied to images.

padding-left

Syntax:

```
<length> ¦ <percentage>
```

Default value: 0
Applies to: All elements
Inherited: No
Percentage values: Refer to parent element's size

Examples:

```
H1 { padding-left: 20px }
```

```
H1 { padding-left: 10% }
```

```
<H1 STYLE="padding-left: 1.2in">
```

See padding-right and margin-right. 'Nuff said.

padding

Syntax:

```
[ <length> ¦ <percentage> ] {1,4}
```

Default value: 0
Applies to: All elements
Inherited: No
Percentage values: Refer to parent element's size

Examples:

```
H1 { padding: 20px 10px 20px 40px }
H1 { padding: 34% 27% }
<H1 STYLE="padding: 1.2in">
```

Like margin, padding is a shorthand property that enables you to set padding-top, padding-right, padding-bottom, and padding-left all at once, and in that order.

Netscape
Navigator

Navigator 4 doesn't support `padding`. You have to use the four individual padding properties instead.

Last
Minute note

A later beta does in fact support `padding`.

border-top-width

Syntax:

```
thin ¦ medium ¦ thick ¦ <length>
```

Default value: `medium`
Applies to: All elements
Inherited: No
Percentage values: N/A

Examples:

```
H1 { border-top-width: thick }
H1 { border-top-width: 8mm }
<H1 STYLE="border-top-width: thin">
```

Each box around an element includes three things, and we've already seen how two of them work. The last is the border, which appears between the padding and the margin of an element. The `border-top-width` property dictates the width of the top border, as its name suggests.

Internet
explorer

Unfortunately, Internet Explorer 3 and 4 don't support any variety of any border property.

Navigator 4 for Windows 95 does in fact support borders, although the Mac version (Preview Release 3) crashes when
trying to display borders. I assume this bug will be fixed with
the final release.

Figure 7.19 shows the keyword values for border-top-width. A thin
border appears above a paragraph of <P> text, a medium border
above <BLOCKQUOTE> text, and a thick border above an image.

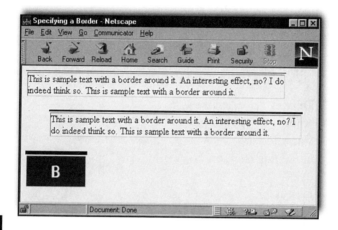

Figure 7.19

*In addition to getting a top border in Navigator, you also get a subtle box
around elements with borders.*

In case you're wondering, border widths can't be negative.

border-bottom-width

Syntax:

thin ¦ medium ¦ thick ¦ <length>

Default value: medium
Applies to: All elements
Inherited: No
Percentage values: N/A

Examples:

```
H1 { border-bottom-width: thick }
H1 { border-bottom-width: 8mm }
<H1 STYLE="border-bottom-width: thin">
```

This property sets the border along the bottom of an element, but is otherwise identical in function to `border-top-width`.

border-right-width

Syntax:

```
thin ¦ medium ¦ thick ¦ <length>
```

Default value: `medium`
Applies to: All elements
Inherited: No
Percentage values: N/A

Examples:

```
H1 { border-right-width: thick }
H1 { border-right-width: 8mm }
<H1 STYLE="border-right-width: thin">
```

This property sets the border along the right side of an element, but is otherwise identical in function to `border-top-width`.

border-left-width

Syntax:

```
thin ¦ medium ¦ thick ¦ <length>
```

Default value: `medium`
Applies to: All elements
Inherited: No
Percentage values: N/A

Examples:

```
H1 { border-left-width: thick }
H1 { border-left-width: 8mm }
<H1 STYLE="border-left-width: thin">
```

This property sets the border along the left side of an element, but is otherwise identical in function to border-top-width. Are we having fun yet?

border-width

Syntax:

```
[ thin ¦ medium ¦ thick ¦ <length> ] {1,4}
```

Default value: Not defined
Applies to: All elements
Inherited: No
Percentage values: N/A

Examples:

```
H1 { border-width: thick medium thick thick }
H1 { border-width: 8mm 16mm }
<H1 STYLE="border-width: thin">
```

border-width is a shorthand property for setting the four various border widths all at once. Like margin and padding, you can include up to four values. If you include four, they appear in this order: border-top-width, border-right-width, border-bottom-width, border-left-width. You can also list fewer than four values, and they will be interpreted similarly to what we saw with margin.

border-color

Syntax:

```
<color> {1,4}
```

Default value: The value of the `color` property
Applies to: All elements
Inherited: No
Percentage values: N/A

Examples:

```
H1 { border-color: #ff0000 }
```

```
H1 { border-color: olive green blue }
```

```
<H1 STYLE="border-color: white">
```

Use `border-color` to define the color given to any or all of the four borders around an element. You can use any color name or value that was discussed in Chapter 6. You can list one color to be used for the entire border, or up to four colors, which will be interpreted in this order: top border color, right, bottom, left.

Note
> Navigator 4 for Windows 95 doesn't support multiple colors for borders. It recognizes only the first color listed.

If no `border-color` is listed, then the border will take on the color of the element it surrounds.

border-style

Syntax:

```
[ none ¦ dotted ¦ dashed ¦ solid ¦ double ¦ groove ¦ ridge ¦ inset ¦
outset ] {1,4}
```

Default value: none
Applies to: All elements
Inherited: No
Percentage values: N/A

Examples:

```
H1 { border-style: solid }
H1 { border-style: inset }
<H1 STYLE="border-style: none">
```

In the ideal browser (of which there are none), you can even define the style of the border itself. Just as with border-color, you can set one style for all the sides of the border, or set each side individually.

The initial value is none, which means that no border will ever be visible unless you set this property.

Here's a key to the keywords:

➡ none—no border is displayed at all, even if there is a border-width value

➡ dotted—a dotted line

➡ dashed—a dashed line

➡ solid—a solid line

➡ double—two lines; the sum of the two lines and the space between them equals the value on border-width

➡ groove—a 3D groove in colors based on the value of border-color

➡ ridge—a 3D ridge in colors based on the value of border-color

➡ inset—a 3D inset in colors based on the value of border-color

➡ outside—a 3D outset in colors based on the value of border-color

Netscape
Navigator

> Navigator 4 supports several (but not all) of the values for
> `border-style`. Figure 7.20 shows them. (It also supports a
> value of `none`.)

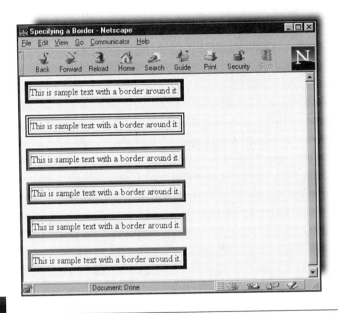

Figure 7.20

From top to bottom: solid, double, groove, ridge, inset, *and* outset
borders.

border-top

Syntax:

`<border-top-width>` ¦¦ `<border-style>` ¦¦ `<border-color>`

Default value: Not defined
Applies to: All elements
Inherited: No
Percentage values: N/A

Examples:

```
H1 { border-top: thin solid blue }
H1 { border-top: dotted red }
<H1 STYLE="border-top: 8mm">
```

`border-top` is a shorthand property for defining all aspects of just the *top* border. You can include from one to three values. If you include fewer than three, then the other aspects take on their default values.

Because all the keywords involved are unique, the order of the values isn't important.

Navigator 4 doesn't support `border-top`. And it doesn't support `border-bottom`, `border-right`, or `border-left` either.

border-bottom

Syntax:

```
<border-bottom-width> ¦¦ <border-style> ¦¦ <border-color>
```

Default value: Not defined
Applies to: All elements
Inherited: No
Percentage values: N/A

Examples:

```
H1 { border-bottom: thin solid blue }
H1 { border-bottom: dotted red }
<H1 STYLE="border-bottom: 8mm">
```

`border-bottom` works just like `border-top`; it's a shorthand property for defining all aspects of just the *bottom* border. The same guidelines apply.

border-right

Syntax:

```
<border-right-width> ¦¦ <border-style> ¦¦ <border-color>
```

Default value: Not defined
Applies to: All elements
Inherited: No
Percentage values: N/A

Examples:

```
H1 { border-right: thin solid blue }
H1 { border-right: dotted red }
<H1 STYLE="border-right: 8mm">
```

border-right can be used to define all aspects of just the *right* border.

border-left

Syntax:

```
<border-left-width> ¦¦ <border-style> ¦¦ <border-color>
```

Default value: Not defined
Applies to: All elements
Inherited: No
Percentage values: N/A

Examples:

```
H1 { border-left: thin solid blue }
H1 { border-left: dotted red }
<H1 STYLE="border-left: 8mm">
```

border-left can be used to define all aspects of just the *left* border.

border

Syntax:

```
<border-width> ¦¦ <border-style> ¦¦ <border-color>
```

Default value: Not defined
Applies to: All elements
Inherited: No
Percentage values: N/A

Examples:

```
H1 { border: thin solid blue }
H1 { border: dotted red }
<H1 STYLE="border: 8mm">
```

And here's the final border property. With `border`, you can define all aspects of the entire border. The only stipulation is that all four sides of the border will be identical if you use this property. Whatever values you state will be used for the entire border.

> **Note**
> Navigator 4 doesn't support the shorthand `border` property.

width

Syntax:

```
<length> ¦ <percentage> ¦ auto
```

Default value: `auto`
Applies to: Block-level and replaced elements
Inherited: No
Percentage values: Refer to parent element's size

Examples:

```
H1 { width: 200px }
```

```
H1 { width: 150% }
<H1 STYLE="width: auto">
```

For specifying the width of an element, we're familiar with the HTML WIDTH attribute. The width property works much the same way. With it, you can force text or an image to a certain dimension, using either length values or percentage values (see Appendix A for details on these units).

Internet Explorer 3 does not yet support width.

Navigator is also not up to the task.

Explorer 4, however, gives us some hope. It supports width for replaced elements, though not for text (see Figure 7.21).

Figure 7.21

The original image, followed by images with greater width.

continues

> The first image shows the original image size. The second is set to 100 pixels wide. The third is set to 50%. Percentage values are relative to the size of the browser window; thus, the image is half as wide as the entire window.

In an ideal browser, when you set `width` on an image, that image is stretched to fit the declared space. It stretches out of proportion, so the height of the image will not change.

> Explorer 4, however, will always increase an image's size proportionally if only the width or the height is set.

However, if you set the `height` property to `auto` (see the next section), then the height will indeed change proportionally to the change in width.

Theoretically, all of this also works on block-level text elements.

height

Syntax:

```
<length> | auto
```

Default value: `auto`
Applies to: Block-level and replaced elements
Inherited: No
Percentage values: Refer to parent element's size

Examples:

```
H1 { height: 200px }
H1 { height: 1.2in }
<H1 STYLE="height: auto">
```

Just like `width`, `height` can force text or an image to a certain dimension.

Explorer 3? No.

Navigator 4? No.

Explorer 4? Yes! Again, height works only for replaced elements, not for text. Length values work, and so do percentage values (which are relative to the height of the current browser window).

If you want to scale an object out of proportion, use height and width in conjunction. In Figure 7.22, height is set to 150 pixels and width is set to 400 pixels. Lovely, no?

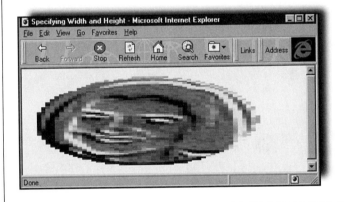

Figure 7.22

Set both height *and* width *to stretch images.*

By the way, if you set both height and width to auto, the element will revert to its default, unadjusted size.

No negative values are allowed for either width or height. (Try it and watch Explorer 4 crash mightily.)

Note

There are also `width` and `height` properties that impact absolute positioning. These are discussed separately in the next chapter.

float

Syntax:

```
left ¦ right ¦ none
```

Default value: `none`
Applies to: All elements
Inherited: No
Percentage values: N/A

Examples:

```
H1 { float: right }
```

```
H1 { float: none }
```

```
<H1 STYLE="float: left">
```

The `float` property also has a companion in HTML. You use `float` like you'd use the `ALIGN` attribute on the `<IMG>` tag: to flow text around an element (in style sheets, this element can be an image or block-level text).

With a `float` value of `none`, an element would appear as it normally does in the text. But with a value of `left`, an element appears on the left side of the browser window, and the text wraps around it on the right.

```
<HTML>
 <STYLE TYPE="text/css">
 <!--
  BODY { background: white }
  .a   { float: left }
 -->
 </STYLE>
```

```
<HEAD>
 <TITLE>Specifying Float</TITLE>
</HEAD>
<BODY>
 <SPAN CLASS=a><IMG SRC="../graphics/woods.jpg"></SPAN>
 <H2>The float property also has a companion in HTML. You use float
like you'd use the ALIGN attribute on the IMG tag: to flow text
around an element (in style sheets, this element can be an image or
block-level text).</H2>
 <SPAN CLASS=a><H1>This is floating H1 text!</H1></SPAN>
 <H2>The float property also has a companion in HTML. You use float
like you'd use the ALIGN attribute on the IMG tag: to flow text
around an element (in style sheets, this element can be an image or
block-level text).</H2>
</BODY>
</HTML>
```

Figure 7.23 shows this in action. Text flows nicely around the
floating image, as we'd expect.

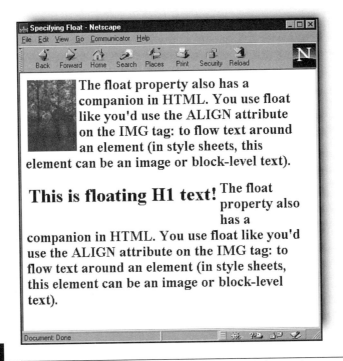

Figure 7.23

Yes! Navigator supports float *for images and for text!*

> Explorer 3 and 4 do not support `float`.

What's new (from traditional HTML) is the capability to float text around *other text*. Any block-level element, such as the `<H1>` here, can be made to float. And if you don't want just one line of floating text, you can easily break it with `<BR>`s within the block-level text (see Figure 7.24). An obvious use: pull-quotes from articles. This could also be used as poor-man's initial caps.

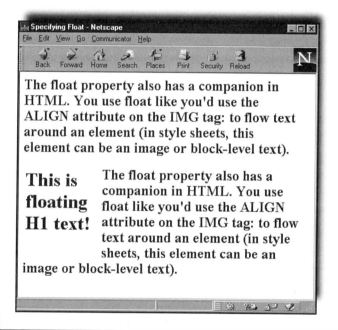

Figure 7.24

Add line breaks and a little `padding` (`margin` *seems to cause trouble) to make floating text blocks more useful and attractive.*

What happens if two floating elements float too close together? The same thing that would happen with two images that are `ALIGN=left` and near each other: they'd get staggered (see Figure 7.25).

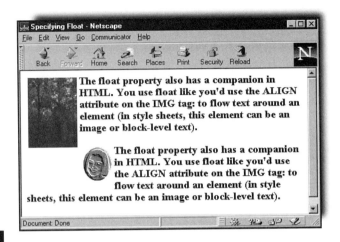

Figure 7.25

A second floating image "floats around" a first.

By the way, if you keep floating elements next to each other, they can easily continue right off the edge of the browser window. They won't usually rewrap until you tell them to do so.

Netscape
Navigator

> Be careful when floating things `right`. Occasionally Navigator will cut off parts of images that float right, so you end up with the right-hand side of the image missing.

Another thing to experiment with is negative margins, which floating elements are allowed to have. As you might expect, the result is the freedom to overlap elements.

clear

Syntax:

none ¦ left ¦ right ¦ both

Default value: none
Applies to: All elements
Inherited: No
Percentage values: N/A

Examples:

```
H1 { clear: right }

H1 { clear: none }

<H1 STYLE="clear: both">
```

Finally, the `clear` property is the equivalent of using `<BR CLEAR=x>` in HTML—only like `float`, `clear` can be used with text as well as with replaced elements such as images.

Basically, this property enables you to specify if an element will allow floating elements to its right or left. Normally, if you use `float` on an element, text and images will wrap around that element. But what if you don't want certain elements to wrap around? `clear` is your solution.

`clear` does not work in Explorer.

For example, check out the following code. The woods image is floated left, so the next two paragraphs of text wrap nicely around it on the right side (see Figure 7.26).

```
<HTML>
 <STYLE TYPE="text/css">
 <!--
  BODY { background: white }
  .a    { float: left }
 -->
 </STYLE>
<HEAD>
 <TITLE>Specifying Float</TITLE>
</HEAD>
<BODY>
 <SPAN CLASS=a><IMG SRC="../graphics/woods.jpg"></SPAN>
 <H2>Basically, this property enables you to specify if an element
will allow floating elements to its right or left. Normally, if you
use float on an element, text and images will wrap around that
element.
```

```
</H2>
 <H2>But what if you don't want certain elements to wrap around?
clear is your solution. Basically, this property enables you to
specify if an element will allow floating elements to its right or
left. Normally, if you use float on an element, text and images will
wrap around that element.</H2>
</BODY>
</HTML>
```

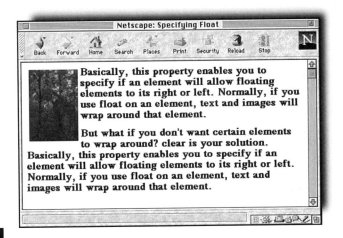

Figure 7.26

The default: both paragraphs wrap around a floating element.

But what if you wanted only the first paragraph to wrap, and then have the second paragraph begin *below* the image? You could try to add a couple of
s but that would be no guarantee. Instead, simply add a clear: left style to the second paragraph. That will tell the browser not to display the second paragraph until its left side is clear of all floating elements. The result is what you want (see Figure 7.27).

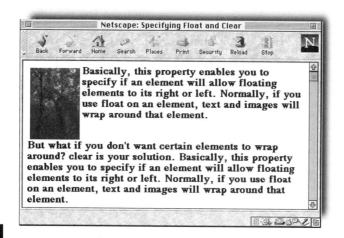

Netscape: Specifying Float and Clear

Basically, this property enables you to specify if an element will allow floating elements to its right or left. Normally, if you use float on an element, text and images will wrap around that element.

But what if you don't want certain elements to wrap around? clear is your solution. Basically, this property enables you to specify if an element will allow floating elements to its right or left. Normally, if you use float on an element, text and images will wrap around that element.

Figure 7.27

Using clear, *you can decide what wraps and what doesn't.*

As you might have guessed, a value of both for clear means that the browser will make sure the right *and* left sides of an element are clear of floating elements. A value of none means that floating elements are allowed on either side.

Beware of occasional problems when trying to use clear on images. For example, if I take the Web page shown in Figure 7.23, which shows two left-floating elements, and try to add clear: left to the face image so that it's displayed directly below the woods image, the result (in Navigator at least) isn't what I'd hoped (see Figure 7.28).

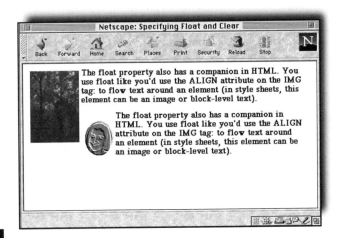

Figure 7.28

Even though the face image is cleared left, it doesn't seem to work in Navigator.

CHAPTER 8

Layout, Part II

This chapter wasn't in the original outline for this book. But when folks at Netscape *and* Microsoft (and Hewlett-Packard, by the way) co-authored a document called "Positioning HTML Elements with Cascading Style Sheets," and then the World Wide Web Consortium published it on its site as a working draft, my curiosity was piqued. And when I heard both Netscape *and* Microsoft promising support for this new spec in their 4.0 browsers, I became interested enough to start reading it. And when I read the document itself and saw what it had to offer, I became entranced.

"Positioning HTML Elements with Cascading Style Sheets" is a kind of sequel to Cascading Style Sheets, level 1. It's an extension to style sheets that enables exciting new positioning capabilities: positioning elements in the horizontal and vertical directions, *and* positioning them in a specific display order so that you can easily layer elements on top of each other. This kind of thing is somewhat possible using the style sheet properties we've already looked at, but it's not as easy, not as flexible, and not as supported by the browsers as the properties we're about to discover.

Really, these properties are an extension of the previous chapter. There, we looked at how to shape text and replace elements that exist as positioned elements. Here, we focus on how to actually position those elements on the page. The two chapters (and the properties within each one) complement each other.

Note

Keep in mind that unlike Cascading Style Sheets, level 1, which is now a finished document, this new document and its properties are a work in progress as I write this. Exact details may shift slightly, so make sure to test everything in the latest browsers.

You can always find the latest version of the official positioning spec from here: `http://www.w3.org/pub/WWW/Style/`.

Internet
explorer

Also keep in mind that because these are newer properties, Version 3 of Internet Explorer doesn't support any of them. Version 4 does. That's important to consider when you evaluate whether you should use them on your site or not.

position

Syntax:

`absolute ¦ relative ¦ static`

Default value: `static`
Applies to: All elements
Inherited: No
Percentage values: N/A

Examples:

`H1 { position: relative }`

`H1 { position: static }`

`<H1 STYLE="position: absolute">`

`position` is the property that opens new doors for controlled page layout. Finally we can more accurately define where any element (text or replaced element) appears onscreen. There are two ways to use `position`:

➡ `absolute` positioning enables you to precisely position elements independently of any other elements around them.

➡ `relative` positioning involves specifying the position of elements relative to their natural position in the document's flow.

Regardless of which method you use, `position` establishes an exact coordinate system on the page for placing child elements. This coordinate system is what makes `position` so different and powerful.

Absolute Positioning

When you position an element with `absolute`, you give it a specific rectangular area that will contain the contents of the element. This new rectangle can be controlled independently of any other element on the page—which means you can place it anywhere you want.

How do you control this placement? By combining the `position` property with the `left` and `top` properties, which we'll talk about more later.

This newfound capability begs for examples:

```
<HTML>
 <STYLE TYPE="text/css">
 <!--
  BODY { background: white }
  DIV  { position: absolute;
         left: 40px;
         top: 70px }
  P    { position: absolute;
         left: 200px;
         top: 100px }
 -->
 </STYLE>
<HEAD>
```

```
<TITLE>Absolute Positioning</TITLE>
</HEAD>
<BODY>
Here is some body text that appears after BODY but before
any other HTML tags. Standard stuff.
<DIV>Now I've started a division, and the text you see
here is within DIV. It gets positioned independently,
based on the coordinate system defined by BODY.
<P>And here is P text within the DIV. It's positioned
independently based on DIV's coordinate system.</P>
</DIV>
</BODY>
</HTML>
```

Here's what's happening in Figure 8.1: When I set <DIV> text to be positioned absolutely, the browser creates a new coordinate system based on its parent element, <BODY>. It then begins <DIV> text (the "box" around <DIV>, actually) at a point that is 40 pixels from the left edge of <BODY>'s normal display area, and 70 pixels down from the top. Similarly, when the browser sees that <P> is a child of <DIV>, it creates yet another coordinate system for <P> that is based on the starting point of <DIV> text (the upper-left corner of the box that surrounds the <DIV> element). So, from that point it goes across 200 pixels and down 100 pixels, and then begins to display <P> text. (By the way, if <P> had a child element, <P>, too, would have its own coordinate system.) I've marked up the screen in Figure 8.2 so that you can see the various coordinate systems and measurements the browser creates.

Internet explorer

For some reason, Explorer 4 positions the <DIV> text correctly, but *not* the <P> text. The <P> text appears to be absolutely positioned but not according to the units specified. It seems that you can't *nest* absolutely positioned elements. That is, you can't absolutely position something if it is a child of an element that is itself absolutely positioned.

I'm hopeful that this is a bug in the beta version that will be fixed before the final 4.0 release.

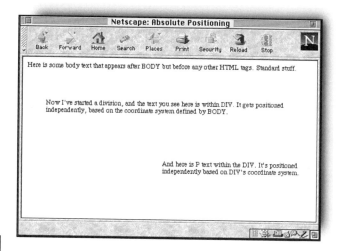

Figure 8.1

Absolute positioning means you can control layout according to coordinate systems.

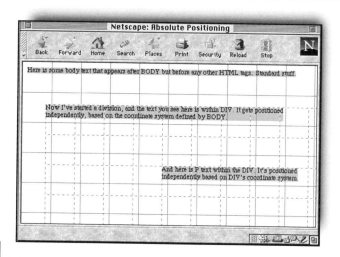

Figure 8.2

Here is the positioning going on behind the scenes. You can see the boxes for each element, and the two coordinate systems (solid lines for <BODY>'s, dashed lines for <DIV>'s).

No matter how much text appears within each element, the positions of the other elements don't change (see Figure 8.3). They're independently placed. Absolutely placed objects "know" nothing about any other objects, and so ignore them entirely. In fact, anything with a position of absolute totally falls outside of the standard style sheets formatting model (see Chapter 7); it's not block-level, inline, or floating. It's instead treated independently of anything else. (It does, however, retain its other non-layout-related attributes, such as default font.)

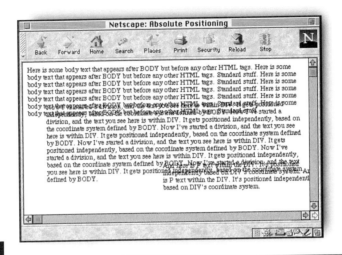

Figure 8.3

No matter what you do, elements positioned absolutely won't budge—even if that means the browser has to overlap elements.

Netscape
Navigator

As you can see, Navigator 4 is sometimes a bit buggy regarding positioning and wrapping text. The third paragraph in the figure should wrap using the same right margin as the other paragraphs; instead a few words flow off the screen.

Last Minute note

As of beta 3, this bug is fixed. Text wraps correctly.

Internet explorer

Explorer 4 has similar behavior. Any text that is positioned absolutely will not automatically wrap to fit into the browser window as you would normally expect. Instead it will extend beyond the window—sometimes with no scrollbar appearing, so therefore there's no way to view it.

Can absolute positioning be used on replaced elements such as images? Absolutely. Can you use small or negative values for purposeful overlap? Absolutely. Witness this example:

```
<HTML>
 <STYLE TYPE="text/css">
 <!--
   BODY { background: black;
          color: white }
   .a   { position: absolute;
          left: 300px;
          top: 0px }
   P    { position: absolute;
          left: -40px;
          top: 80px }
 -->
 </STYLE>
<HEAD>
 <TITLE>Absolute Positioning</TITLE>
</HEAD>
<BODY>
 <H2>Muir Woods: Your Path to Peace</H2>
 <SPAN CLASS=a><IMG SRC="woods.jpg">
 <P>Stepping into Muir Woods is like stepping into the
 quietest part of your soul. The wind in the trees slows
 the racing mind...</P>
 </SPAN>
</BODY>
</HTML>
```

Figure 8.4 shows the magic happening. The image is positioned 300 pixels from the left edge of <BODY> (which is also the edge of the browser window). Because the top value is set to 0 pixels, it's brought to the top edge of the window (definitely something difficult to do in standard HTML!). Then, the line of <P> text is positioned based on the coordinate system the image creates: 80 pixels down from the top of the image, and −40 pixels to the right (that is, 40 pixels to the left) of the image's left edge.

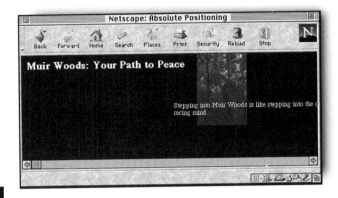

Figure 8.4

Absolute positioning with images and negative values can create interesting results.

When layering occurs while you're using position, the child elements always appear on top of their parents. That's why the text is displayed on top of the image in Figure 8.4.

Internet
explorer

Unfortunately, I can't get Explorer 4 to absolutely position images. Again, I hope this bug will be fixed.

Relative Positioning

When you position an element with relative, it's placed relative to its parent element, more or less like we're used to in HTML. But even though the element does retain its natural formatting on the page, it can receive some of the special abilities that absolute offers. For example, you can position child elements relative to it, and you can also use it to layer with other elements.

```
<HTML>
 <STYLE TYPE="text/css">
 <!--
  BODY { background: white }
  I    { position: relative;
         left: 10px;
         top: 50px }
 -->
```

```
</STYLE>
<HEAD>
 <TITLE>Relative Positioning</TITLE>
</HEAD>
<BODY>
 <H4>Here's some normal body text.
 <I>When you position an element with relative, it's placed relative
to its parent element, more or less like we're used to in HTML. But
even though the element does retain its natural formatting on the
page, it can receive some of the special abilities that absolute
offers.
 </I></H4>
</BODY>
</HTML>
```

In this example, the browser is told to position the italicized text relative to the regular text. Specifically, the instructions are to begin displaying the italicized text 10 pixels across and 50 pixels down from *where it would otherwise be displayed* by default (see Figure 8.5). There is a coordinate system at work here, but the coordinates begin *not* at the beginning of an element, but at the "end." So, after the period after "text," the browser goes down 50 pixels and across 10 before displaying the other text.

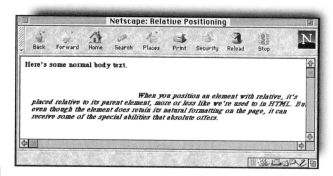

Figure 8.5

Relative positioning moves the element from the position it would otherwise occupy.

Notice how the other lines in the italicized section continue to wrap (more or less) like the first, using its left margin. That's because the text continues to be formatted like its parent. That's the difference between relative and absolute.

Netscape
Navigator

> Navigator lets a few words run off the screen again, but otherwise displays this effect properly.

Last
Minute note

> Again, as of beta 3, this bug is fixed.

Internet
explorer

> The first beta of Explorer 4 does not support relative positioning.

Let's look at a more complicated example to see how multiple relatively positioned objects interact:

```
<STYLE TYPE="text/css">
<!--
  BODY { background: white;
         margin-top: 60px }
  I    { position: relative;
         left: 0px;
         top: -40px }
  B    { position: relative;
         left: 0px;
         top: 20px }
  .a   { position: relative;
         left: -100px;
         top: 0px }
-->
</STYLE>
<HEAD>
<TITLE>Relative Positioning</TITLE>
</HEAD>
<BODY>
<P>Here's some normal body text.
<I>When you position an element with relative, it's placed relative
to its parent element, more or less like we're used to in HTML. It
flows naturally.</I>
<B>But even though the element does retain its natural formatting on
the page, it can receive some of the special abilities that absolute
offers.</B>
<SPAN CLASS=a><IMG SRC="../graphics/face.gif"></SPAN>
</P>
```

```
</BODY>
</HTML>
```

The rule to remember is this: Relatively positioned elements are always placed relative to where they *should* have been if they hadn't been positioned at all. So, in our example we see that the italicized text is continued 40 pixels above where it should have been. No problem (see Figure 8.6).

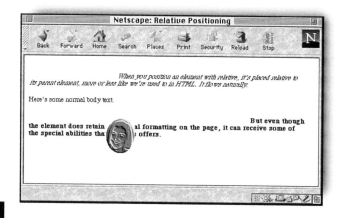

Figure 8.6

The more relative *positions, the more confusing things get.*

But it gets more tricky when we look at the bold text. It's supposed to be 20 pixels down from the end of the italicized text, right? Well, not exactly. And in fact onscreen it certainly looks like more than 20 pixels. In fact, the bold text begins 20 pixels below the point where the italicized text *would* have ended if the italicized text were not styled at all.

The same is true for the image, which should be displayed 100 pixels left *not* from the actual end of the bold text, but from the end of where the bold text *would* have been displayed if it weren't styled at all. We can now see why more than one line of text is covered by the image: from the image's "point of view," that text shouldn't be there.

By the way, the same rules we're already familiar with apply regarding layering. Yes, layering is permitted, and child elements are always displayed on top of parent elements.

So what happens when absolute and relative positions interact?

```
<HTML>
<STYLE TYPE="text/css">
<!--
  BODY { background: white }
  SPAN { position: relative;
        font-family: arial }
  I    { position: absolute;
        left: 0px;
        top: 100px }
-->
</STYLE>
<HEAD>
<TITLE>Relative and Absolute Positioning</TITLE>
</HEAD>
<BODY>
<H3>Here's some normal H3 text.
<SPAN>When you position an element with relative, it's placed rela-
tive to its parent element, more or less like we're used to in HTML.
<I>It flows naturally.</I>
But even though the element does retain its natural formatting on
the page, it can receive some of the special abilities that absolute
offers.</SPAN>
</H3>
</BODY>
</HTML>
```

On this page, text within <SPAN> is relatively placed but not reposi-
tioned, so all that changes is the font face. But the italicized text is
absolutely positioned. Its parent is <SPAN>, so it positions itself according to the top-left corner of the <SPAN> element. That's why
the italicized text appears 100 pixels straight down from the
words that begin the <SPAN> section (see Figure 8.7).

Static Positioning

The final value for position is static, which is identical to what
HTML normally does without any style sheets present. A static
element cannot be positioned, nor does it define a coordinate
system by which some other child element could be positioned.
static text is just normal, everyday text.

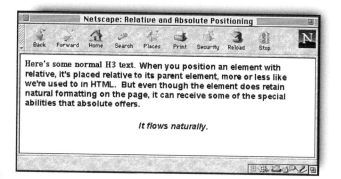

Figure 8.7

You can put both absolute *and* relative *into the mixture.*

A quick example: If you were to take the previous Web page, and declare <SPAN> static instead of relative, you'd get what you see in Figure 8.8. Because <SPAN> is static, it can no longer provide a co-ordinate system for any child elements such as <I>. Thus, the browser instead uses <BODY>'s coordinate system to display <I>, which means the italicized text begins right along the edge of the browser window, 100 pixels down from the top.

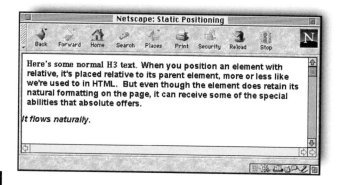

Figure 8.8

static *elements "just say no" to any involvement in positioning.*

left

Syntax:

```
<length> ¦ <percentage> ¦ auto
```

Default value: `auto`
Applies to: All elements with the `position` property
Inherited: No
Percentage values: Refer to parent element's width

Examples:

```
H1 { left: 2in }
```

```
H1 { left: 40% }
```

```
<H1 STYLE="left: auto">
```

As I already mentioned, `left` is what you use with `position` to tell the browser where to place an element horizontally, either with absolute or relative positioning. You can't use `left` unless `position` is also present.

The `left` property accepts any length units (see Appendix A), though pixels are safest to use across browsers and platforms at this time. `left` also accepts percentage values, which refer to the parent element's width.

Explorer 4 associates these percentage values with the size of the browser window. A `left` value of `50%` means the element will begin halfway across the browser window.

For elements with absolute positioning, `left` is relative to the upper-left corner of the box of the nearest parent element, assuming that parent element itself has a `position` value of `absolute` or `relative`.

For elements with relative positioning, `left` is relative to the normally rendered position of the element, as discussed in the previous section.

The default value for `left` is `auto`, which simply means the element will get its normal position, as if it were not styled at all.

> Explorer 4 translates `auto` as 0 pixels, meaning that the element will be aligned with the edge of the browser window.

top

Syntax:

`<length> ¦ <percentage> ¦ auto`

Default value: `auto`
Applies to: All elements with the `position` property
Inherited: No
Percentage values: Refer to parent element's height

Examples:

`H1 { top: 2in }`

`H1 { top: 40% }`

`<H1 STYLE="top: auto">`

The `top` property is just like `left`, except everything is vertical instead of horizontal. Refer to the previous section.

width

Syntax:

`<length> ¦ <percentage> ¦ auto`

Default value: `auto`
Applies to: All elements with `position` of `absolute`
Inherited: No
Percentage values: Refer to parent element's width

Examples:

```
H1 { width: 5in }
```

```
H1 { width: 60% }
```

```
<H1 STYLE="width: auto">
```

I touched on the `width` property in the previous chapter, but it has other uses here in the context of `absolute` positioning. (It will have no effect on elements that are positioned `relative` or `static`.)

The `auto` value is what we've already seen when positioning elements. If you don't specify any width for an element, the browser assumes you mean `auto`, and the result is that text flows the same width (to the same right margin) that its parent does. That's what you saw in Figure 8.1.

But if you set a `width` value, the text is forced into that horizontal distance, so it will no longer assume the right margin of the parent element. Give the element a `width` of 200 pixels, and it will wrap to the next line after 200 pixels from where it starts, regardless of what any parent element is doing, and regardless of where the browser window ends.

```
<HTML>
 <STYLE TYPE="text/css">
 <!--
  BODY { background: white }
  DIV { position: absolute;
        left: 80px;
        top: 90px;
        width: 200px }
 -->
 </STYLE>
<HEAD>
 <TITLE>Absolute Positioning with Width</TITLE>
```

```
</HEAD>
<BODY>
Here is some body text that appears after BODY but before
any other HTML tags. Standard stuff.
<DIV>Now I've started a division, and the text you see
here is within DIV. It gets positioned independently,
based on the coordinate system defined by BODY.
</DIV>
</BODY>
</HTML>
```

In this example, the text within <DIV> is positioned with absolute, and then declared to have a width of 200px. As a result, the browser wraps the text so that no line exceeds 200 pixels horizontally (see Figure 8.9).

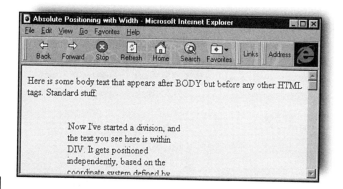

With width *you can constrain the horizontal size of a text box.*

Internet
explorer

More evidence of a bug I mentioned earlier: In Explorer 4, if text runs off the screen because of absolute positioning, you can't scroll to view it. The scrollbar appears but doesn't function.

You can use any length or percentage units for width. (Percentage in Explorer 4 refers to the width of the browser window.)

height

Syntax:

```
<length> ¦ <percentage> ¦ auto
```

Default value: auto
Applies to: All elements with position of absolute
Inherited: No
Percentage values: Refer to parent element's height

Examples:

```
H1 { height: 5in }
```

```
H1 { height: 60% }
```

```
<H1 STYLE="height: auto">
```

height works like width, though it obviously specifies vertical dimension instead of horizontal. See the previous section.

| height doesn't work in Explorer 4. |

| height doesn't work in Navigator 4 either. |

clip

Syntax:

```
<shape> ¦ auto
```

Default value: auto
Applies to: All elements with position of absolute
Inherited: No
Percentage values: N/A

Examples:

```
H1 { clip: rect(10px 20px 30px 40px) }
```

```
H1 { clip: rect(25% auto 5% auto) }
```

```
<H1 STYLE="clip: rect(auto)">
```

The `clip` property enables you to control the clipping of elements (text or replaced elements). That is, you can define which part of an element is visible, and which part should be clipped off and not displayed. This affects the display only, *not* the layout. The clipped part of the element is still there; you just can't see it.

For the shape of the clipping region, the spec proposes `rect` as the only option for now, though more clipping shapes could evolve later. `rect` is defined by length measurements like so:

```
H1 { clip: rect(10px 20px 30px 40px) }
```

The first value is for the top of the clipping region, the second is for the right side, the third for the bottom, and the last for the left side. These coordinates are with respect to the element's origin. You can use any length or percentage units.

You can use `auto` for any coordinate, which means that coordinate will match what the element would normally be if unstyled. The default value for `clip` is auto on all four coordinates; the clipping value thus covers the entire element, making the whole thing visible.

By the way, negative clipping values are permitted.

Navigator 4 doesn't support `clip`.

Explorer 4 doesn't support `clip` either.

overflow

Syntax:

```
none ¦ clip ¦ scroll
```

Default value: none
Applies to: All elements with position of absolute or relative
Inherited: No
Percentage values: N/A

Examples:

```
H1 { overflow: clip }
```

```
H1 { overflow: scroll }
```

```
<H1 STYLE="overflow: none">
```

What happens if an element's contents ever exceed its specified width or height? With the overflow property, you can decide instead of letting the browser do so for you.

Set overflow to none, and all of the element will be displayed, even if it goes outside of its declared boundaries. Nothing will be clipped off.

Set this property to clip, and the browser will clip off whatever part of the elements "goes over the line," so to speak. If line three of a given paragraph goes past the defined height, then that line of text will be cut off and you'll see only the top half or so of the words.

Use scroll, and the excess element will be clipped, just as with clip, but this time the browser will invoke a scrolling mechanism. The result is similar to a frame in a Web page in which there's more text than display area; a scrollbar appears so you can scroll to see the other part of the content.

Of course, even if you have overflow set to none, the browser will still clip the element on its own if the element's contents go outside of the browser window.

Navigator 4 doesn't support overflow.

Explorer 4 doesn't support overflow either.

z-index

Syntax:

```
auto ¦ <integer>
```

Default value: auto
Applies to: All elements with position of absolute or relative
Inherited: No
Percentage values: N/A

Examples:

```
H1 { z-index: 2 }
```

```
H1 { z-index: auto }
```

```
<H1 STYLE="z-index: 1">
```

With z-index, you can control the order in which elements are layered, as long as those elements are absolutely or relatively positioned. Normally, elements are layered with the parent element always below its child element. z-index enables you to change this default.

Explorer 4 (at least in beta form) does not support z-index.

Let's see this in action:

```
<HTML>
 <STYLE TYPE="text/css">
 <!--
  BODY { background: white }
  .a   { position: absolute;
          left: 0px;
          top: 0px }
   .b   { position: absolute;
          left: 150px;
          top: 110px;
          z-index: 2 }
    B    { position: absolute;
          left: 100px;
          top: 70px;
          z-index: 1 }
  -->
 </STYLE>
<HEAD>
 <TITLE>Specifying Layering Order</TITLE>
</HEAD>
<BODY>
 <DIV CLASS=a>
 <IMG SRC="../graphics/world.jpg">
 <SPAN CLASS=b><IMG SRC="../graphics/face2.gif"></SPAN>
 <B><IMG SRC="../graphics/woods.jpg"></B>
 </DIV>
</BODY>
</HTML>
```

Here's what we've got: a large image positioned to the edge of the
browser window, and two smaller images, both of which are child
elements of the larger (which is contained in a <DIV>). These two
"sibling" elements would normally be layered in the order they
appear in the HTML: the face image first, the woods photo second and thus on top. However, with z-index in play, that order is
reversed. The face gets a higher z-index than the woods image, and
so the face appears on top (see Figure 8.10).

Figure 8.10

Among sibling elements, higher z-index values get you on top.

You can also give elements a negative z-index value. They will then be layered below even their parent element.

Netscape
Navigator

Navigator 4 works fine with positive integer values, but not negative. There's no way to layer a child element so it's displayed below its parent.

The layering order between two elements that aren't siblings and aren't direct parent and child can be figured out by evaluating the previous rules for the elements' ancestors.

Remember, z-index works only with elements that have a position property. You can't control the layering order of elements that have been overlapped using negative margins.

visibility

Syntax:

```
inherit ¦ visible ¦ hidden
```

Default value: `inherit`
Applies to: All elements
Inherited: If value is `inherit`
Percentage values: N/A

Examples:

```
H1 { visibility: visible }
```

```
H1 { visibility: hidden }
```

```
<H1 STYLE="visibility: inherit">
```

The `visibility` property enables you to decide the initial display state of an element: Do you want the element to be visible or invisible? `visibility` affects the appearance of a page, but it doesn't affect the layout. The element is still there; you just can't see it. It's effectively transparent (see Figures 8.11 and 8.12).

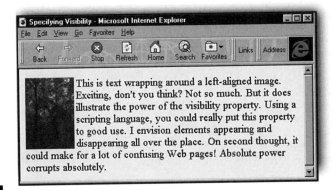

Figure 8.11

Now you see it. Text wrapping around an image.

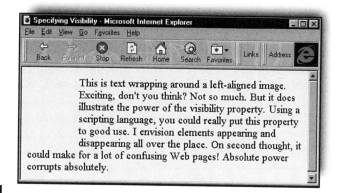

Figure 8.12

Now you don't. The image is set to hidden, *but the text still wraps around it.*

Why would you want to make an element invisible? Practical uses involve scripting: You could dynamically display or not display an element based on user action (such as rolling the mouse pointer over an element), for instance. Maybe this is something JavaScript Style Sheets would be useful for (see Chapter 1).

By default, visibility is set to inherit, meaning it will inherit its display state from its parent. The other possible values are self-explanatory: visible will keep the object visible, and hidden will make it invisible.

Netscape **Navigator**

Navigator 4 for Windows 95 supports hidden, but not visible or inherit. The Mac version supports none of the above.

CHAPTER 9

Classification

The remaining properties that are part of the original style sheets specification aren't really about defining specific visual effects. These properties classify elements into particular categories, that can then be formatted as you wish.

Unfortunately, browser support for the following properties is less than stellar. But in the hopes that upcoming versions of Navigator and Explorer will improve, I give you the details anyway for future reference.

display

Syntax:

```
block ¦ inline ¦ list-item ¦ none
```

Default value: `block`
Applies to: All elements
Inherited: No
Percentage values: N/A

Examples:

```
H1 { display: list-item }

H1 { display: none }

<H1 STYLE="display: block">
```

The `display` property enables you to declare if or how an element is treated and displayed. That is, should the item be a block-level element, an inline element, or an item in a list? Or should it be displayed at all?

Traditionally, all HTML tags come with built-in assumptions about what they are. As we've talked about previously, tags such as `<P>` and `<H1>` are block-level, because they automatically create their own new line breaks, and thus their own "box," as defined in the style sheet formatting model (see Chapter 7, "Layout, Part I"). Meanwhile, other HTML tags are automatically treated as inline elements, such as `<I>` and `<CODE>`. They define styles within a line instead of starting a new line. Then there are list-item HTML tags, such as `<LI>`, which are essentially block-level elements with a marker (typically a bullet character) added.

With the `display` property, you can override these defaults if you want. You can make `<P>` an inline element, or `<I>` a block-level element, or whatever.

If you give an element a `display` value of `block`, the browser will treat it like it does any other block-level element: The element will get its own box, and be appropriately positioned relative to other boxes on the page—via padding, border, and margin. Here's an example:

```
<HTML>
 <STYLE TYPE="text/css">
 <!--
  BODY { background: white;
        font-size: 20px }
  B    { display: block }
 -->
 </STYLE>
<HEAD>
 <TITLE>Specifying Display Classification</TITLE>
</HEAD>
<BODY>
 <P>Welcome to the <B>display property</B>, which enables you to
 set how an element is treated by a browser.</P>
</BODY>
</HTML>
```

In this simple example, I've declared that `<B>` should be a block-level element, although it normally is not. When displaying bold text, the browser should give the text its own line, just as it would for an `<H1>` or other such block-level element (see Figure 9.1).

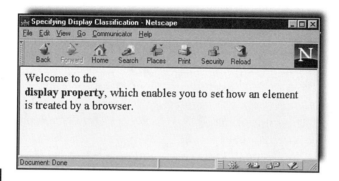

`<B>` is now a block-level element to do with as I wish.

Note   Navigator 4 inserts a line break before the new `block` element, but as you can see, it doesn't do so after the element as it also should.

Note   Explorer 3 and 4 don't support the `display` property at all.

Similarly, you can force elements to become inline or list-item elements:

```
<HTML>
 <STYLE TYPE="text/css">
 <!--
  BODY { background: white;
        font-size: 20px }
  H1   { display: inline }
  .a   { display: list-item }
 -->
 </STYLE>
<HEAD>
 <TITLE>Specifying Display Classification</TITLE>
```

```
</HEAD>
<BODY>
 <P>Welcome to the <H1>display property</H1>, which enables you to
 set how an element is treated by a browser.</P>
 <SPAN CLASS=a><IMG SRC="face.gif"></SPAN>
 <SPAN CLASS=a><IMG SRC="face.gif"></SPAN>
 <SPAN CLASS=a><IMG SRC="face.gif"></SPAN>
</BODY>
</HTML>
```

Without styles, this page would consist of three blocks of text, then three inline graphics in the next line. But because I've declared <H1> an inline element, there should be only one paragraph of text. And because I've declared the graphics as list items, they should each be on their own lines and with preceding bullet symbols (see Figure 9.2).

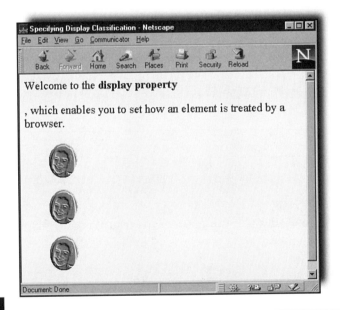

Figure 9.2

Navigator displays the newly defined items as it should, with a few flaws though.

Finally, you can set display to none, which means that the given element won't display *at all*. This also affects all child elements. This capability could be useful in scripting situations, when you want an element to suddenly pop into being at a certain time or based upon a certain user action. It can also be useful for designing styled pages that degrade well, as discussed in Chapter 3. You could add some text and hide it using `display`, and it would then be visible only in non-style-sheet browsers.

 Note | Navigator 4 supports `none` strangely. In the previous example, if I set `<H1>` to `none`, Navigator refuses to display `<H1>` text *and* all the text that follows! Also, `none` doesn't seem to work on images; they display anyway.

By the way, you'll note that the default `display` value is `block`, but in reality the browsers have their own default values for how they treat each unique HTML tag.

white-space

Syntax:

```
normal ¦ pre ¦ nowrap
```

Default value: `normal`
Applies to: Block-level elements
Inherited: Yes
Percentage values: N/A

Examples:

```
H1 { white-space: pre }
```

```
H1 { white-space: nowrap }
```

```
<H1 STYLE="white-space: normal">
```

As we all know, when browsers come upon a bunch of spaces in traditional `<P>` HTML text, they collapse that white space. The only way we can guarantee those spaces are displayed is to use the `<PRE>` tag (in which case your font changes to a usually ugly monospaced font face) or to insert a bunch of special character entities ( ) that could backfire in older browsers.

With the white-space property, you can finally instruct the browser on exactly what it should do when it comes across white space within an element. If it's set to normal, space will collapse as it normally does. Set it to pre, and all extra spaces will be respected, as if you'd used the <PRE> tag. Using nowrap tells the browser *not* to wrap to a new line unless it comes across a <BR> tag.

The default value is normal, but obviously this depends on the HTML tag. <PRE> has a default value of pre, for example.

A quick example of all three in action:

```
<HTML>
 <STYLE TYPE="text/css">
 <!--
  BODY { background: white;
        font-size: 17px }
  .a   { white-space: normal }
  .b   { white-space: pre }
  .c   { white-space: nowrap }
 -->
 </STYLE>
<HEAD>
 <TITLE>Specifying How White Space Is Handled</TITLE>
</HEAD>
<BODY>
 <P CLASS=a>Check out the    many    spaces in this    line.</P>
 <P CLASS=b>Check out the    many    spaces in this    line.</P>
 <P CLASS=c>Check out the    many    spaces in this    line.
 And for this one I'll add even more text so that it doesn't
 wrap until right<BR>here.</P>
</BODY>
</HTML>
```

Figure 9.3 shows the result in Navigator. Check out how the spaces are preserved in the second line. That can come in handy sometimes.

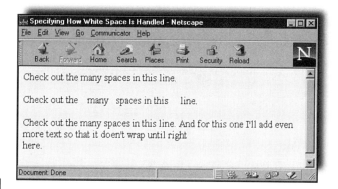

Figure 9.3

With white-space, *tell the browser exactly what to do with those spaces you have in your HTML.*

Note

From the previous figure, you can see that Navigator supports pre, but not nowrap. It shouldn't have wrapped that text at all until that final word.

Note

Explorer 3 and 4 don't support the white-space property at all.

list-style-type

Syntax:

```
disc ¦ circle ¦ square ¦ decimal ¦ lower-roman ¦ upper-roman ¦
lower-alpha ¦ upper-alpha ¦ none
```

Default value: disc
Applies to: Elements with display set to list-item
Inherited: Yes
Percentage values: N/A

Examples:

```
H1 { list-style-type: square }

H1 { list-style-type: upper-roman }

<H1 STYLE="list-style-type: circle">
```

Want to change the symbol that displays before items in a list? This is the way to do it. Keep in mind that you can use this property only if you also use the `display` property on the same element, and it is set to `list-item`.

 Navigator 4 supports all the `list-style-type` values except `none`, which it renders as a circle.

 Explorer 3 or 4 don't support `list-style-type`.

list-style-image

Syntax:

```
<url> ¦ none
```

Default value: `none`
Applies to: Elements with `display` set to `list-item`
Inherited: Yes
Percentage values: N/A

Examples:

```
H1 { list-style-image: url(../graphics/bullet.gif) }

H1 { list-style-image: none }

<H1 STYLE="list-style-image: url(http://www.mulder.com/dot.png)">
```

What if you don't want to use one of the pre-specified symbols to precede your list items, but instead use your own GIF image? With style sheets, you can. Just throw an absolute or relative URL at the `list-style-image` property, and your own custom graphic can serve as the bullet symbol. (For a reminder of how to use URLs in style sheet rules, see the discussion under "`background-image`" in Chapter 6.) You can use any graphic or image file you wish.

If this property is set to `none`, or if the browser fails to load the image specified, then the browser will use the value of `list-style-type` instead.

Netscape **Navigator**

> Navigator 4 does not support `list-style-image`.

Internet explorer

> Explorer 3 and 4 don't support `list-style-image` either.

list-style-position

Syntax:

```
inside ¦ outside
```

Default value: `outside`
Applies to: Elements with `display` set to `list-item`
Inherited: Yes
Percentage values: N/A

Examples:

```
H1 { list-style-position: inside }
```

```
<H1 STYLE="list-style-position: outside">
```

The `list-style-position` property enables you to dictate to the browser how it draws the list item marker or symbol or graphic with regard to the content of the list.

If you set the property to `outside`, the bulleted text appears like we're used to. The bullet (or other symbol) appears "outside" the lines of text, like so:

➡   This is some
    sample text.

➡   This is more
    sample text.

But if you use the `inside` setting, the text "wraps around" the symbol more, like this:

➡   This is some
sample text.

➡   This is more
sample text.

In my opinion, `outside` is more attractive, but it's up to you.

Navigator 4 does not support `list-style-position`.

Explorer 3 and 4 don't support `list-style-position` either.

list-style

Syntax:

```
<keyword> ¦¦ <position> ¦¦ <url>
```

Default value: Not defined
Applies to: Elements with `display` set to `list-item`
Inherited: Yes
Percentage values: N/A

Examples:

```
H1 { list-style: square outside }

H1 { list-style: disc url(images/red-dot.gif) }

<H1 STYLE="list-style: upper-roman inside">
```

`list-style` is another one of those shorthand properties that enables you to set a number of different properties all at once. In this case, the properties include `list-style-type`, `list-style-image`, and `list-style-position`. Whatever values you could use for those properties, you can use here, too.

Tip

It's often wiser to use these `list-style` properties on `<OL>` or `<UL>`, not on `<LI>` itself, if you have more than one type of list on a particular Web page.

Netscape **Navigator**

Navigator 4 does not support `list-style`.

Internet explorer

Explorer 3 and 4 don't support `list-style` either.

CHAPTER 10

Style Sheets Gallery

Okay, you know the syntax. You know the possibilities. You know the rules. And you know the browser support (or lack thereof). What's the best way to learn more and discover new, creative uses of style sheets? From the Web, of course.

We're all used to viewing source code of other Web sites to find out just how somebody did something cool. The same strategy works with style sheets. That's what this chapter is all about: checking out interesting uses of style sheets on the Web and dissecting how they are put together. The code is here for your perusal.

Style sheets is a very new technology, so there aren't as many examples out there as I expected when I wrote this. But as word of the power of style sheets gets out, you can be sure that more and more great styled sites will be popping up every week. So keep an eye out!

Note

The code you see in this chapter is essentially unchanged from the original page, though I did close up page-wasting vertical and horizontal spaces when I could. In some cases, I also cut code or text from the page if it wasn't relevant to the styles or to the screen capture of the site shown.

ESPNET SportsZone: 1996 Olympics

http://espnet.sportszone.com/editors/atlanta96/

Font size with backup <FONT SIZE> HTML tag

Font face and leading

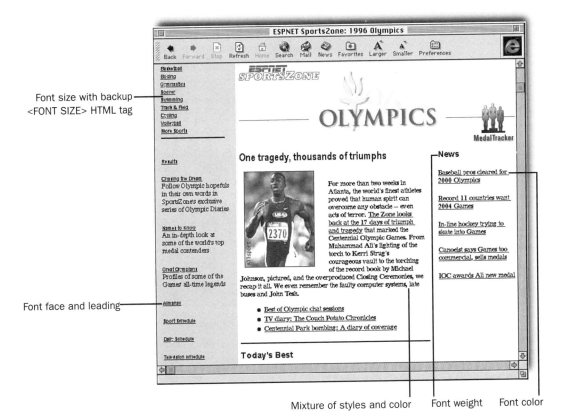

Mixture of styles and color   Font weight   Font color

```html
<html>
<head><title>ESPNET SportsZone: 1996 Olympics</title>
<style type="text/css">
<!--
    BODY    {font: 11pt/13pt "times roman";
             color: black}
```

```
     A        {color: navy;
              font-weight: bold}
     H1       {font: 18pt/18pt "arial narrow", sans-serif;
              font-weight: bold;
              color: black}
     H2       {font: 14pt/16pt "arial", sans-serif;
              font-weight: bold;
              color: black}
     H4       {font: 8.5pt/9pt "arial", sans-serif;
              font-weight: bold}
     A.WHITE  {font: 8.5pt/10pt "arial";
              color: black;
              font-weight: normal}
     A.SILVER {font: 8.5pt/10pt "arial";
              color: gray;
              font-weight: normal}
-->
</style>
</head>
<body background="/img/sportpaperneutral.gif">
<table border="0" align="left">
<tr>
<td width="125" rowspan="3" valign="top">
<font size="-1">
<a href="/editors/atlanta96/sports/bask/index.html" class="WHITE">
Basketball</a><br>
<a href="/editors/atlanta96/sports/box/index.html" class="WHITE">
Boxing</a><br>
<a href="/editors/atlanta96/sports/gym/index.html" class="WHITE">
Gymnastics</a><br>
<a href="/editors/atlanta96/sports/soc/index.html" class="WHITE">
Soccer</a><br>
<a href="/editors/atlanta96/sports/swim/index.html" class="WHITE">
Swimming</a><br>
<a href="/editors/atlanta96/sports/track/index.html" class="WHITE">
Track & Field</a><br>
<a href="/editors/atlanta96/sports/cycle/index.html" class="WHITE">
Cycling</a><br>
<a href="/editors/atlanta96/sports/voll/index.html" class="WHITE">
Volleyball</a><br>
<a href="/editors/atlanta96/sports.html" class="WHITE">
More Sports</a>
<hr width="110" align="left">
<br clear="all"><br>
```

```
<a href="http://medaltracker-espnet.sportszone.com/editors/
atlanta96/medaltracker/scripts/sportindex.idc" class="WHITE">
Results</a><p>
<a href="/editors/atlanta96/diaries/archive.html" class="WHITE">
Chasing the Dream</a><br>
Follow Olympic hopefuls in their own words in SportsZone's exclusive
series of Olympic Diaries
<p>
<a href="/editors/atlanta96/features/names/namesindex.html"
class="WHITE">Names to Know</a><br>
An in-depth look at some of the world's top medal contenders
<p>
<a href="/editors/atlanta96/features/greatindex.html" class="WHITE">
Great Olympians</a><br>
Profiles of some of the Games' all-time legends
<p>
<a href="/editors/atlanta96/almanac/index.html" class="WHITE">
Almanac</a><p>
<a href="/editors/atlanta96/schedule/sportsked.html" class="WHITE">
Sport Schedule</a><p>
<a href="/editors/atlanta96/schedule/dailysked.html" class="WHITE">
Daily Schedule</a><p>
<a href="/editors/atlanta96/preview/nbcsked.html"class="WHITE">
Television schedule</a><p>
</font>
</td>

<td width="8" rowspan="3"></td>

<td colspan="3" valign="top">
<a href="/img/olyfront.map">
<img src="/img/olympic3.gif" border=0 ISMAP></a>
<br clear="all"><br><br>
</td>
</tr>

<tr>
<td valign="top" width="325">
<h1>One tragedy, thousands of triumphs</h1>

<img src="/editors/media/photo/olympics/0729m400.jpg" height=160
width=120 hspace=8 align=left alt="Michael Johnson">
```

```
<b>For more than two weeks in Atlanta, the world's finest athletes
proved that human spirit can overcome any obstacle -- even acts of
terror. <a href="/editors/atlanta96/review/index.html">The Zone
looks back at the 17 days of triumph and tragedy</a> that marked the
Centennial Olympic Games. From Muhammad Ali's lighting of the torch
to Kerri Strug's courageous vault to the torching of the record book
by Michael Johnson, pictured, and the overproduced Closing
Ceremonies, we recap it all. We even remember the faulty computer
systems, late buses and John Tesh.

<ul>
<li><a href="/editors/atlanta96/features/0804bestchat.html">
Best of Olympic chat sessions</a>
<li><a href="/editors/atlanta96/features/tvarch.html">
TV diary: The Couch Potato Chronicles</a>
<li><a href="/editors/atlanta96/blast.html">
Centennial Park bombing: A diary of coverage</a></b>
</ul>

<hr>
<H2>Today's Best</H2>
<a href="/editors/atlanta96/features/0804vincent.html">
<b>Vincent: Games finish on spirited note</b></a><br>
The Zone's Charlie Vincent finds testaments to the human spirit in
an Olympic marathoner and the American women who dominated in
Atlanta.<p>
<a href="/editors/atlanta96/features/0804drury.html">
<b>Drury: Making sense (or cents) of Centennial Olympiad</b></a><br>
The Zone's Bob Drury muses about steroid charges, stunted Dominiques
and John Tesh.<p>
</td>

<td valign="top" width="10"></td>

<td width="135" valign="top">
<p>
<H2>News</H2>
<a href="/editors/atlanta96/sports/base/960921baseball.html">
<b>Baseball pros cleared for 2000 Olympics</b></a><p>
<a href="/editors/atlanta96/0815bid.html">
<b>Record 11 countries want 2004 Games</b></a><p>
```

```
<a href="/editors/atlanta96/0809hockey.html">
<b>In-line hockey trying to skate into Games</b></a><p>
<a href="/editors/atlanta96/0805medals.html">
<b>Canoeist says Games too commercial, sells medals</b></a><p>
<a href="/editors/atlanta96/0803ali.html">
<b>IOC awards Ali new medal</b></a><P>
</td>
</tr>
<tr><td colspan="5">
</td></tr></table>
</body>
</html>
```

Insight: from the World Wide Web Consortium Site

http://www.w3.org/pub/WWW/Style/css/msie/insight3.htm

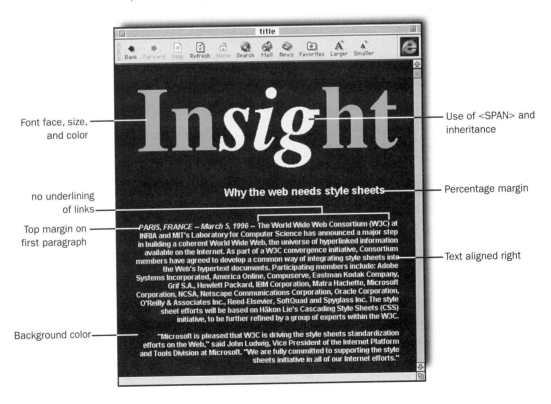

Font face, size, and color

Use of <SPAN> and inheritance

no underlining of links

Percentage margin

Top margin on first paragraph

Text aligned right

Background color

```
<HTML>
<HEAD>
<TITLE>title</TITLE>
<STYLE TYPE="text/css">
  BODY {
    color: #FFA;
    background: black;
    margin-left: 5%;
    margin-right: 5%;
    font-family: "arial", "helvetica", sans-serif; }
  H1 {
    color: #7AF;
    margin-top: 10px;
    text-align: right;
    font: 150px charter, times, serif; }
  H1 SPAN {
    font-style: italic;
    color: #BFF; }
  P SPAN { font-weight: bold; font-style: italic }
  H2 {
    color: #BFF;
    margin-left: 30%;
    margin-right: 5%;
    margin-top: 10px;
    text-align: right; }
  P {
    text-align: right;
    font-weight: bold; }
  P.initial {
    margin-top: 10px; }
  A:link { text-decoration: none }
  A:visited { text-decoration: none }
</STYLE>
</HEAD>
<BODY>
<H1>In<SPAN>sig</SPAN>ht</H1>
<H2>Why <A HREF="http://www.w3.org/">the web</A> needs style sheets
</H2>
<P CLASS=INITIAL><SPAN>PARIS, FRANCE -- March 5, 1996 --</SPAN>
```

```
The <A href="http://www.w3.org/">World Wide Web Consortium (W3C)</A>
at <A href="http://www.inria.fr/">INRIA</A> and MIT's <A href=
"http://www.lcs.mit.edu/">Laboratory for Computer Science</A> has
announced a major step in building a coherent World Wide Web, the
universe of hyperlinked information available on the Internet.
As part of a W3C convergence initiative, <A HREF=
"http://www.w3.org/pub/WWW/Consortium/Member/List.html">Consortium
members</A> have agreed to develop a common way of integrating style
sheets into the Web's hypertext documents. Participating members
include: Adobe Systems Incorporated, America Online, Compuserve,
Eastman Kodak Company, Grif S.A., Hewlett Packard, IBM Corporation,
Matra Hachette, Microsoft Corporation, NCSA, Netscape Communications
Corporation, Oracle Corporation, O'Reilly &amp; Associates Inc.,
Reed-Elsevier, SoftQuad and Spyglass Inc. The style sheet efforts
will be based on H&aring;kon Lie's <A HREF=
"http://www.w3.org/pub/WWW/TR/WD-css1.html">Cascading Style
Sheets (CSS)</A> initiative, to be further refined by a group of
experts within the W3C.

<P>"Microsoft is pleased that W3C is driving the style sheets
standardization efforts on the Web," said John Ludwig, Vice
President of the Internet Platform and Tools Division at Microsoft.
"We are fully committed to supporting the style sheets initiative in
all of our Internet efforts."
</BODY>
</HTML>
```

the Web Newsletter: from the Microsoft CSS Gallery

```
http://www.microsoft.com/truetype/css/gallery/slide3.htm
```

Style sheets combined with tables

Font weight
and style

Absolute margins

Font face, size, and leading

Text color

Negative margins

```
<HTML>
<HEAD>
<TITLE>WWLive CSS demo 1</TITLE>
<STYLE  TYPE="text/css">
<!--
BODY { background: coral }
.copy { color: Black;
    font-size: 11px;
    line-height: 14px;
    font-family: Verdana, Arial, helvetica, sans-serif }
A:link { text-decoration: none;
    font-size: 20px;
```

```
      color: black;
      font-family: Comic Sans MS, Arial Black, Arial, helvetica,
      sans-serif }
.star { color: white;
      font-size: 350px;
      font-family: Arial, Arial, helvetica, sans-serif }
.subhead { color: black;
      font-size: 28px;
      margin-top: 12px;
      margin-left: 20px;
      line-height: 32px;
      font-family: Impact, Arial Black, Arial, helvetica, sans-serif }
.what { color: black;
      font-size: 22px;
      margin-left: 20px;
      font-weight: bold;
      font-style: italic;
      font-family: Times New Roman, times, serif }
.quott { color: black;
      font-size: 120px;
      line-height: 120px;
      margin-top: -24px;
      margin-left: -4px;
      font-family: Arial Black, Arial, helvetica, sans-serif }
.quotb { color: black;
      font-size: 120px;
      line-height: 120px;
      margin-right: -1px;
      margin-top: -33px;
      font-family: Arial Black, Arial, helvetica, sans-serif }
.quote { color: red;
      font-size: 24px;
      line-height: 28px;
      margin-top: -153px;
      font-family: Impact, Arial Black, Arial, helvetica, sans-serif }
.footer { color: cornsilk;
      background: red;
      font-size: 22px;
      margin-left: 20px;
      margin-top: 16px;
      font-family: Impact, Arial Black, Arial, helvetica, sans-serif }
.headline { color: black;
      font-size: 80px;
```

```
      line-height: 90px;
      margin-left: 20px;
      font-family: Impact, Arial Black, Arial, helvetica, sans-serif }
.mast { color: cornsilk;
      font-size: 90px;
      font-style: italic;
      font-family: Impact, Arial Black, Arial, helvetica, sans-serif }
-->
</STYLE>
</HEAD>
<BODY>
<CENTER>
<TABLE BGCOLOR=cornsilk WIDTH=730 CELLPADDING=0 CELLSPACING=0
BORDER=0>
    <TR>       .
    <TD VALIGN=TOP ALIGN=LEFT> </TD>
    <TD COLSPAN=2></TD>
    <TD VALIGN=TOP ALIGN=RIGHT> </TD>
    </TR>
    <TR>
    <TD COLSPAN=4 VALIGN=TOP>
        <TABLE CELLPADDING=0 CELLSPACING=0 BORDER=0>
        <TR><TD WIDTH=20></TD>
        <TD WIDTH=340 ALIGN=CENTER BGCOLOR=red>
        <DIV CLASS=mast>the Web </DIV></TD>
        <TD></TD>
        <TD WIDTH=330 VALIGN=TOP>
    <DIV CLASS=what>Style sheets give you the ability to control
    the presentation of a Web document without compromising its
    underlying structure </DIV>
        </TD>
        </TR>
        </TABLE>
    </TD>
    </TR>

    <TR>
    <TD COLSPAN=4>
    <DIV CLASS=headline>STYLE SHEETS ARRIVE!</DIV>
    <DIV CLASS=subhead>WWW GETS EXTRA STYLE THANKS TO CASCADING
    STYLE SHEETS</DIV>
    </TD>
    </TR>
```

```
<TR>
<TD COLSPAN=4 VALIGN=TOP ALIGN=CENTER>

     <TABLE CELLPADDING=5 CELLSPACING=0 BORDER=0>
     <TR>
     <TD WIDTH=228 VALIGN=TOP>
<DIV CLASS=copy><BR><B>The World Wide Web Consortium describe CSS1
as &#145;a simple style sheet mechanism that allows authors and
readers to attach style to HTML documents.&#146;</B><BR>

   According to its authors CSS1 uses &#145;common desktop
publishing terminology&#146; which should make it easy for
professional as well as untrained designers to make use of its
features. This page introduces some of the basic concepts and
describes the font related features of CSS1. For full details of the
CSS1 specification please see the official W3C Cascading Style
Sheets page. <BR>

   CSS1 provides the designer with various ways of
specifying style for a Web page. Style information can be stored in
an external file and referenced by any number of Web pages, or the
attributes can be applied to a specific section of text within the
body of a page. The method described below involves including style
information within a STYLE section in the HEAD part of a particular
HTML file. Style properties can be applied to HTML elements at the
block level and at the text or <BR></DIV>
     </TD>

     <TD WIDTH=228 VALIGN=TOP><DIV CLASS=copy><BR>
inline level. Block level elements are those that usually cause
paragraph breaks.</DIV>

<DIV CLASS=quott>&#147;</DIV>
<DIV ALIGN=RIGHT CLASS=quotb>&#148;</DIV>
<DIV ALIGN=CENTER CLASS=quote>
         
USES COMMON<BR>DESKTOP PUBLISHING<BR>TERMINOLOGY
        </DIV>
```

```
<DIV CLASS=copy><BR><BR>These include H1 to H6 (headings), P
(paragraphs), and LI (list items). Text level elements include EM,
STRONG and CITE as well as B, I and A (hypertext anchors). In CSS1
HTML elements are known as selectors. <BR>

   CSS1 supports 35 different properties which can be
applied to selectors. Properties include background (color or
graphic), font-size, font-weight, line-height (leading or
interlinear spacing), font-family, letter-spacing and word-spacing.
A property and its associated value is known as a declaration.</DIV>
        </TD>

        <TD WIDTH=228 VALIGN=TOP><DIV CLASS=copy></DIV>
            <TABLE WIDTH=212 HEIGHT=263 CELLPADDING=0 BORDER=1>
            <TR>
            <TD BACKGROUND="/truetype/css/gallery/hakon.gif"></TD>
            </TR>
            </TABLE>
</TD></TR></TABLE>
    </TD>
    </TR>
    <TR>
    <TD COLSPAN=4 HEIGHT=10></TD>
    </TR>
    </TABLE>
</CENTER>
</BODY>
</HTML>
```

IntraOffice Communication: from the Microsoft CSS Gallery

```
http://www.microsoft.com/gallery/files/styles/icc.htm
```

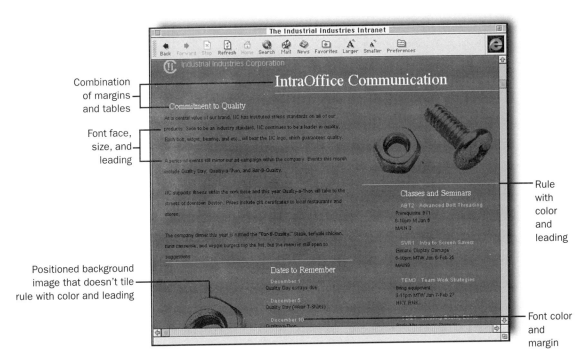

Combination of margins and tables

Font face, size, and leading

Positioned background image that doesn't tile rule with color and leading

Rule with color and leading

Font color and margin

```html
<html>
<title>The Industrial Industries Intranet</title>
<style type="text/css">
<!--
body {font: "arial";
    color: black;
    background: url(images/bg_bolts.jpg) repeat-x ; }
hr {color: "#FF9933";
    margin-left: 0px;
    margin-right: 0px;
    line-height:5pt; }
.company {font: 14pt "arial";
    color: "#FF9933";
    margin-left: 15px; }
.h1 { font: 30pt "times roman";
    margin-left: 33%;
    color: white; }
.h2 {font: 16pt/7pt "times roman";
    color: white;
    margin-left: 10px; }
.h3 {font: 10pt "arial";
    color: "#FF9933";
    margin-left: 10px; }
```

```
.copy { font: 9pt/20pt "arial";
    margin-left: 10px;
    margin-right: 10px; }
.copy2 { font: 9pt/12pt "arial";
    margin-left: 10px;
    margin-right: 10px; }
.credit { font: 9pt/12pt "arial";
    color: "#FF9933";
    margin-left: 20px; }
.classdesc { font: 9pt/14pt "arial";
    margin-left: 64px; }
.logobg { background: url(images/logo_bolts.gif) 50% 25% no-repeat;
    }
-->
</style>
<body topmargin=0 bgcolor="#336666">
<br><span class=company><img src="images/sm_logo_bolts.gif"
align=middle>Industrial Industries Corporation</span>

<table width=700>
<tr><td class=h1 colspan=2>IntraOffice Communication
 <hr size=1> </td></tr>
<tr><td colspan=2> </td></tr>
<tr><td valign=top>

<!-- ************** Left table ************** -->
<table class=logobg>
<tr>
<td class=copy colspan=2>
<span class=h2>Commitment to Quality</span><br>
As a central value of our brand, IIC has instituted stress standards
on all of our products. Soon to be an industry standard, IIC
continues to be a leader in quality. Each bolt, widget, bearing, and
etc., will bear the IIC logo, which guarantees quality.<br><br>

A series of events will mirror our ad campaign within the company.
Events this month include Quality Day, Quality-a-Thon, and
Bar-B-Quality.<br><br>

IIC supports fitness within the work force and this year
Quality-a-Thon will take to the streets of downtown Boston. Prizes
include gift certificates to local restaurants and stores.<br><br>
```

```
The company dinner this year is named the "Bar-B-Quality." Steak,
teriyaki chicken, tuna casserole, and veggie burgers top the list,
but the menu is still open to suggestions<br><hr size=1><br>
</td>
</tr>

<tr>
<td width=50% align=center><img src="images/big_bolt.gif"></td>
<td class=copy2 valign=top>
<span class=h2>Dates to Remember<br><br></span>
<span class=h3>December 1</span><br>
Quality Day essays due<br><br>

<span class=h3>December 5 </span><br>
Quality Day (Wear T-Shirts)<br><br>

<span class=h3>December 10 </span><br>
Quality-a-Thon<br><br>

<span class=h3>December 11</span><br>
Quality Gift Wrap<br><br>

<span class=h3>December 15 </span><br>
Bar-B-Quality<br><br>

<span class=h3>December 20 </span><br>
Santa-Quality<br><br>

<span class=h3>December  25-29 </span><br>
Holiday<br><br>
</td></tr></table>
</td>

<!-- ************** Right table **************-->
<td>
<table>
<tr><td><img src="images/two_bolts.gif"><br><hr size=1></td></tr>
<tr><td class=classdesc>
<span class=h2>Classes and Seminars<br><br></span>
```

```
<span class=h3>ABT2     Advanced Bolt Threading</span><br>
        Prerequisite BT1<br>
        6-10pm M Jan 6<br>
        MAIN 3<br><br>
<span class=h3>SVR1     Intro to Screen Savers</span><br>
        Elimate Display Damage<br>
        6-10pm MTW Jan 6-Feb 26<br>
        MAIN9<br><br>
<span class=h3>TEM3     Team Work Strategies</span><br>
        Bring equipment<br>
        9-11pm MTW Jan 7-Feb 27<br>
        HKY RNK<br><br>
<span class=h3>GBQ1     Creating Quality Ethics</span><br>
        Basic Management Strategies<br>
        6-10pm MTW Jan 6,7,8<br>
        MAIN 5<br><br>
<span class=h3>RCY1     Recycling</span><br>
        Office recycling strategies<br>
        6-10pm MTW Jan 6-Feb 26<br>
        DSPSL 3<br>
<hr size=1>
</td></tr>
</table>
</td>
</tr>
<tr><td colspan=2><hr size=1></td></tr>
</table>
<span class=credit>Page layout and design by <a href="http://
www.girvindesign.com">Tim Girvin Design</a><span>
</body>
</html>
```

yo flava 23 magazine: from the Microsoft CSS Gallery

```
http://www.microsoft.com/truetype/css/gallery/4d.htm
```

Wingdings font
for circles

Font face, size,
and style

Negative margin
for overlap

color

Absolute margins

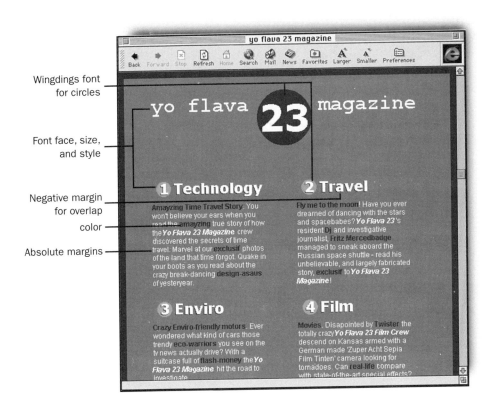

```
<HTML>
<HEAD>
<TITLE>yo flava 23 magazine</TITLE>
<STYLE>
<!--
BODY { background: darkblue;
    color: black}
P { color: black;
    font-size: 12px;
    font-family: Arial, sans-serif }
.copy { color: white;
    margin-left: -4px;
    margin-right: 6px;
    margin-top: 10px;
    font-size: 12px;
    font-family: Arial, sans-serif }
.plus { color: white;
    margin-left: -200px;
    margin-right: -200px;
```

```
                     font-size: 33px;
                     font-family: Courier New }
    .logo1 { color: darkblue;
                margin-top: -17px;
                font-size: 160px;
                font-weight: bold;
                font-family: Wingdings; }
    .logo2 { color: azure;
                margin-top: -131px;
                margin-right: -3px;
                font-size: 62px;
                font-weight: bold;
                font-family: Verdana; }
    .logo3 { color: azure;
                font-size: 35px;
                font-weight: bold;
                font-family: Courier New; }
    .ball { color: deepskyblue;
                font-size: 44px;
                font-weight: bold;
                font-family: Wingdings; }
    .subhead { color: darkblue;
                margin-left: 8px;
                margin-top: -39px;
                font-size: 24px;
                font-weight: bold;
                font-family: Verdana; }
    .subhead2 { color: white;
                margin-left: 9px;
                margin-top: -30px;
                font-size: 24px;
                font-weight: bold;
                font-family: Verdana; }
    B { color: darkblue }
    I { font-weight: bold }
    A:link { font-size: 10px;
                text-decoration: none;
                color: #AAAAAA;
                font-family: Verdana; }
    A:visited { font-size: 10px;
                text-decoration: none;
                color: #AAAAAA;
                font-family: Verdana; }
```

```
-->
</STYLE>
</HEAD>
<BODY LINK=#AAAAAA VLINK=#AAAAAA>
<CENTER>
<TABLE WIDTH=560 CELLPADDING=0 CELLSPACING=0 BORDERCOLORDARK=black
 BORDERCOLORLIGHT=red BORDER=0 BGCOLOR=steelblue>
<TR><TD COLSPAN=5 ALIGN=CENTER>

<TABLE WIDTH=550 CELLPADDING=0 CELLSPACING=0>
<TR><TD WIDTH=220 VALIGN=TOP><P><BR> 
<DIV ALIGN=RIGHT CLASS=logo3>yo flava</DIV></TD>
<TD WIDTH=110 ALIGN=CENTER><DIV CLASS=logo1>l</DIV>
<DIV CLASS=logo2>23</DIV></TD>
<TD WIDTH=220 VALIGN=TOP><P ALIGN=RIGHT><BR> 
<DIV ALIGN=LEFT CLASS=logo3>magazine</DIV>
</TD></TR></TABLE></TD></TR>

<TR>
<TD WIDTH=50 VALIGN=TOP> </TD>
<TD WIDTH=200 VALIGN=TOP>
<DIV CLASS=ball>l</DIV>
<DIV CLASS=subhead>1 Technology</DIV>
<DIV CLASS=subhead2>1 Technology</DIV>
<DIV CLASS=copy><B>Amayzing Time Travel Story</B>. You won't believe
your ears when you read the <B>amayzing</B> true story of how the
<I>Yo Flava 23 Magazine</I> crew discovered the secrets of time
travel. Marvel at our <B>exclusif</B> photos of the land that time
forgot. Quake in your boots as you read about the crazy break-
dancing <B>design-asaus</B> of yesteryear.</DIV>
</TD>

<TD ROWSPAN=3 WIDTH=50> </TD>

<TD WIDTH=200 VALIGN=TOP>
<DIV CLASS=ball>l</DIV>
<DIV CLASS=subhead>2 Travel</DIV>
<DIV CLASS=subhead2>2 Travel</DIV>
<DIV CLASS=copy><B>Fly me to the moon</B>! Have you ever dreamed of
dancing with the stars and spacebabes? <I>Yo Flava 23</I>'s resident
<B>Dj</B> and investigative journalist, <B>Fritz Mercedbadge</B>
managed to sneak aboard the Russian space shuttle - read his
unbelievable, and largely fabricated story, <B>exclusif</B> to
```

```
<I>Yo Flava 23 Magazine</I>!</DIV>
</TD>

<TD WIDTH=50 VALIGN=TOP> </TD></TR>

<TR><TD COLSPAN=5 VALIGN=TOP> </TD></TR>

<TR><TD WIDTH=50 VALIGN=TOP> </TD>

<TD WIDTH=200 VALIGN=TOP>
<DIV CLASS=ball>l</DIV>
<DIV CLASS=subhead>3 Enviro</DIV>
<DIV CLASS=subhead2>3 Enviro</DIV>
<DIV CLASS=copy><B>Crazy Enviro-friendly motors</B>. Ever wondered
what kind of cars those trendy <B>eco-warriors</B> you see on the
tv news actually drive? With a suitcase full of <B>flash-money</B>
the <I>Yo Flava 23 Magazine</I> hit the road to investigate.</DIV>
</TD>

<TD WIDTH=200 VALIGN=TOP>
<DIV CLASS=ball>l</DIV>
<DIV CLASS=subhead>4 Film</DIV>
<DIV CLASS=subhead2>4 Film</DIV>
<DIV CLASS=copy><B>Movies</B>. Disapointed by <B>Twister</B> the
totally crazy <I>Yo Flava 23 Film Crew</I> descend on Kansas armed
with a German made 'Zuper Acht Sepia Film Tinten' camera looking for
tornadoes. Can <B>real-life</B> compare with state-of-the-art
special effects? You be the judge.<BR><BR> </DIV>
</TD>

<TD WIDTH=50 VALIGN=TOP> </TD></TR>
</TABLE>
</CENTER>
</BODY>
</HTML>
```

Team TrueType: from the Microsoft CSS Gallery

http://www.microsoft.com/truetype/css/gallery/4a.htm

Spaces were
used for colored
table cells

Negative margins
for overlap

Font face,
size and style

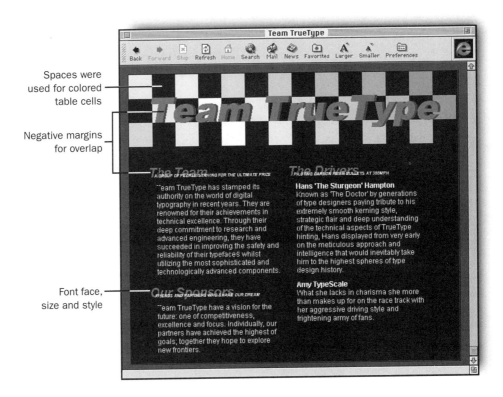

```
<HTML>
<HEAD>
<TITLE>Team TrueType</TITLE>
<STYLE>
<!--
BODY { background: darkslategray;
    color: black}
P { color: black;
    font-size: 12px;
    font-family: Arial, helvetica, sans-serif; }
.copy { color: white;
    margin-left: -4px;
    margin-right: 6px;
    margin-top: 10px;
    font-size: 12px;
    font-family: Arial, helvetica, sans-serif; }
.logo1 { color: darkred;
    margin-left: 8px;
    margin-top: -124px;
```

```
        font-size: 58px;
        line-height: 84px;
        font-style: Italic;
        font-family: Arial Black, Impact, Arial, Helvetica, Sans-serif;}
.logo2 { color: red;
        margin-top: -84px;
        font-size: 58px;
        line-height: 84px;
        font-style: Italic;
        font-family: Arial Black, Impact, Arial, Helvetica, Sans-serif;}
.subhead { color: red;
        margin-top: 15px;
        margin-left: -15px;
        font-size: 22px;
        font-weight: bold;
        font-style: italic;
        font-family: Arial, sans-serif; }
.suboverlay { color: white;
        margin-top: -12px;
        margin-left: -6px;
        font-size: 7px;
        font-weight: bold;
        font-style: italic;
        text-decoration: underline;
        font-family: Arial, sans-serif; }
A:link { font-size: 10px;
        text-decoration: none;
        color: #AAA;
        font-family: Verdana, Arial, sans-serif; }
A:visited { font-size: 10px;
        text-decoration: none;
        color: #AAA;
        font-family: Verdana, Arial, sans-serif; }
-->
</STYLE>
</HEAD>
<BODY>
<TABLE WIDTH=564 CELLPADDING=0 CELLSPACING=0 BORDERCOLORDARK=black
 BORDERCOLORLIGHT=darkred BORDER=1 BGCOLOR=black>
<TR><TD COLSPAN=5 VALIGN=TOP>

<TABLE WIDTH=560 HEIGHT=120 CELLPADDING=0 CELLSPACING=0 BORDER=0
BGCOLOR=black>
<TR>
```

```
<TD WIDTH=40 HEIGHT=40 BGCOLOR=#EEEEE> </TD><TD WIDTH=40></TD>
<TD WIDTH=40 BGCOLOR=#EEEEEE> </TD><TD WIDTH=40></TD>
<TD WIDTH=40 BGCOLOR=#DDDDDD> </TD><TD WIDTH=40></TD>
<TD WIDTH=40 BGCOLOR=#CCCCCC> </TD><TD WIDTH=40></TD>
<TD WIDTH=40 BGCOLOR=#BBBBBB> </TD><TD WIDTH=40></TD>
<TD WIDTH=40 BGCOLOR=#AAAAAA> </TD><TD WIDTH=40></TD>
<TD WIDTH=40 BGCOLOR=#999999> </TD><TD WIDTH=38> </TD>
</TR>
<TR>
<TD WIDTH=40 HEIGHT=40></TD><TD WIDTH=40 BGCOLOR=#EEEEEE> </TD>
<TD WIDTH=40></TD><TD WIDTH=40 BGCOLOR=#FFFFFF> </TD>
<TD WIDTH=40></TD><TD WIDTH=40 BGCOLOR=#EEEEEE> </TD>
<TD WIDTH=40></TD><TD WIDTH=40 BGCOLOR=#DDDDDD> </TD>
<TD WIDTH=40></TD><TD WIDTH=40 BGCOLOR=#CCCCCC> </TD>
<TD WIDTH=40></TD><TD WIDTH=40 BGCOLOR=#BBBBBB> </TD>
<TD WIDTH=40></TD><TD WIDTH=40 BGCOLOR=#999999> </TD>
</TR>
<TR>
<TD WIDTH=40 HEIGHT=40 BGCOLOR=#DDDDDD> </TD><TD WIDTH=40></TD>
<TD WIDTH=40 BGCOLOR=#EEEEEE> </TD><TD WIDTH=40></TD>
<TD WIDTH=40 BGCOLOR=#FFFFFF> </TD><TD WIDTH=40></TD>
<TD WIDTH=40 BGCOLOR=#EEEEEE> </TD><TD WIDTH=40></TD>
<TD WIDTH=40 BGCOLOR=#DDDDDD> </TD><TD WIDTH=40></TD>
<TD WIDTH=40 BGCOLOR=#CCCCCC> </TD><TD WIDTH=40></TD>
<TD WIDTH=40 BGCOLOR=#BBBBBB> </TD><TD WIDTH=40></TD>
</TR>
</TABLE>

<DIV CLASS=logo1 ALIGN=CENTER>Team TrueType</DIV>
<DIV CLASS=logo2 ALIGN=CENTER>Team TrueType</DIV>
<P><BR>
</TD>
</TR>

<TR>
<TD WIDTH=50 VALIGN=TOP> </TD>
<TD WIDTH=220 VALIGN=TOP> </TD>
<TD WIDTH=20 VALIGN=TOP> </TD>
<TD WIDTH=220 VALIGN=TOP> </TD>
<TD WIDTH=50 VALIGN=TOP> </TD>
</TR>

<TR>
<TD WIDTH=50 VALIGN=TOP> </TD>
```

```
<TD WIDTH=220 VALIGN=TOP><DIV CLASS=subhead>The Team</DIV>
<DIV CLASS=suboverlay>A GROUP OF PEOPLE STRIVING FOR THE ULTIMATE
PRIZE</DIV>
<DIV CLASS=copy>Team TrueType has stamped its authority on the world
of digital typography in recent years. They are renowned for their
achievements in technical excellence. Through their deep commitment
to research and advanced engineering, they have succeeded in
improving the safety and reliability of their typefaces whilst
utilizing the most sophisticated and technologically advanced
components.</DIV>

<DIV CLASS=subhead>Our Sponsors</DIV>
<DIV CLASS=suboverlay>FRIENDS AND PARTNERS WHO SHARE OUR DREAM</DIV>
<DIV CLASS=copy>Team TrueType have a vision for the future: one of
competitiveness, excellence and focus. Individually, our partners
have achieved the highest of goals; together they hope to explore
new frontiers.<BR> </DIV>
</TD>

<TD WIDTH=20 VALIGN=TOP> </TD>

<TD WIDTH=220 VALIGN=TOP>
<DIV CLASS=subhead>The Drivers</DIV>
<DIV CLASS=suboverlay>PILOTING CARBON FIBER BULLETS AT 300MPH</DIV>
<DIV CLASS=copy><B>Hans 'The Sturgeon' Hampton</B><BR>Known as
'The Doctor' by generations of type designers paying tribute to his
extremely smooth kerning style, strategic flair and deep
understanding of the technical aspects of TrueType hinting, Hans
displayed from very early on the meticulous approach and
intelligence that would inevitably take him to the highest spheres
of type design history.</DIV>

<DIV CLASS=copy><B>Amy TypeScale</B><BR>What she lacks in charisma
she more than makes up for on the race track with her aggressive
driving style and frightening army of fans.<BR> </DIV>
</TD>

<TD WIDTH=50 VALIGN=TOP> </TD>
</TR>
<TR></TR></TABLE>
</CENTER>
</BODY>
</HTML>
```

Notscape: Fun with Styles

```
http://www.eastax.com/eastax/stylefun.html
```

I don't have the room here to print all the code behind this page, but I had to include it in this chapter for its sheer cleverness! Someone with a lot of patience has re-created the Netscape Navigator interface using an amazing combination of style sheet properties. There is not one single graphic on this Web page. Wow.

See if you can spot some of the creative uses of absolute and negative margins, background and foreground colors, indents, leading, creative font faces such as Wingdings and Marlett, and so on. And the whole page is only 9K.

Units

Throughout the book you've seen style sheet rules that use a variety of units for their values: pixels, ems, percentages, and so on. This appendix explains what each unit represents and what values are allowed for each unit. It also reveals which ones actually work or don't work in the various browsers. Coverage includes units for:

➡ Absolute dimensions

➡ Relative dimensions

➡ Percentages

Absolute Dimensions

Absolute dimensions are the units of measurement we're most used to in the physical world: inches, centimeters, points, picas, and so on. Here are the available units and how they look within style sheet rules:

➡ Inches: `H1 { margin: 1.5in }`

➡ Centimeters: `H1 { line-height: 4cm }`

➡ Millimeters: `H1 { word-spacing: 4mm }`

➡ Points: `H1 { font-size: 14pt }`

➡ Picas: `H1 { font-size: 1pc }`

Netscape is apparently dead set against any kind of absolutes on the Internet because Navigator 4 supports *none* of these values. That's right, no inches, no centimeters, no millimeters, no points, no picas. No luck.

And if you use one of these units, Navigator ignores the unit and treats the number as if you mean *pixels*. Yes, this can get ugly. Try to indent 1 inch, and Navigator translates that into 1 pixel. Try to indent 30 millimeters, and Navigator indents 30 pixels. Try to define a text size of 1 inch, and Navigator displays the text 1 pixel tall. Gross.

Internet Explorer does it right. It supports *all* of these units. In beta 3, Navigator supports all of these units except pica.

Here are some helpful translation formulas (numbers are approximate):

➡ 1 in = 2.54 cm = 25.4 mm = 72 points = 6 picas

➡ 1 cm = .39 in = 10 mm = 28.1 points = 2.34 picas

➡ 1 mm = .039 in = .1 cm = 2.81 points = .234 picas

➡ 1 point = .0139 in = .0353 cm = .353 mm = .0833 picas

➡ 1 pica = .167 in = .424 cm = 4.24 mm = 12 points

Unfortunately, such absolute precision is just about impossible, because an inch or centimeter in the digital world is fairly meaningless. There's a good chance that what takes up an inch on my screen doesn't take up exactly an inch on yours—especially across platforms.

This is worth showing. Figures A.1 and A.2 show exactly the same Web page. Each line is indented so many inches, centimeters, and so on. The rows of squares serve as a kind of ruler, so we can compare what an inch on a Mac screen is to an inch on a PC screen.

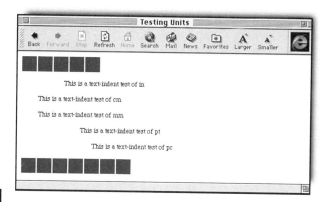

Text and squares on a Mac monitor.

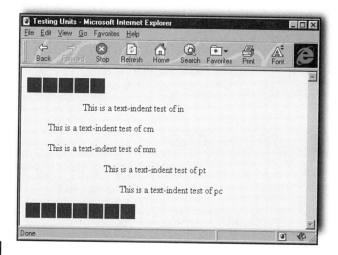

The exact same page on a PC monitor.

The differences are obvious. The first line of text is indented exactly 1 inch. But an inch on a PC is apparently longer than an inch on a Mac. The same goes for the other units. This is a big deal when designing Web sites. If this comparison doesn't make you want to test every single page you ever design on both platforms, nothing will!

Keep in mind that you can also specify these values as *negative*
units. That is, the following rule would specify a negative margin:

```
H1 { margin: -1.5in }
```

Not all browsers support negative values, so use at your own risk
(see Chapters 5 and 7 for more details). Browsers that don't
support negative values will find the nearest value that they do
support (probably 0). You can also put a plus sign (+) in front of
values, but since the plus is already assumed, you aren't required
to do so.

If the browser simply can't display something at a specified absolute value, then it will approximate to come as close as it can.

Relative Dimensions

Relative lengths can be flexible and powerful within style sheets.
They specify a dimension that's relative to the dimension of another property. The relative dimension units available under style
sheets include:

➡ Em: `H1 { margin: 1.5em }`

(An em is a unit of distance equal to the point size of a font.
In 14-point type, an em is 14 points wide. An em is relative
to font size.)

➡ X-Height: `H1 { margin: 1ex }`

(X-height refers to the height of the lowercase letters [not
including ascenders or descenders, such as "h" or "p" have]
of a font. X-height is relative to font size.)

➡ Pixels: `H1 { font-size: 12px }`

(A pixel is the smallest discrete unit of a display screen or printed page. It is relative to the resolution of the "canvas.")

Note

Explorer 3 and 4 for Windows 95 do not support `em` or `ex` values. (If you use `em` or `ex`, Explorer 3 assumes you mean pixels instead!)

The Mac version *does* support both `em` and `ex`.

And *both* versions support `px` values.

Note

Navigator supports pixels (`px`). But it appears to only sometimes support `em` and `ex`. (In my tests, Navigator recognized `em` and `ex` when used for `text-indent` but not when used for `font-size`. Very odd.

Tip

The bottom line? Though no unit can be guaranteed to work in all situations across all browsers and platforms, the pixel comes the closest at this time.

We're used to measuring by pixels, of course, and we rely on them for more consistent and predictable measurement for on-screen display, because most monitors are 72 ppi (pixels per inch). But I've also seen 96 ppi monitors. And if you were to print the Web page to a 300 dpi laser printer, all hell would break loose. It doesn't, fortunately, because good Web browsers rescale pixel values when they print (Explorer 3 for Windows, however, doesn't do this). Otherwise everything would be very tiny on paper. But remember that pixels are always measured relative to the size of the canvas (most often a monitor in our case, but TV set-top boxes and Web phones are on the way, so look out!). The style sheets specification recommends a "reference pixel" that is the "visual angle of one pixel on a device with a pixel density of 90 dpi and a distance from the reader of an arm's length." My question is: Whose arm? :-)

Style sheets that use relative units will more easily scale from one medium to another, so keep this in mind as you design. Style rules that use ems for unique letterspacing, for example, will remain more true to original intent than rules that use centimeters for letterspacing. When you print the document, ems will scale from a computer monitor to a printer; centimeters (and other absolute measurements) might not.

As with absolute units, relative units can occur in negative values. Simply append a minus sign (-). The plus sign (+) is the default. Browsers that don't support negative values will find the nearest value that they do support.

Also, if browsers can't support the specified value, they will approximate to do the best they can. For all style sheet properties, any further computations or inheritance should be based on this approximated value, not the original one.

One important thing to note about how relative units are inherited in style sheets: Child elements inherit the *computed* value, not the relative value.

```
<HTML>
 <STYLE TYPE="text/css">
 <!--
  P { font-size: 14pt;
      text-indent: 2em }    /* i.e., 28pt */
  B { font-size: 18pt }
 -->
 </STYLE>
<HEAD>
 <TITLE>Inheritance and Relative Units</TITLE>
</HEAD>
<BODY>
 <P>This is normal text indented 28 points.</P>
 <P><B>What am I? Also indented 28 points, even though my size
 is different.</B></P>
</BODY>
</HTML>
```

As Figure A.3 shows, the `text-indent` value of anything within `<B>` displays at 28 points, not 36 points. The indent as originally calculated for `<P>` "trickles down" to all the child elements, and isn't recalculated when the browser hits `<B>`.

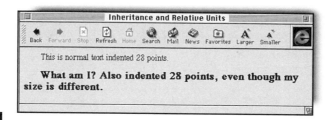

Figure A.3

Computed values of relative units endure throughout the style sheet.

Percentages

Percentage values are straightforward: They always represent a value relative to a length unit. To specify a percentage value, just include a number (with or without a decimal point) that is immediately followed by %:

```
H1 { line-height: 140% }
```

You can use percentage values only with certain properties, and each of these properties also defines what length unit is referred to by the percentage. (See the actual listings in Chapters 4 through 9 for which properties support percentage values.)

In all style sheet properties, child elements inherit the result, not the percentage value.

```
<HTML>
 <STYLE TYPE="text/css">
 <!--
  P { font-size: 14pt;
      line-height: 200% }    /* i.e., 28pt */
  B { font-size: 24pt }
 -->
 </STYLE>
<HEAD>
```

```
<TITLE>Inheritance and Percentage Units</TITLE>
</HEAD>
<BODY>
<P>This is normal text with a line-height of 28 points. I'll
add more text here so you can see it wrap and get a feel for
the leading.</P>
<P><B>What am I? Also with a line-height of 28 points, even
though my text size is different. And here's more text so you
can see it wrap.</B></P>
</BODY>
</HTML>
```

This code combined with Figure A.4 should make this point clear. Percentage units like that for line-height are calculated once for the entire document, not calculated multiple times for different selectors.

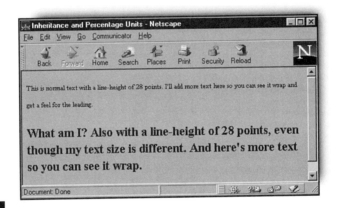

Figure A.4

Computed values of percentage units endure throughout the style sheet.

Font Faces

The details of specifying fonts were discussed in Chapter 4. There we looked at all the possible values of font-style (normal, italic, oblique), font-variant (normal, small-caps), font-weight (normal, bold, bolder), and so on.

But in Chapter 4 I didn't go into all the possible values of font-family, because they're too numerous and too difficult to nail down. As you remember, there is no sure-fire way to guarantee that visitors will have on their systems the font face you specify. You can of course specify that rare but cool font anyway, and pray that visitors have it and can view it. Or you can play it safe and use a font that you're pretty sure all visitors will have.

Here I want to talk about what those fonts might be—both the "sure bet" fonts and the "best guess" fonts.

"Sure Bet" Fonts

Thank goodness, there are some fonts that come with every computer. These are the fonts you know will be there when you want to specify a font-family. Unfortunately, those fonts aren't the same for Macintosh as they are for Windows. (Nope, I'm not even going to go into Unix.)

> **Note**
>
> Keep in mind for all the fonts in this chapter that when used in style sheets, they should be all lowercase (`helvetica`, `times new roman`, for example).

The fonts that ship with new Mac systems these days include:

➡ Chicago

➡ Courier

➡ Geneva

➡ Helvetica

➡ Monaco

➡ New York

➡ Palatino

➡ Symbol

➡ Times

➡ Zapf Dingbats

If your audience is all on Macs, then using any of these fonts is a safe bet.

The fonts that ship with Windows 95, Windows 3.1x, and Windows NT include:

➡ Arial

➡ Comic Sans

➡ Courier New

➡ Modern

➡ MS Sans Serif

➡ Symbol

➡ Times New Roman

➡ WingDings

 Note

For some reason, Navigator doesn't display Comic Sans, MS Sans Serif, or WingDings, regardless of how they're spelled. And it likes `courier`, but not `courier new`. (Explorer displays all of these just fine.)

Finally, Windows 97 ships with all of the same fonts as Windows 95, with many more as part of the Windows 97 Value Pack. A few fonts worth noting are:

➡ Baskerville Old Face

➡ Book Antiqua

➡ Bookman Old Style

➡ Century Schoolbook

➡ Cooper Black

➡ Copperplate Gothic

➡ Eras

➡ Eurostile

➡ Franklin Gothic

➡ Garamond

➡ Gill Sans

➡ Goudy Old Style

➡ Impact

➡ Lucida

➡ Lucida Sans

➡ Stencil

Note

> There are a lot of font faces that Navigator *should* display, but does not (especially on the Mac). Test often, and try not to get too discouraged!

And what do all these systems have in common? What are the fonts that you can always use on any page and never have to worry? The master list:

→ Arial and Helvetica (they look alike; make sure to name both for each use)

→ Courier

→ Symbol

→ Times

Note

> Fortunately, Courier and Times work across platforms even though the names vary slightly. If you use `times` as the value of `font-family`, the Windows browser recognizes it as Times New Roman. But to be safe among the many browsers out there, you might still wish to refer to both `times` and `times new roman`, and do the same for `courier` and `courier new`.

Three fonts to choose from for text (I'm not including the Symbol font). Not exactly a lot of flexibility. This is why Microsoft, Adobe, and others are racing to develop new type standards such as OpenType (and dynamic fonts—see upcoming sections), which will enable Web designers to transfer actual *font information* right along with Web pages, so visitors can see fonts even if they don't have them installed on their systems. Very cool.

In the meantime, we have to abandon "sure bet" fonts much of the time and make some guesses.

"Best Guess" Fonts

Okay, here is where you have to be willing to take some risks. If visitors don't have the font you specify, what will they see? Refer back to Chapter 4 to find out. Make sure you know before taking the leap, and make sure you test and test and test before going to sleep at night.

Internet Explorer Fonts

If your audience is using Internet Explorer, your options expand a bit. Internet Explorer 3 for Windows 95 ships with these fonts included:

➡ Arial Black

➡ Comic Sans MS

➡ Impact

➡ Verdana

The final version of Explorer 4.0 will ship with these fonts as well, if not more.

Meanwhile, the full version of Internet Explorer 3 for Macintosh ships with these fonts:

➡ Arial

➡ Arial Black

➡ Comic Sans MS

➡ Courier New

➡ Georgia

➡ Impact

➡ Times New Roman

➡ Trebuchet

➡ Verdana

➡ Wingdings

So if your audience is definitely using Explorer, you can add most of these font faces to your "sure bet" column.

Netscape's Dynamic Fonts

Netscape licensed technology from Bitstream Inc. has another way to try to get around the problem of limited font choices. Built into Navigator 4.0 is the capability of displaying fonts even if those fonts *aren't* on the user's system. This technology, called TrueDoc, maintains the look and feel of any font across all platforms, including onscreen display and printing. It even anti-aliases the font, so there are no ugly jaggies.

Basically, here's how it works: You specify any font you want to in your style sheet. When a visitor comes to your page, the browser checks your system for the font. If it's there, great. If not, True-Doc's font processors will closely approximate the font for temporary use. That is, the visitor will see the font onscreen and be able to print it, but will be unable to keep the font for other uses. When the page is gone, so is the font.

Of course, keep in mind that this dynamic font technology gives you font freedom only if your audience is entirely using Navigator. (Unfortunately, as of this writing, this dynamic font technology is not yet part of the Navigator 4 beta. But Netscape promises it will be part of the final version.)

OpenType

This is a good time to mention OpenType, which is a font initiative somewhat like TrueDoc. OpenType is currently being co-developed by Microsoft and Adobe. The very fact that these two companies are teaming up for something means that OpenType stands a good chance at becoming a standard.

OpenType is a new font format, a superset of existing TrueType and Type 1 fonts, which will allow for fast downloading of font information over the Web. It will enable Web designers to embed specific fonts into a Web page, so that even visitors without those fonts installed will be able to view them temporarily. These high-quality on-screen fonts and font technology will be cross-platform and (many of us pray) cross-browser as well.

Details on OpenType are still sketchy at this point. Neither browser supports OpenType in their 4.0 versions. But it's definitely something to watch for in the future!

Microsoft Office Fonts

Everyone's got Microsoft Office, right? Or at least Microsoft Word? Well, no. But a lot of people do. And that might be reason enough to use the following fonts, which ship with various versions of Office (97, 95, NT, 4.3, and 4.2):

Font	97	95	NT	4.3 (Win)	4.2 (Mac)
Algerian	✓	✓	✓	✓	
Arial Black	✓	✓	✓	✓	
Arial MT					✓
Arial Narrow	✓	✓	✓	✓	✓
Arial Rounded Bold	✓	✓	✓	✓	✓
Bauhaus 93					✓
Book Antiqua	✓	✓	✓	✓	✓
Bookman Old Style	✓	✓	✓	✓	✓
Braggadocio	✓	✓	✓	✓	✓
Brittanic Bold	✓	✓	✓	✓	✓
Brush Script MT	✓	✓	✓	✓	✓
Century Gothic	✓	✓	✓	✓	✓

continues

Font	97	95	NT	4.3 (Win)	4.2 (Mac)
Century Schoolbook	✓	✓	✓	✓	
Colonna MT	✓	✓	✓	✓	✓
Courier					✓
Desdemona	✓	✓	✓	✓	✓
Footlight MT Light	✓	✓	✓	✓	✓
Garamond	✓	✓	✓	✓	
Greek Symbols	✓	✓	✓	✓	
Haettenschweiler	✓	✓	✓	✓	
Iconic Symbols ext	✓	✓	✓	✓	
Impact	✓	✓	✓	✓	✓
Kino MT	✓	✓	✓	✓	✓
Math ext	✓	✓	✓	✓	
Matura MT Script Capitals	✓	✓	✓	✓	✓
Mistral					✓
Monotype Corsiva					✓
Monotype Sorts					✓
MS LineDraw	✓	✓	✓	✓	
Multinational ext	✓	✓	✓	✓	
Playbill	✓	✓	✓	✓	✓
Stencil					✓
Times New Roman PS MT					✓
Typographic	✓	✓	✓	✓	
Vivaldi					✓
Wide Latin	✓	✓	✓	✓	✓
Wingdings					✓

Obviously, the fonts that cross all versions of Office are even better guesses of fonts to use on your Web pages. Watch for varying spellings, however (see Chapter 4 for important details).

Free Downloadable Fonts

Another thing we're seeing to increase font choice is the giveaway of fonts. There are many sites that provide free downloadable fonts, and *way* too many fonts to list here. One concern is that many of these free fonts are variations of other, more standard font families. Names vary wildly, so be careful.

Microsoft is pushing hard to make a core set of TrueType fonts freely available at its Typography site (`http://www.microsoft.com/truetype/`). These are solid fonts and are worth adding to your list of options.

The free fonts from Microsoft, which are available for both Mac *and* Windows, include:

➡ Arial

➡ Arial Black

➡ Comic Sans

➡ Courier New

➡ Georgia

➡ Impact

➡ Times New Roman

➡ Trebuchet

➡ Verdana

Yes, some of these already come installed with Windows or Microsoft Office. But these Web versions, Microsoft tells us, contain more characters that future versions of Internet Explorer can take advantage of.

Verdana is fast becoming a font of choice for many Web designers. It was designed specifically for the screen, and so is
very readable, even at small sizes. A lot of sites are using it
already.

Other Guesses

After the fonts previously listed, I'm afraid you're on your own. If
you've got a good feeling that some other particular font is popu-
lar and that many people have it, feel free to take your chance
with it.

A few other fonts that I personally think might be ubiquitous
enough across platforms to use:

➡ Bauhaus 93

➡ Book Antiqua

➡ Bookman Old Style

➡ Brittanic Bold

➡ Brush Script

➡ Century Gothic

➡ Century Schoolbook

➡ Colonna MT

➡ Franklin Gothic

➡ Garamond

➡ Gill Sans

➡ Goudy

➡ Kino

➡ Stencil

Online Resources

Do you want to learn more about style sheets, stay up-to-date on the latest browser support, and see how others are creatively using style sheets? Here's a list to get you started.

Note

If you don't feel like typing URLs, take a trip to this book's Web site, where all these URLs will be ready and waiting for you as links. You'll also find any book updates there. The address is `http://www.hayden.com/internet/style/`.

Technical Information

`http://www.w3.org/pub/WWW/TR/REC-CSS1/`
The official specification of Cascading Style Sheets, level 1, as published at the end of 1996 by the World Wide Web Consortium.

`http://www.w3.org/pub/WWW/Style/`
The official home of style sheets on the World Wide Web Consortium site. Links to the latest style sheet documents and specs, as well as news.

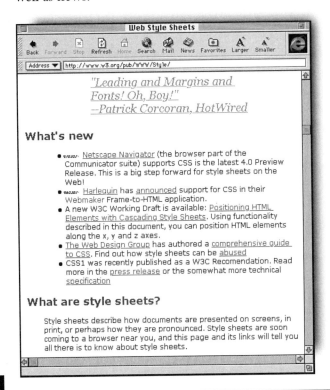

Figure C.1

The birthplace of style sheets: the World Wide Web Consortium.

`http://www.w3.org/pub/WWW/Mail/Lists.html`
Information on the `www-style@w3.org` mailing list (among others), a great (though sometimes rather technical) resource and community.

`comp.infosystems.www.authoring.stylesheets`
A relatively new Usenet newsgroup dedicated to style sheets. Grab a newsreader and check it out!

`http://www.htmlhelp.com/reference/css/`
Web Design Group's complete and helpful guide to style sheets.

`http://www.blooberry.com/html/style/styleindex.htm`
Another excellent style sheets guide, this one from Index DOT Html.

`http://www.peavine.com/CSS/`
Style Sheets Resource Centre. Information, examples, and even a mailing list.

`http://www.microsoft.com/workshop/author/css/css-f.htm`
A User's Guide to Style Sheets. A tutorial from Microsoft's Site-Builder Network.

`http://www.microsoft.com/workshop/author/css/usingcss-f.htm`
Using Cascading Style Sheets. More tips and tricks from the Site-Builder Network.

`http://www.webmonkey.com/webmonkey/teachingtool/`
The Teaching Tool on Webmonkey, which includes some lessons and updates on style sheets.

`http://www.microsoft.com/MIND/1096/CASCADING/CASCADING.HTM`
An article on style sheets with some cool examples.

`http://www.microsoft.com/truetype/content.htm`
The Microsoft Typography page. Full of font news, style sheets examples, and more.

Browser and Tool Support

http://www.shadow.net/~braden/nostyle/
Braden N. McDaniel's research on Internet Explorer 3 for Windows 95/NT and its support (or lack thereof) of style sheets.

http://www.cwru.edu/lit/homes/eam3/css1/css1.html
Eric A. Meyer's findings on style sheets support in Macintosh browsers, including Explorer and Navigator.

http://www.microsoft.com/truetype/css/gallery/cssinf5.htm
Creation tools that support style sheets.

Creative Uses

http://www.microsoft.com/truetype/css/gallery/entrance.htm
Microsoft's CSS Gallery. The first stunning examples on the Web showing some of the potential of style sheets.

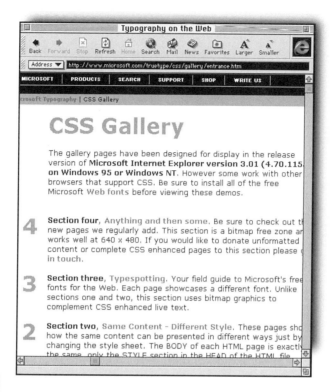

Figure C.2

The entrance to the Microsoft CSS Gallery. Inspiring examples await you.

http://www.cwebdev.com/css/

CSS in Action. Links to many sites using style sheets.

http://www.microsoft.com/gallery/files/styles/

The Microsoft Style Sheets Gallery. Style sheets you can freely download and use.

http://www.razorfish.com/bluedot/typo/

typoGRAPHIC, an amazing interactive refresher course on type and typography. Not specific to style sheets, but worth the trip.

Style Sheets Quick Reference

If you're like me, having a quick cheat sheet to all this style sheet information is a life-saver. That's the reason for this appendix, which is an all-in-one guide to all the style sheet properties and their current browser support.

Note | I'll be keeping an up-to-date version of this quick reference on this book's companion Web site, so drop by often for the latest changes: `http://www.hayden.com/internet/style/`.

Here's a quick guide to the symbols and abbreviations used:

IE: Internet Explorer

NN: Netscape Navigator

(W): Windows 95

(M): Macintosh

● Complete (or near-complete) browser support (just a few bugs or no bugs at all)

▶ Partial browser support (many bugs)

○ No browser support

Style Sheet Syntax

Syntax	IE3(W)	IE3(M)	IE4(W)	NN4(W)	NN4(M)
Embedded styles	●	●	●	●	●
Linked styles	●	●	●	●	●
Imported styles	○	○	○	○	○
Inline styles	●	●	●	●	●
Grouping	●	●	●	●	●
Inheritance	●	●	●	●	●
Classes	●	●	●	●	●
IDs	●	●	●	●	●
Contextual selectors	●	●	●	●	●
Pseudo-Classes, etc.					
A:link	●	●	●	○	○
A:visited	○	◗	●	○	○
A:active	○	○	●	○	○
first-letter	○	○	○	○	○
first-line	○	○	○	○	○
/* Comments */	●	●	●	●	●
! important	○	○	○	○	○

Style Sheet Properties

Property	IE3(W)	IE3(M)	IE4(W)	NN4(W)	NN4(M)
Fonts					
font-family	●	●	●	●	●
<font-family>	●	●	●	●	●
serif	●	○	●	●	○
sans-serif	●	○	●	●	○
cursive	●	○	●	○	○
fantasy	●	○	●	○	○
monospace	●	●	●	●	○
font-size	●	●	●	●	◗
<absolute-size>	●	●	●	●	○
<length>	○	◗	○	◗	◗
<percentage>	◗	◗	●	●	○
xx-small	●	●	●	○	○
x-small	●	●	●	○	○
small	●	●	●	●	○
medium	●	●	●	●	○
large	●	●	●	●	○
x-large	●	●	●	●	○
xx-large	●	●	●	●	○
smaller	○	○	●	●	○
larger	○	○	●	●	○

continues

Property	IE3(W)	IE3(M)	IE4(W)	NN4(W)	NN4(M)
Fonts					
font-style	◗	◗	●	●	●
normal	○	○	●	●	●
italic	●	●	●	●	●
oblique	○	○	●	●	●
font-weight	◗	◗	●	◗	○
extra-light	●	●	●	○	○
light	●	●	●	○	○
demi-light	●	●	●	○	○
medium	●	●	●	○	○
normal	○	○	●	●	○
demi-bold	●	●	●	○	○
bold	●	●	●	●	○
extra-bold	●	●	●	○	○
bolder	○	○	●	○	○
lighter	○	○	●	○	○
100-900	○	○	◗	●	◗
font-variant	○	○	●	○	○
normal	○	○	○	○	○
small-caps	○	○	●	○	○
text-transform	○	○	●	●	●
capitalize	○	○	●	●	●
uppercase	○	○	●	●	●
lowercase	○	○	●	●	●
none	○	○	●	●	●

text-decoration	◐	◐	●	◐	◐
none	●	●	●	●	●
underline	●	●	●	●	●
overline	○	○	●	○	○
line-through	●	●	●	●	●
blink	○	○	○	●	●
font	◐	◐	●	●	◐

Typography

word-spacing	○	○	○	○	○
normal	○	○	○	○	○
<length>	○	○	○	○	○
letter-spacing	○	○	●	○	○
normal	○	○	●	○	○
<length>	○	○	●	○	○
line-height	◐	◐	●	●	●
<number>	◐	◐	●	●	●
<length>	●	●	●	●	●
<percentage>	●	●	●	●	●
text-align	◐	◐	◐	●	●
left	●	●	●	●	●
right	●	●	●	●	●
center	●	●	●	●	●
justify	○	○	○	●	●

continues

Property	IE3(W)	IE3(M)	IE4(W)	NN4(W)	NN4(M)
Fonts					
vertical-align	○	○	◗	○	○
baseline	○	○	○	○	○
sub	○	○	●	○	○
super	○	○	●	○	○
top	○	○	○	○	○
text-top	○	○	○	○	○
middle	○	○	○	○	○
bottom	○	○	○	○	○
text-bottom	○	○	○	○	○
<percentage>	○	○	○	○	○
text-indent	●	●	●	●	●
<length>	●	●	●	●	●
<percentage>	●	●	●	●	●
Colors and Backgrounds					
color	●	●	●	●	●
background-color	○	○	●	◗	◗
transparent	○	○	●	○	○
<color>	○	○	●	●	●
background-image	○	○	●	●	●
<url>	○	○	●	●	●
none	○	○	●	●	●
background-repeat	○	○	○	●	●
repeat	○	○	○	●	●
repeat-x	○	○	○	●	●
repeat-y	○	○	○	●	●

no-repeat	○	○	○	●	●
background-attachment	○	○	○	○	○
scroll	○	○	○	○	○
fixed	○	○	○	○	○
background-position	○	○	○	○	○
<percentage>	○	○	○	○	○
<length>	○	○	○	○	○
top	○	○	○	○	○
center	○	○	○	○	○
bottom	○	○	○	○	○
left	○	○	○	○	○
right	○	○	○	○	○
background	●	●	◗	◗	◗
transparent	●	●	●	○	○
<color>	●	●	●	●	●
<url>	●	●	●	●	●
none	●	●	●	●	●
repeat	●	●	○	●	●
repeat-x	●	●	○	●	●
repeat-y	●	●	○	●	●
no-repeat	●	●	○	●	●
scroll	●	●	○	○	○
fixed	●	●	○	○	○
<percentage>	●	●	○	○	○
<length>	○	○	○	○	○

continues

Property	IE3(W)	IE3(M)	IE4(W)	NN4(W)	NN4(M)
Colors and Background					
top	●	●	○	○	○
center	●	●	○	○	○
middle	●	●	○	○	○
bottom	●	●	○	○	○
left	●	●	○	○	○
right	●	●	○	○	○
Layout (CSS level 1)					
margin-top	◐	●	○	●	●
<length>	◐	●	○	●	●
<percentage>	●	●	○	●	●
auto	○	○	○	○	○
margin-bottom	◐	○	○	●	●
<length>	◐	○	○	●	●
<percentage>	◐	○	○	●	●
auto	○	○	○	○	○
margin-right	●	●	●	●	●
<length>	●	●	●	●	●
<percentage>	●	●	●	●	●
auto	○	○	○	○	○
margin-left	●	●	◐	◐	◐
<length>	●	●	◐	◐	◐
<percentage>	●	●	◐	◐	◐
auto	○	○	○	○	○

margin	◗	◗	◗	◖	◗
<length>	○	○	○	◗	◗
<percentage>	●	●	●	◗	◗
auto	○	○	○	○	○
padding-top	○	○	○	●	●
<length>	○	○	○	●	●
<percentage>	○	○	○	●	●
padding-bottom	○	○	○	●	●
<length>	○	○	○	●	●
<percentage>	○	○	○	●	●
padding-right	○	○	○	◗	◗
<length>	○	○	○	◗	◗
<percentage>	○	○	○	◗	◗
padding-left	○	○	○	◗	◗
<length>	○	○	○	◗	◗
<percentage>	○	○	○	◗	◗
padding	○	○	○	◗	◗
<length>	○	○	○	◗	◗
<percentage>	○	○	○	◗	◗
border-top-width	○	○	○	●	○
border-bottom-width	○	○	○	●	○
border-right-width	○	○	○	●	○
border-left-width	○	○	○	●	○
border-width	○	○	○	●	○
border-color	○	○	○	●	○

continues

Property	IE3(W)	IE3(M)	IE4(W)	NN4(W)	NN4(M)
Layout (CSS level 1)					
`border-style`	○	○	○	◗	○
`border-top`	○	○	○	○	○
`border-bottom`	○	○	○	○	○
`border-right`	○	○	○	○	○
`border-left`	○	○	○	○	○
`border`	○	○	○	○	○
`width`	○	○	◗	●	●
<length>	○	○	◗	●	●
<percentage>	○	○	◗	●	●
auto	○	○	◗	●	●
`height`	○	○	◗	○	○
<length>	○	○	◗	○	○
<percentage>	○	○	◗	○	○
auto	○	○	◗	○	○
`float`	○	○	○	●	●
left	○	○	○	●	●
right	○	○	○	●	●
none	○	○	○	●	●
`clear`	○	○	○	◗	◗
none	○	○	○	●	●
left	○	○	○	◗	◗
right	○	○	○	◗	◗
both	○	○	○	◗	◗

Layout (Positioning/Layers)

position	○	○	◗	●	●
absolute	○	○	◗	●	●
relative	○	○	○	●	●
static	○	○	◗	●	●
left	○	○	●	●	●
<length>	○	○	●	●	●
<percentage>	○	○	●	●	●
auto	○	○	●	●	●
top	○	○	●	●	●
<length>	○	○	●	●	●
<percentage>	○	○	●	●	●
auto	○	○	●	●	●
width	○	○	●	●	●
<length>	○	○	●	●	●
<percentage>	○	○	●	●	●
auto	○	○	●	●	●
height	○	○	○	○	○
<length>	○	○	○	○	○
<percentage>	○	○	○	○	○
auto	○	○	○	○	○
clip	○	○	○	○	○
overflow	○	○	○	○	○
z-index	○	○	○	●	●
auto	○	○	○	●	●
<integer>	○	○	○	●	●

continues

Property	IE3(W)	IE3(M)	IE4(W)	NN4(W)	NN4(M)
Layout (Positioning/Layers)					
visibility	○	○	●	◐	○
inherit	○	○	●	○	○
visible	○	○	●	○	○
hidden	○	○	●	●	○
Classification					
display	○	○	○	◐	◐
block	○	○	○	◐	◐
inline	○	○	○	●	●
list-item	○	○	○	●	●
none	○	○	○	◐	◐
white-space	○	○	○	◐	◐
normal	○	○	○	●	●
pre	○	○	○	●	●
nowrap	○	○	○	○	○
list-style-type	○	○	○	●	●
list-style-image	○	○	○	○	○
list-style-position	○	○	○	○	○
list-style	○	○	○	○	○

Style Sheet Units

Unit	IE3(W)	IE3(M)	IE4(W)	NN4(W)	NN4(M)
in (inch)	●	●	●	●	●
cm (centimeter)	●	●	●	●	●
mm (millimeter)	●	●	●	●	●
pt (point)	●	●	●	●	●
pc (pica)	●	●	●	○	○
em (em)	○	●	○	◗	◗
ex (x-height)	○	●	○	◗	◗
px (pixel)	●	●	●	●	●
% (percentage)	●	●	●	●	●
Color names	●	●	●	●	●
Hex numbers	●	●	●	●	●
RGB values	○	○	●	●	●

INDEX

Symbols

@import command in external style sheets, 31-32

A

<A> tag classes
A:active, 40-43
A:link, 40-43
A:visited, 40-43
A:active class, <A> tag, 40-43
A:link class, <A> tag, 40-43
A:visited class, <A> tag, 40-43
absolute dimensions
browser support, 307-310
centimeters, 307-310
defined, 307-310
inches, 307-310
millimeters, 307-310
picas, 307-310
points, 307-310
translation formulas, 308-309
absolute keywords in font style sheets, 99-101
absolute positioning
clip property, 260-261
CSS, 244-245
defined, 245
height property, 260
HTML elements, 245-250
HTML examples, 245-250

I

J - K - L

JavaScript-Accessible Style Sheets
features, 13-14
Web browser support, 13-14

keywords, background position property, 183-186

layout style sheets
border bottom property, 229
border bottom width property, 223-224
border color property, 226
border left property, 230
border left width property, 224-225
border right property, 230
border right width property, 224
border style property, 226-228
border top property, 228-229
border top width property, 222-223
border width property, 225
clear property, 238-241
float property, 235-238
height property, 233-235
margin bottom property, 204-208
margin left property, 212-215
margin property, 215-218
margin right property, 208-212
margin top property, 193-194
    automatic margins, 197-198
    by length, 194-196
    by percentage value, 196-197
    negative margins, 198-204
overview, 189-193
padding bottom property, 219-220
padding left property, 221
padding right property, 220
padding top property, 218-219
quick reference charts, 338-342
width property, 231-233

leading (line height property)
by length value, 134-136
by number, 131-134
by percentage value, 136-137
defined, 128-138

left position property
absolute, 256-257
HTML
    elements, 256-257
    examples, 256-257
relative, 256-257

length units
em, 103-104
ex, 103-104
font style sheets, size property, 103-104

line height property
image overlaps, 137-138
leading, 128-138
    by length value, 134-136
    by number, 131-134
    by percentage value, 136-137
text overlaps, 137-138

<LINK> tag, 29-31

link effects in Web pages, 40-43

linked style sheets, 51-53

linking external style sheets, 28-31

links, underlining, removing, 42-43

list-style property, 279

list-style-image property, 276-277

list-style-position property, 277-278

list-style-type property, 275-276

M

Macintosh
fonts, 316
Internet Explorer fonts, 319–320
style sheet quick reference chart,
331–343

margin bottom property (layout style sheets), 204–208

margin left property (layout style sheets), 212–215

margin property (layout style sheets), 215–218

margin right property (layout style sheets), 208–212

margin top property (layout style sheets)
automatic margins, 197–198
by length, 194–196
by percentage value, 196–197
negative margins, 198–204

matching font style sheets in Web browsers, 83–84

measurement units
absolute dimensions, 307–310
percentage values, 313–314
relative dimensions, 310–313
style sheet quick reference charts, 343

Microsoft CSS Gallery Web site, 328

Microsoft Office, system fonts, 321–322

Microsoft SiteBuilder Network Web site, 327

Microsoft Typography Web site, 327

Microsoft Web site, 32
downloading style sheets, 32

multiple names in font style sheets, 90–91

N

negative margins, 198–204

negative values, absolute positioning of images, 249–250

Netscape Navigator
absolute dimensions, 307–310
absolute keywords in font style sheets, 99–101
background color property, 156–163
built-in style sheets, 2
color style sheets
background attachment property, 175-177
background position property, 177-178
background property, 186-188
background repeat property, 171-174
color name support, 148-150
hexidecimal numbers, 151
RGB values, 152-153
default fonts, 88–89
drop caps style sheet, non-support, 44–45
external style sheets, non-support, 32
first line effects, non-support, 45–46
font style sheets, size property, 95–98
fonts, 320
inline styles, non-support, 32–34
length units in font style sheets, 103–104
percentage units in font style sheets, 105–106
percentage values, 313–314

X - Y - Z

The *Web Designer's Guide to Style Sheets* Web Site

http://www.hayden.com/internet/style/

Make sure to visit the Web site devoted to this book. You'll find the following:

➡ All the example Web pages and style sheet code discussed in this book

➡ The latest book updates and news about style sheets and browser support

➡ Links to other useful style-sheets–related sites

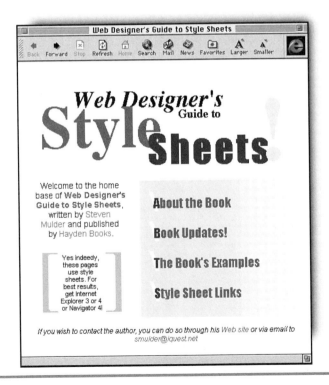